8/03

Courting Disaster

SOCIAL PROBLEMS AND SOCIAL ISSUES

An Aldine de Gruyter Series of Texts and Monographs

SERIES EDITOR

Joel Best, *University of Delaware*

Courting Disaster

Intimate Stalking, Culture, and Criminal Justice

JENNIFER L. DUNN

Aldine de Gruyter
New York

ABOUT THE AUTHOR

Jennifer L. Dunn is Assistant Professor of Sociology at Southern Illinois University, Carbondale.

ALDINE DE GRUYTER
A division of Walter de Gruyter, Inc.
200 Saw Mill River Road
Hawthorne, New York 10532

This publication is printed on acid free paper ⊗

Library of Congress Cataloging-in-Publication Data

Dunn. Jennifer L., 1957-
   Courting Disaster : intimate stalking, culture, and criminal justice / Jennifer L. Dunn
       p. cm. — (Social problems and social issues)
Includes bibliographical references and index.
   ISBN 0-202-30661-5 (cloth : alk. paper) — ISBN 0-202-30662-3 (pbk. : alk. paper)
   1. Stalking.   2. Stalking victims.   3. Man-woman relationships.   4. Conjugal violence.   I. Title.   II. Series
       HV6594 .D86 2002
       364. 15—dc21

2001008755

Manufactured in the United States of America

10 9 8 7 6 5 4 3 2 1

To Tom,
who laughed when I told him the title
and courted me anyway.

Contents

Acknowledgments

First, I would like to thank the many people who helped me at the Valley City District Attorney's Office, especially the Valley City Survivors of Stalking, and the sorority sisters, all of whom made the research possible. This book was a long time in the making, and several people read various portions and versions of it. I wish to remember the help of Joel Best, Kathy Charmaz, Diane Felmlee, John Hall, Lew Hendrix, Joan McDermott, Virginia Oleson, Jim Thomas, John Walton, and Kathy Ward. Special thanks are due to Mary Jackman and Lyn Lofland. Much constructive criticism was offered and the flaws remaining are due to the suggestions I did not take. The University of California Pro Femina Research Consortium and the Southern Illinois University Carbondale Office of Research and Development provided funding for data collection and analysis. Parts of some chapters draw on earlier publications: Jennifer L. Dunn (1999), "What Love Has To Do With It: The Cultural Construction of Emotion and Sorority Women's Responses to Forcible Interaction," *Social Problems* 46(3): 440–459, and Jennifer L. Dunn (2001), "Innocence Lost: The Accomplishment of Victimization in Intimate Stalking Cases," *Symbolic Interaction* 24(3): 285–313.

My loved ones were incredibly patient with me. Thank you all.

1

Pursuing Justice:
Setting the Stage for Intimate Stalking Victimization

This book is about women who are being coerced, intimidated, and stalked by former intimates. It is about the things these women do to manage this situation, and what happens to them as a consequence. Stalking is a behavior that has relatively recently been defined as problematic, and as criminal when violence or the threat of violence occurs. This new category of crime has created a new category of victim, the stalking victim, and this is a story of how some of these new kinds of people come into being, interact with their former partners, and seek help. It is about experiencing stalking victimization and, also, about living through what some women consider a form of secondary victimization by the criminal justice system. We will discover that these are complex and reciprocal processes.

The identity of the stalking victim is not inherent in any person or experience, but is contingent upon interpretation. Thus this book is also an account of the definitional processes that take place as a woman decides that she is a victim of stalking and seeks to convince others of this. It uses a variety of data and methods to examine this phenomenon from the perspectives of both victims and law enforcement agents, and adds to our understanding of attributions of responsibility and blame when violence occurs between intimates. By examining social constructions of this particular type of victimization and the choices stalking victims make, we learn more in general about the forces constraining human decisions.

Stalking victimization is complicated because it is an ongoing process. It often doesn't stop once the criminal justice system is involved. Women who are being stalked by their former partners face a profound dilemma in their efforts to manage their pursuers and to pursue their cases through the criminal justice system. Like all crime victims, they deal with a justice system that traditionally has depended upon them as witnesses, but not given priority to their needs as victims. Like others who fall prey to intimates, in highly gendered crimes, these women describe working particularly hard to establish and maintain their credibility. Unlike other crime victims, however, they must do so even as they face almost unimaginable difficulties simply getting the criminal behavior to cease.

We shall see that the processual, structural, gendered and relational aspects of stalking victimization can lead to more than the usual frustration with the "system." Indeed, stalking's character surely plays a part in these women's sometimes counter-productive efforts in their own behalf. In turn, victims' responses may decrease their credibility or permit stalking to escalate or both. If they then fail to gain the assistance of legal advocates, this amplifies feelings of "secondary victimization"—assertions of revictimization by the criminal justice system—even as primary victimization continues.

The nature of intimate stalking cases provides an opportunity to observe women's strategies for managing interactions with their former partners *and* with law enforcement, and for managing their "victim" identities, over a period of time. We can thus examine an extended relationship between victims, offenders, and law enforcement actors in ways that few other crimes provide, and that allows for relationships between "victims" and "victimizers" that are far from straightforward or unambiguous. This should be of special interest to victimologists and victim advocates.

What makes intimate stalking victimization sociologically interesting are the ways in which these component features of interaction are shaped by the social structures, cultural frameworks, and institutional organizations within which they take place. The stalking itself, the responses of women to their pursuers, the attributions that criminal justice actors make on the basis of these responses, and the consequences of these attributions for these women are not idiosyncratic actions and events. Rather, they are all influenced and constrained by repertoires of possible and "appropriate" action, cognition, and feeling. These are socially derived, maintained, and reproduced. This book tries to show the reader what it is like to be stalked and to have to convince others that one is truly a stalking victim. In addition, it explores some of the social forces that give these experiences their unique character. And because era, culture and power give to victims' lives their frightening textures and bitter flavors, these are examined as well.

Consider the following excerpt[1] from a preliminary hearing in which the victim was being cross-examined by a defense attorney:

> Q: And you've had no intention since that time that you filed the restraining order . . . to ever want to see [the defendant] again, be with him emotionally, physically, or any manner whatsoever, you want the relationship over from that point in time forward, is that correct?
> A: I knew that in the back of my mind.
> Q: You never wanted to see him again; isn't that right?

A: Correct.

Q: And you still felt that way continuously from that day forward all the way to today's date in court; isn't that right?

A: Correct.

Q: So you've never called him anywhere; is that right?

A: I would return. I haven't initialed [sic] the contact.

Q: You say you returned calls?

A: Yes.

Q: Now, you know that it is a violation of the restraining order for you to call him and for him to even speak to you; isn't that correct?

A: For him, yes.

Q: So why do you call him and encourage him to talk to you with those phone calls?

A: When he is calling and threatening my parents, when he is saying he is on his way, I will talk to him.

The defense attorney tried to cast doubt on this woman's claim that she was a stalking victim by questioning her in a way that suggested that she continued to have a voluntary relationship with the defendant even after obtaining a restraining order. Even as she attempted to define herself as being forced to continue interacting with her former partner, he sought to portray her as a willing participant.

When a woman claims that her lover or spouse is victimizing her (whether the crime is battery, sexual assault, or stalking), the intimacy, and all of the cultural meanings that attach to romantic and sexual relationships between men and women, become part of what she and others must take into account when they decide what kind of situation they are facing and what is to be done about it.

A COURSE OF CONDUCT: HISTORICAL, CULTURAL, AND HIERARCHICAL FRAMEWORKS

Before being immersed in the horrors and the struggles of stalking victims, however, some empirical and theoretical background information is necessary. This chapter begins with a general introductory discussion of the new laws criminalizing stalking, paying particular attention to the history of this legislation in California (the first state to enact antistalking statutes), the distinct nature of stalking as a recognized crime, and by comparing the demographics of stalking victimization to domestic violence victimization. Not only is stalking a fairly newly defined crime, but like the gendered crimes of rape and domestic violence, it depends on evidence of victim noncompliance with the defendant and evidence that the victim did not precipitate or encourage the defendant's behavior. This makes the behavior of victims particularly susceptible to "framing" processes, in which their actions in response to stalking come under scrutiny and their character questioned. Prosecution and conviction of stalkers is especially difficult. This, coupled with the ongoing nature of being stalked, may likely make the victim feel twice victimized.

We then review briefly some literature on the social construction of reality and the prosecution of "gender violence" crimes to place intimate stalking into context. This is followed by a description of the research setting and the data from which this study emerged.

The Historical Context for AntiStalking Legislation

Like all social problems, stalking has a history. While behaviors that we now define as stalking may have been occurring as long as there have been intimate relationships, it is only recently that stalking has become framed as "something we should do something about" and then criminalized. Kathleen Lowney and Joel Best (1995) examined media sources and found that it wasn't until 1989, when television actress Rebecca Shaeffer was murdered in the doorway of her apartment building by an obsessed fan, that stalking became a social issue. This well-publicized incident was one of many cases of celebrity stalking that received widespread attention in the popular press and contributed to a new construction of stalking as a social problem. This social problem became institutionalized with the passage of antistalking legislation. However, the legislation, like the enforcement processes I will describe, fails to encompass the complexity of stalking victimization.

After four women, all but one of whom had sought help from authorities[2], were killed by former partners in a six-week period in Orange County in 1990 (Beck 1992), California became the first state in the nation to enact antistalking legislation, followed shortly by 47 additional states and the District of Columbia (Lowney and Best 1995); Maine uses an antiterrorizing statute. According to Lowney and Best (1995) the success of claims about stalking and the resulting legislation in the other states were linked to support by battered women's movements and victims' rights movements, who framed stalking as a form of domestic violence and used their considerable resources to keep stalking a topic for public discourse and action. With the enactment of antistalking legislation, victims had a new resource: "upon criminalizing stalking, the state becomes responsible for investigating the crime, initiating the proceedings, providing the evidence, and seeking punishment" (Morville 1993:927). In spite of continuing concerns about the constitutionality and effectiveness of such legislation,[3] antistalking measures are seen as more effective than the civil remedies they replace, such as injunctions against harassment that require women to hire private attorneys and seek monetary damage but fail to otherwise incapacitate stalkers. Legislation is supported by victims' rights advocates, including the National Organization for Victim Assistance, the National Victims Center, and the National Battered Women's Law Project (Morville 1993).

The largest study to date of stalking incidence and prevalence was conducted by Patricia Tjaden and Nancy Thoennes (1998a) as part of the federally funded National Violence Against Women Survey for November 1995 through May 1996. In their description of their findings, Tjaden and Thoennes describe stalking as follows:

> Stalking generally refers to harassing or threatening behavior that an individual engages in repeatedly, such as following a person, appearing at a person's home or place of business, making harassing phone calls, leaving written messages or objects, or vandalizing a person's property. These actions may or may not be accompanied by a credible threat of serious harm, and they may or may not be precursors to an assault or murder (1998a:1)

Stalking is typically defined by the statutes as "willful, malicious, and repeated following and harassing of another person" (National Criminal Justice Association 1993:13). Some states additionally proscribe "lying in wait," nonconsensual communication, and "surveillance." A "pattern of conduct" is required by most states to establish that stalking has occurred, meaning that a series of acts occurs, and many insist that a "reasonable fear" for safety or of death or bodily injury exists. California, like most states, has the narrowly constructed requirement that a "credible threat" be made by the stalker, "with the intent to place [the victim] in reasonable fear of death or great bodily injury or of the death or great bodily injury of his or her immediate family." This threat does not have to be a verbal threat, but can include conveying threat using other symbolic means (National Institute of Justice 1996:6).

Initially, there were numerous and problematic variations in the language of these statutes that made them extremely difficult to enforce, leading to congressional hearings resulting in the Project To Develop a Model Antistalking Code for States (National Criminal Justice Association 1993). The National Institute of Justice, through Police Executive Research Forums, surveyed police chiefs in 248 local, county, and state police agencies, as well as in the largest cities in ten states with no Forum, and criminal justice agencies and police agencies in Australia, Canada, and the United Kingdom. Thirteen percent of the respondents in states with stalking laws in place said their laws offered inadequate intervention options, stating that "specific actions should be defined as stalking to avoid confusion with other charges" and that their laws were "too vague, overly broad, or too difficult to prove and prosecute" (National Criminal Justice Association 1993:40). In addition, the researchers found the language of "credible threat" to be problematic, noting that it "might be construed as requiring an actual verbal or written threat," that many stalkers engage in conduct that is threatening, and that, therefore, this language referring to such behavior ought not to be included in the model code (National Criminal Justice Association 1993:45).

Several writers have drawn attention to problems associated with the credible threat provision of much antistalking legislation. Michele Ingrassia (1993), reporting in *Newsweek*, described the ineffectiveness of stalking laws in deterring some offenders, in cases that don't appear to meet the law's requirements and in which victims are thus unable to obtain protective orders. These cases, Ingrassia says, "underscore the difficulty of creating laws to deal with the murky issues of stalking . . . the most difficult problems lie in discerning a credible threat from a casual remark" (1993:28). She goes on to say that 75 to 80 percent of cases involve people who were once married or dating, complicating the ability of observers to adjudicate contested claims about statements the alleged stalker makes. Lieutenant John Lane of the Los Angeles Police Department's Threat Management Unit, in his testimony before the U.S. Senate, had this to say:

> The one hurdle that we have trouble with in meeting the standards of our stalking law is the credible threat issue. The first element is simply to establish a pattern of willful, malicious conduct wherein a suspect follows and annoys and basically establishes a pattern of fear. But it also has to rise to a standard of where that suspect makes a credible threat, an overt threat, a communication to do them great bodily injury or death . . . It has been our experience to date that many of our suspects don't do that. They do everything but, and they scare the heck out of our victims . . . they don't come right out and—I mean, it is implied by many of their acts and behaviors, but they don't actually communicate that direct threat. (U.S. Senate 1993:72)

Lieutenant Lane suggests that the language of the California antistalking legislation be modified to eliminate the credible threat standard in favor of a "reasonable fear" standard, in which stalking behaviors create a reasonable fear in a reasonable person that he or she is in danger. Even this standard may be problematic, however; according to Joan Zorza of the National Battered Women's Law Project, "Courts often look at the 'reasonable' man standard [b]ut what might not be terrifying to a reasonable man *is* terrifying to a reasonable woman" (cited in Furio 1993:91).

Zorza's statement suggests a perception of male bias in legal definitions, and there continue to be struggles over constructions of the imaginary person in legal discourse (Woody and Viney 1996). Several critics of the presumably gender neutral "reasonable person" standard (that has begun to replace the "reasonable man") argue that even this hypothetical is usually male, and that a "reasonable *woman*" standard is more appropriate in highly gendered crimes such as rape and in sexual harassment cases (Ehrenreich 1990; Forell and Matthews 2000; Leland 1994; Pinkston 1993; Scheppele 1991). In the case of stalking, Forell and Matthews argue that this crime is "viewed through a male-focused lens" (2000:123) that circumscribes reasonableness, and thus stalking laws "remain an inadequate remedy" (2000: 129). They conclude:

> Applying the reasonable woman standard in determining what conduct creates reasonable fear explicitly incorporates the perspective of women, the group most commonly stalked and the group with the most to fear when they are stalked. This gendered standard will help decision makers recognize that the "reasonable" fear of bodily injury that must be shown for a stalking remedy should be women's fear, not men's. (2000:129)

Others find problems associated with the "reasonable woman" standard; for example, Eisenman (1995) claims the standard is "culture-bound" and biased against men.

The National Institute of Justice, in drafting model antistalking legislation, tried to address issues of overbreadth and vagueness, as well as problems associated with due process (ambiguously worded statutes may not provide individuals with "fair notice" of the types of behavior proscribed by the law), the restriction of movement, proportionality in sentencing, double jeopardy, and the right to bail. Despite the efforts of this group, both the adequacy and constitutionality of even the model legislation continues to be problematic (Faulkner and Hsiao 1994). The American Civil Liberties Union (as well as the National Organization for Men) has expressed concerns that overzealous prosecutors could use the laws to "suppress the rights of political dissidents and others" (Morville 1993). In sum, it appears to be extremely difficult to draft legislation that is sufficiently inclusive to encompass the range of dangerous behaviors in which stalkers engage, and at the same time excludes behavior protected by the First and Fifth Amendments.

The National Institute of Justice project members "expressed concern and serious reservations about the current trend in this country of 'federalizing' any high-profile or topical crime issue in this country" and they concluded that Congress "should not enact a federal antistalking law states and local governments are best situated to formulate and enforce laws that proscribe stalking behavior" (National Criminal Justice Association 1993: 12). The federal government did, however, distribute the Model Antistalking Legislation to the States, and with the help of the National Criminal

Justice Association, conducted a series of regional seminars to assist the States in developing and implementing legislation (National Institute of Justice 1996). Many states have since revised their antistalking legislation to address the issues described above. However, findings from the National Violence Against Women Survey led Tjaden and Thoennes (1998a) to conclude that credible threat requirements should be eliminated entirely from antistalking statutes, as fewer than half of the women they identified as stalking victims had been explicitly threatened by their stalkers.

Stalking As Intimate and Gendered Violence

We will see that "credible threat" represents only one ambiguous aspect of intimate stalking when we examine actual cases. Another aspect is intimacy. What is the relationship between stalking and other forms of intimate violence? The National Violence Against Women Survey cited above provides useful data in this regard, not only because a representative sample of 8000 men and 8000 women was obtained, but also because respondents were questioned about physical assault, rape, and stalking. Stalking is more common than rape but less common than physical assault. According to the survey, annually in the United States approximately 1.9 million women are physically assaulted, 1,006,970 women are stalked, and 302,100 women are raped (Tjaden and Thoennes 1998a, 1998b).

As in the case of rape and physical assault, women are significantly more likely than men to be victimized by a partner than by a stranger. A current or former intimate was the perpetrator in 76 percent of the cases in which women were either raped or physically assaulted or both as adults, compared with 18 percent of the cases where the victims were men; 59 percent of the women, but only 30 percent of the men, reporting stalking said former intimates were the perpetrators (Tjaden and Thoennes 1998a, 1998b). And, importantly, women who are being stalked by a former intimate are much more likely than other women to have been raped or physically assaulted by that person. "Husbands or partners who stalk their partners are four times more likely than husbands or partners in the general population to physically assault their partners, and they are six times more likely to sexually assault their partners" (Tjaden and Thoennes 1998a).

As in other forms of intimate violence, stalking violence is primarily male violence perpetrated against female victims. Ninety-three percent of women raped or physically assaulted as adults were attacked by men, a figure almost identical (94 percent) to the proportion of women being stalked by men (Tjaden and Thoennes 1998a, 1998b). Eighty percent of stalking victims are women, and 87 percent of stalkers are men. Even male victims are more likely to be stalked by men than by women; 60 percent of male victims reported male stalkers (Tjaden and Thoennes 1998a). In sum, the success of victims' advocates' efforts to link stalking with domestic violence in public perceptions (Best 1999; Lowney and Best 1995) appears to rest in part on people's recognition of their own everyday experience, not just that of celebrities, as problematic. And if gender shapes perceptions of domestic violence, by the same token it is likely to influence representations and interpretations of intimate stalking.

The Cultural Context for Law Enforcement Responses to Intimate Stalking

If the recognition of stalking as a social problem, and the development of legislative remedies, are fairly recent phenomena, how does this influence victims' experience of stalking and of seeking help? And how *does* the gendered and intimate character of stalking shape these processes? To understand these sometimes subtle but always complex interrelationships between legal, structural, and cultural arrangements and actors' lived experience, two things are helpful. The first is to think of the reality of stalking victimization as socially constructed through ongoing, interactive processes of attribution and subsequent decision making. The second is to place these processes into context. To do this, I briefly explore the usefulness of an interactionist and social constructionist sociological framework and of research on the prosecution of other crimes involving gender and intimates.

Symbolic Interaction and the Social Construction of "Victims"

I approach the study of intimate stalking from a symbolic interactionist perspective in which identities—in this case, "victim" identities—are socially constructed rather than inherent in the people to whom they are imputed (Blumer 1969). Like all attributes, identities are consequential, because we act—can only act—on the basis of the meanings we ascribe to people and situations (Blumer 1969). And, importantly, we attribute identities in interactive processes with all of the other relevant actors involved in the situation, making identities "interactionally constituted" (Holstein and Miller 1991). This interactional property of identities gives them a fluid rather than static character; identities are "social productions more situated than substantial, constructed rather than objective, and reflexive of symbolic process" (Altheide 2000:3–4). Importantly, people seek to achieve "preferred identities" (Charmaz 1987:283) but always face the possibility of having the identity claims they make called into question (Goffman 1959, 1963). Identities can thus be "spoiled" whenever there is a discrepancy between normative expectations or stereotypes and what Goffman refers to as "actual identity" (1963:2). Spoiled identity confers stigma; we devalue stigmatized people and "reduce [their] life chances" (Goffman 1963:5). Simply put, I only successfully present myself as the type of person I claim to be to the degree that you accept my claim, and how you treat me depends utterly on the legitimacy you afford me. But your acceptance can falter, if I do anything at any time to belie the impression, the self, that I am trying to create and maintain. And social interaction is replete with possibilities for questioning, for erring, for violating expectations. When this happens, you see me differently and act accordingly.

Specifically, I approach the idea of the "stalking victim" as an identity conferring process in which people must compete for access to limited legal and advocacy resources, so that "victim contests" occur (Holstein and Miller 1991). These contests are quintessentially moral in Goffman's (1963) sense; successful presentation of victimization obligates the audience to treat the "victim" accordingly. Women in this situation struggle to make their claims heard, to negotiate and maintain and manage victim identities. They face a multitude of hazards in the process, precisely *because* stalking is a continuing process and shapes their decisions to comply with (or resist) the demands former intimates make for continued interaction. The actions they take to manage the emotions of their stalkers—while claiming to be stalked—can violate our everyday understandings of who true "victims" are and discredit them in the eyes of these crucial others. Moreover, even those who successfully establish their claims to victimization often become frustrated because they perceive a lack of sufficient advocacy. Subsequently, they may interact with their advocates in ways that also complicate successful maintainance of the identities they have achieved.

Also, even for the "winners" in these contests an unintended consequence of victimization can be stigma. This happens because to be a victim is, by definition, to potentially be discrepant—to violate normative expectations (Goffman 1963). Candace Clark says, "having a problem that warrants sympathy can also qualify a person for a deviant label, a loss of social credit" (1997:198). Similarly, Donileen Loseke argues that although our cultural morality of individualism and personal autonomy has changed in ways that foster an increase in victim claims, "it remains the case that our culture prizes *strength* and *personal responsibility* while the category of victim is about *weakness* and personal *non-responsibility*" (1999:141, emphasis in original). The fulcrum of the definitional see-saw for stalking victims centers on the issues of agency and accountability, of innocence and responsibility. The efforts of victims to define themselves as such, and, consequently, to redefine themselves as "survivors," bear witness to these dilemmas.

Gender, Culture, and the Prosecution
of Intimate Violence

The struggle of stalking victims to claim (and, sometimes, disavow) victimization take place within historical, cultural, and organizational contexts shaped by multiple perspectives on what it means to be a "true" victim. Stalking victims must meet the criteria held by relevant actors in the criminal justice system, if they are to get help. These actors determine whether or not (1) a prosecutable crime has occurred, (2) the victim is credible, and (3) the victim needs and merits the services provided by law enforcement actors. In some cases these actors also make attributions resulting in the choice of some victims, rather than others, to serve as lay advocates for stalking victims. These attributions do not take place in an organizational vacuum. Rather, they are shaped by everyday (and social science) understandings of victimization as well as legal understandings.

Included in these understandings are the ideas of "victim precipitation" (Amir 1971), on the one hand, and "victim blaming" (Best 1997; Felson 1991; Kennedy and Sacco 1998; Ryan 1971), on the other. Criminologists have argued that victims sometimes play a role in their own victimization, while victim advocates (including social scientists) have charged that this conceptualization deflects responsibility from where it truly lies—with perpetrators of crimes. Both frameworks have gained currency. Best, for example, argues that a widespread "ideology of victimization" has permeated legal arenas. This ideology frames the law itself as an institution that "discourages victims, blames them for their suffering, forces them to humiliate themselves, and then fails to deliver justice" (Best 1997:14). This villianizing of legal institututions is possible in part because the victim ideology constructs victimization as "morally unambiguous" and victims as "innocent" (Ibid:11). Best claims that even those involved in exploitative relationships may see complexities that advocates miss (Ibid:11). From this perspective, those who criticize the concept of victim precipitation and its use by victimologists to explain victimization—and defense attorneys to excuse defendants—might be characterized as "sympathetic" and as "accept[ing] elements of the ideology of victimization" (Best 1997:14).

Others argue that, in criminal justice systems and the everyday world, victim precipitation is the hegemonic ideology governing the ways in which various actors make sense of and respond to victimization. In this view, the notion leads to victim blaming and inevitably results in further victimization of "victim/witnesses" by the criminal justice system itself. Stanko (1981) was one of the first analysts to describe the relative importance of crime victims' character and credibility in prosecutors' decisions about whether to pursue a specific case. She points out that when prosecutors face the problem of allocating finite resources within organizational constraints privileging convictability, they try to predict how juries will react to particular victims.

> and they often base these predictions on a common-sense evaluation of how judge and jury will assess a victim's life-style and moral character, and derivatively [her] honesty and trustworthiness as [a] witness (Stanko 1981:229)

Moreover, according to Stanko, prosecutors draw upon their understandings of stereotypical notions of what *type* of person is credible. In later work, Stanko (1982) extends this analysis to female victims, arguing that gender stereotypes color prosecutors' assessments of convictability and thereby shape their decision making. Women are particularly likely to suffer as a consequence: "Questions about a particular victim's provocation or consent are influenced by assumptions about the 'proper' woman's behavior in that situation" (Stanko 1982:78).

Analyses of rape victims' experiences of participation during prosecution illuminate tensions between the legal and organizational constraints that criminal justice system personnel must take into consideration and the rape victims' needs and perceived interests (Frohmann 1994; Holmstrum and Burgess 1983; Kerstetter 1990; Kerstetter and Van Winkle 1990; Konradi 1996, 1997; Madigan and Gamble 1989; Martin and Powell 1994; Rose and Randall 1982; Stanko 1982). Prosecutors' careers depend upon their careful selection of and devotion to "winnable" cases. Thus they must attend to features of victims and cases that distinguish "real" rapes and "worthy" victims. They do this by subjecting the claims of victims to an intense and often skeptical regard, questioning the legitimacy of victims' claims as a procedural matter. Researchers and advocates argue that in this process, victims come to feel as if they, not the defendants, are on trial (Frohmann 1994; Holmstrum and Burgess 1983; Kerstetter 1990; Kerstetter and Van Winkle 1990; Konradi 1996, 1997; Madigan and Gamble 1989; Martin and Powell 1994; Rose and Randall 1982; Stanko 1982).

Frohmann (1994) describes how, in their concern with convictability (conviction rates serving as the basis for promotion in the district attorney's office she studied), prosecutors rely on stereotypical assumptions about gender, relationships, and sexuality to find discrepancies between victims' accounts and typifications of "real" rape. Thus they actively seek to discredit victims. Similarly, Martin and Powell examine legal and medical processors of rape victims and find that organizational conditions subordinating victims' needs to the state's lead even sympathetic staff to "frame and treat victims in ways that give priority to organizational interests over victims' interests [and] treat victims poorly" (1994:858). Revictimization, sometimes called the "second assault" (Williams and Holmer 1981) consists of questioning the legitimacy of victims' claims: "Processing organization staff subject rape victims to various tests to ascertain their truthfulness and worthiness: Does she merit our trust, time, effort, and involvement?" (Martin and Powell 1994:879–880). Martin and Powell explicitly associate what they term "responsive processing" with "empowering" victims and admonish institutions to "avoid blaming the victim" (Ibid: 862).

More recently, Amanda Konradi explored how prosecutors prepare rape victims for court appearances, actively constructing them as credible and as typifying "real" rape victimization (1996, 1997). She extends previous researchers' analyses of secondary victimization from prior to charging into what she calls the "continued betrayal of the victim through the trial process" (Ibid: 7), detailing the same sorts of resource allocation based on predictions of stereotypical judge and jury decision making (Ibid: 36–37). Konradi describes revictimization as a likely consequence of inadequate preparation for court coupled with treating women in accordance with stereotypes, and suggests that the "responsiveness" advocated by Martin and Powell (1994) be broadened to include precourt preparation of victim / witnesses. Others hold little hope for significant reform and suggest that victim participation in the criminal justice system serves victims little if at all (Elias 1990).

Stalking, like sexual assault, is a highly gendered crime. Like other crimes in which women are mostly the victims and relationships as well as people are on trial, victimization is not a given, but must be constructed. Moreover, as Loseke argues, in order for us to construct a person as a victim, we must deem her worthy of our sympathy, and this only happens if we don't consider her responsible for the harm that befalls her (Loseke 1999:76). In order for a woman to convince others that she is being stalked, and deserves help, she must demonstrate that she has done nothing to bring her troubles upon herself, and that she is not encouraging the attentions of her former partner or sending "mixed messages." We must believe that she is genuinely afraid. If so, we believe that she is truly in need of what we have to offer.

Both Clark (1997) and Holstein and Miller (1997) elaborate the role that other actors play in these definitional processes: Clark describes "sympathy brokers" and "sympathy entrepreneurs" who work to "create moral boundaries distinguishing the sympathy-worthy from those undeserving of sympathy" (1997:42, 125); Holstein and Miller define in some detail the "social problems work" of various actors in community mental health, social control, and human service settings who "constitute" victimization by labeling others as victims (1990:117). This is where legal actors, particularly victim advocates, enter the stage. Their name suggests the significance of what they do; in the prosecutor's office, they present the women whose stories they believe, and about whom they genuinely care, in ways that are actively designed to enlist the interest and energy of the attorneys.

Thus, there are complex interactive processes taking place that enable (or prevent) women from establishing and sustaining the "fact" of their victimization. What follows is a description of how I went about studying these processes in a criminal justice setting, and the kinds of data collected there. I also introduce the people with whom I became involved and who shared their experiences with me in the course of the study—victims, advocates, and prosecutors—to bring them to life and give a sense of who they are, of what their lives and constraints are like, and of the real-life criminal justice system within which they must cope with intimate stalking. I explain some of the constraints under which prosecutors and advocates work so that the obstacles presented by stalking cases can be understood within the context of the work accomplished in the organization. Each of these groups, and victims, see intimate stalking and their roles within the system somewhat differently, and it is in their differing perspectives that we can begin to trace and explore some of the tensions and dilemmas that occur here.

PURSUING JUSTICE: STUDYING THE ORGANIZATION OF VICTIMS AND THEIR ADVOCATES

The data for this project were gathered from several sources, beginning with the survey of undergraduate sorority women who will be described in chapter four. Most of the data, however, come from a Domestic Violence Unit (DVU) in a large metropolitan district attorney's office in the western United States. I had read an article about stalking that described how Laura Lennox,[4] the supervising deputy district attorney (DDA) in the DVU, obtained a Department of Justice grant to hire a specialized prosecutor to handle stalking cases. When I called the district attorney's office to enquire about researching stalking cases, I was quickly referred to the supervising victims' advocate cited in the article, the woman I call Eliza Nash. Eliza had compiled a few statistics about some of the stalking cases prosecuted in the DVU and she was eager to have a systematic review take place. Later I learned that as an advocate, Eliza was actively involved in the work of establishing stalking victimization as a serious social problem and felt that the DVU could be doing significantly more to help victims. She believed that my research would contribute to her efforts.

Thus, Eliza made every possible accommodation to my needs in the setting. She introduced me to Laura Lennox, as well as to various attorneys and advocates. She found a series of spaces for me to work in, each better than the last in terms of being centrally located and near her. She made certain that I not only had my own phone, but that I had business cards with my number and title ("Researcher") printed up to distribute to victims and other participants in the study. She invited me to staff meetings, called victims to request interviews, facilitated the gathering of case files, got me security clearance, and gave me access to office supplies and machines. In essence, she helped to create the role of "stalking researcher" for me, and legitimized not only my presence in the office, but also the activities in which I engaged.

Despite Eliza's efforts on my behalf, it took several months to establish sufficient rapport with DVU staff and records gatekeepers to gain access to all of the case files and victim participants I eventually gathered into my web. Donna D'Amato, the victim advocate hired to work with stalking victims, was initially extremely protective of her charges even as she expressed support for the project. Her concerns arose primarily out of her perception of the stalking victims with whom she was working as particularly vulnerable, emotionally fragile women—possibly at risk of increased effects of post traumatic stress disorder triggered by my interviews. She had interviewed some of her clients, using a semi-structured interview guide I constructed in the early stages of the project. This methodology ensures that all interviewees are asked identical or similar questions and the guide can be used by more than one interviewer. I later abandoned this technique, in part because of the difficulties that came up for Donna. Two of the clients interviewed in this fashion reported severe flashbacks and distress as a result of being interviewed. As a consequence I decided that I alone would do any interviewing, and that I would use the most sensitive of "intensive" interviewing methodologies.[5]

Eventually, after many discussions in Donna's office and during her daily "smoke breaks," she decided that I was (1) a careful interviewer who could be trusted to be gentle with victims, rather than someone who was greedy for data and thus overly intrusive, and (2) that I was, politically, a woman after her own heart—that is, in the DVU not merely to do research, but to do research that had the potential to serve victims and their advocates. As I believed both of these impressions to be true, and because they helped tremendously to facilitate the research, I did nothing to discourage them. I then became a "sounding board" for Donna, who experienced great frustration from the beginning of her tenure at the district attorney's office, and who was often severely sanctioned for her aggressive and outspoken tactics on behalf of victims and advocates. The rapport we established greatly facilitated my understanding of the workings of the DVU from the perspective of the victim advocates, and made it possible for me gain access to data I never would have encountered otherwise.

I collected data over a two-year period beginning in May 1996 and ending in May of 1998. I began by using a computer-generated list of cases in which stalking had been charged, to identify cases and retrieve them from storage. As misdemeanor cases are held for only ninety days before being "purged," I restricted myself to the felony cases resolved between January 1995 and December 1997 (for a period encompassing three years). Thirty-seven of these could not be found, but I was able to read a total of 130 cases. Two of these were not domestic violence cases, and are not included in my analysis. An additional case, a homicide, is also not included because there were no victim narratives in the file.

Prosecutors' case files vary tremendously in their contents; among other things, they depend on how serious the charges are, how much evidence exists, and how conscientious the prosecuting attorneys are. A case that was resolved quickly, for example, might contain little more than a crime report or two. Other files included declarations; chronologies and letters written by victims; cards and letters sent by stalkers to victims; victim, suspect, and law enforcement "narratives" in crime reports, and transcriptions of telephone messages, conversations, and courtroom testimony. For this reason, and because I was most interested in the *meanings* various actors attached to stalking, a qualitative analysis appeared best suited to these data. I did record case, defendant, and victim characteristics and how many times different kinds of stalking behaviors and victim responses were reported for 123 of the 130 cases, however, and I describe these in order to give a general sense of their incidence in these cases.[6]

When I began the research, I was given a desk in a corner of the DVU, in a space shared by a succession of legal and victim advocate interns. I quickly became part of the scenery as I pored over the files, many of them several inches thick. Often, as I sat there, the advocates and deputy district attorneys whom I came to know would stop and talk with me, and I expanded my data collection to include many of these conversations. I took field notes describing interactions I observed (and in which I was involved) in the office, at staff meetings, and in court. After gaining Donna's trust, I was able to engage in participant observation in the support group I call the "Valley City Stalking Survivors" (VCSS), which met monthly at that time in the Unit, after hours. Donna and Eliza also made it possible for me to interview six stalking victims in intensive interviews ranging from ninety minutes in one sitting to several hours over an extended time period. Three of these women were members of VCSS; one member of the group disappeared before I was able to interview her. I talked to another woman, Winnie Newton, whom Donna introduced to me during observations in court. I was also able to interview seven undergraduate women from the university where I conducted the survey research about problematic dating experiences, and their stories also contribute to this study. One of these young women, Lee Ann Yamamoto, had been involved in criminal prosecution of her former boyfriend.

In the intensive interviews with stalking victims and undergraduate women (audiotaped for later analysis), I recorded detailed accounts of how these women defined their situations, their responses to the situations, and their understanding of what happened to them as a result. I asked questions that probed their understanding of and feelings about their experiences as they developed. I explored these women's interactional strategies with both their former partners and with law enforcement actors, particularly those involving emotion management. I looked for themes and commonalities in these interviews, and I developed preliminary coding schema for the case file narratives based on the patterns I observed.

I approached the other data somewhat differently, for the following reasons. Although virtually everyone in the DVU knew that I was a researcher, I believe that my continued presence there and my primary association with victim advocates and certain high-profile victims gave me an identity as a sort of quasi-advocate. This role gave me access to far more than case files and victims; it also gave me access to the advocates' perspectives on victims and their own roles in the DVU. At the same time, I retained my master status (Hughes 1945) as a researcher in the eyes of Eliza Nash, the supervising victim advocate, and the Deputy District Attorneys. Laura Lennox, the lead attorney in the DVU, asked me to present findings at staff meetings and at conferences she attended and held. Thus, I had access to attorneys' perspectives as well, and I may have been treated with a little more respect, as well as wariness, than were the advocates, who ranked low in the DVU hierarchy. One attorney asked me if I would be willing to provide "expert witness" testimony in a stalking case, and the attorneys in general were probably more cautious in my presence about what they said, especially when it was clear that I was taking notes.

The vantage point enabled by the multiple roles I played is important; not only was I able to learn about the DVU and the stalking cases from multiple perspectives, but I became sensitized to the tensions and conflicts between the interests and needs of these varied groups. When meanings and identities are contested, as they are in the DVU and in the courtroom, it is especially useful to hear from, to identify with, and to develop rapport with as many of the participants as possible. While this book emphasizes the stories told by victims, my analysis of them is shaped by all of the people who talked to me so freely. Following, I describe the DVU, its structure, some of what normally occurs there, and some of the central actors in this account.

THE VALLEY CITY DISTRICT ATTORNEY'S OFFICE DOMESTIC VIOLENCE UNIT

The district attorney's office where most of this research took place was located on the edge of the downtown commercial areas of Valley City. It was across the street from the County Court House, down the street from the Sheriff's Department, and a few blocks from the County Jail. As I walked toward the office, there was often a steady stream of people somehow involved with the Court: police officers in uniform, attorneys with their briefcases, clients and victims often looking uncomfortable in their dress clothing, women and children headed for the Temporary Restraining Order Workshops held daily at the District Attorney's office, and other employees of the office and the Court. When I entered the building, the first thing I noticed was a small, linoleum-tiled lobby with no furnishings other than a couple of inhospitable chairs, a bulletin board with posters advertising the costs of drunk driving and instructing minor miscreants how to deal with the court system, and a large convex mirror placed in the corner of the ceiling to reflect every inch of the lobby back to the personnel behind the counters. The reception counter extended a few feet into the lobby, and was divided along its length by sheets of bullet-proof Plexiglas with small circular openings to speak through and slots at the bottom to push documents through. Behind the Plexiglas were the receptionists, heavily made-up, laconic women who viewed each claimant to entrance with unconcealed suspicion, and who had red "panic buttons" next to their computers in case their suspicions were confirmed. Not everyone who entered had legitimate business there, and occasionally a "street person" or angry spouse might show up.

Midway through the research, Valley City police officers were hired to stand behind the receptionists during business hours, making visual contact with persons who proceeded into the interior of the building without talking to the receptionists. This was a right of passage held only by employees, who were given a code to punch in to an electronic system that unlocks the doors restricting access. Often, however, when two or more employees arrived at the same time, one person keyed in his or her code and the rest simply followed after. When this happened, if the police officer did not recognize all the parties coming through the door, she would apprehend any stranger and ask for identification. At the same time this policy went into effect, the women who came daily to fill out restraining orders were required to wear stick-on labels marked "visitor," as were any other nonemployees having business at the office. When I questioned the institution of this new policy, I was told of a rumor that the District Attorney had received a death threat, but I was unable to verify this.[7]

Once beyond the lobby, I entered a maze of offices and a highly stratified system that was mirrored in the distribution of offices. On the first floor were the social workers in the Victim-Witness program, the clerical staff, and the process servers. The prosecutors' offices were on the second, third, and fourth floors. When I first began my research, the Domestic Violence Unit was on the second floor, a reflection of its low status within the district attorney's office. It was staffed mostly by women, and I was told early on by Donna D'amato that DV was just a stepping stone toward more prestigious assignments in Major Crimes, Career Criminals, and at the top of the hierarchy (occupying the fourth floor next to the district attorney herself), Homicide. When Laura Lennox managed to acquire substantial grant monies to fund eight additional Deputies for the DVU, as well as increased investigative and clerical staff to support the Domestic Violence Home Court[8] that came into being in July of 1997, the entire Unit moved upstairs to the third floor. The symbolic impact of the move was clearly articulated in delighted discussion among the advocates of how "pissed off" the Deputies in other units were at being moved. They attributed the annoyance of the latter not only to the inconvenience of moving, but also to the increased attention to domestic violence by the district attorney and the media, attention being equated with importance and thus status.

Within the DVU itself, there were additional layers of power, esteem, and access to offices with windows. Offices encircled a central, carpeted lobby furnished like a living room, with inexpensive but comfortable donated couches, side tables, a coffee table, soothing floral prints in pastel colors, and silk plants and flowers completing the effect. Interns (legal and victim advocate) occupied cubicles walled off by movable, neutral toned screens on either side of the lobby. Next in rank were the clerical staff, who were literally seated in the hallways extending out from the lobby. The victim advocates had windowless offices adjoining the lobby, and the lower-status deputies had similar spaces adjoining the hallway. At the time of much of this research, Eliza Nash, Laura Lennox, Sam Negri (a lead deputy), and Cassie Turner (the stalking deputy) had window offices adjoining the lobby and the hallway. Position within the hierarchy was demarcated literally as well as symbolically by these arrangements.

Laura Lennox supervised two lead deputies, one in charge of the seven trial deputies and the other responsible for the Superior Court Review (SCR), where, following the institution of the Home Court, most domestic violence cases were resolved by negotiated plea bargains in lieu of hearings. In addition to the stalking deputy and another specialized prosecutor, Laura was responsible for the intake deputy (who determined from police reports if charges could be filed), victim advocates including Eliza and Donna, criminal investigators and two investigative assistants, interns, and administrative and secretarial staff. After the intake deputy reviews cases referred to the DVU by the Valley City Police Department and the Sheriff's Office, Laura assigned the cases to the other deputies. When I began the study, there were too many domestic violence cases for the deputies in the DVU to prosecute, and some were assigned to other units. With the advent of the Home Court, however, additional deputies were hired and this no longer occurred.

Prosecutors only charged domestic violence defendants with felonies about a third of the time, and of these more serious charges, very few were stalking charges. For example, in 1995, the year in which I began collecting data, the DVU reviewed 4,238 cases referred to them by the Valley City Police Department or Valley City Sheriff's office. About 20 percent of the cases were rejected, usually for insufficient evidence. Thus of the total reviewed,

2,067 (about half) were filed as misdemeanors and 1,332 (31 percent) were filed as felonies. One-third of these, or 435 cases, stayed in the DVU. Felony stalking was charged at intake in 86 of the total cases reviewed, constituting about six percent of the felonies.

This pattern is corroborated by data collected with the inception of the Domestic Violence Home Court. In the first six months of its operation, from July 1997 through December 1997, analysts reviewed the 861 domestic violence cases resolved by DVU Deputies (this represents only about 30 percent of an average six-month case load, but cases were still being processed in other units at this time). About half of these were felonies. All charges were dismissed in about one-third of the cases. Of the remainder, the vast majority were resolved with negotiated plea bargains; this can occur in the Superior Court Review or following a preliminary hearing, and only one percent of the cases handled in the DVU went to a jury trial. It is also important to note that a large proportion of domestic violence cases (20 percent) are resolved by means of converting criminal charges into violations of probation. About half the time, the defendant is already on probation for some other offense, and domestic violence victims are often reluctant to testify. During this time period, according to DVU data, only 10 of the 861 defendants were charged with stalking at intake, and 5 of them were convicted.[9]

Prosecutor and Advocate Roles and Responsibilities

There is a substantial body of research on the organizational constraints within which prosecutors decide how to manage the cases that come their way (Frohmann 1994; Holmstrum and Burgess 1983; Kerstetter 1990; Kerstetter and Van Winkle 1990; Konradi 1996, 1997, 1999; Martin and Powell 1994; Rose and Randall 1982; Stanko 1981, 1982). As Amanda Konradi puts it:

> [A]rrests and charging decisions made by police and prosecutors often reflect their efforts to conserve the resources of their respective departments. They seek to weed out unwinnable cases before time and effort is invested in making arrests, charging, and follow-up investigation. (1997:5)

Convictions are the goal, and while prosecutors devote the most time and energy to cases that will go to a preliminary hearing or a trial, trials are risky and any conviction is better than none. A deputy moves up in the hierarchy of the DVU or the district attorney's office by winning high-profile or "major" cases, resolving a high volume of cases, and having a high proportion of convictions. For these reasons, the vast majority of cases are resolved with negotiated pleas in the SCR. Stalking was considered particularly difficult to prosecute, because of the "course of conduct," "credible threat," and specific intent elements of the charge. Frequently, the stalking deputy would negotiate a "no contest" or (less often) a guilty plea to felonies that carried equal penalties but that were easier to prove (e.g., spousal assault or making a terrorist threat).

"Who Wants To Do Misdo Trials?": The Dilemmas of the Deputies

The reality of these "organizational principles" (Konradi 1997) created some contradictions and conflicts for prosecutors. For example, in a three-page memo to DVU attorneys, Laura Lennox outlined guidelines for deciding "appropriate case resolution proposals" in a "comprehensive yet organized process," noting that " [w]hile case preparation for trial will require more in-depth preparation, certain basic procedures are fundamental to arriving at any proposed resolution." In the memo Laura instructs the deputies to review offense reports of the current and any past domestic violence offenses; familiarize themselves with the defendant's criminal history; examine physical evidence as needed to "assess the severity of the circumstances, credibility of witnesses, and the provability of the crimes,"; obtain medical records if applicable; contact the victim or discuss contact of the victim by the victim advocate or review her notes; evaluate merits of the defense, request supplemental investigation as needed; communicate with probation/parole if there is a history of violations of probation/parole; identify aggravating factors, sentencing exposure, restitution needs, and sentencing objectives; communicate with victims regarding proposed dispositions "to the extent feasible;" communicate with key staff, discuss significant or sensitive cases with supervisors; evaluate whether a presentence investigation should be conducted; discuss the case with any defense attorneys; and, finally, " [m]ake a resolution offer if warranted." There are additional instructions for case handling after resolution.

If this is the standard for cases that do not go to trial, it is not surprising that Sam Negri's response to an argument that repeated restraining order violations (a misdemeanor) constituted stalking (even if the felony was not charged) was "Who here wants to do misdo [misdemeanor] trials?" When several of the deputies in this particular staff meeting raised their hands, he looked surprised and asked, "Who wants to see these upgraded to felonies?" At this, more deputies raised their hands, because in the calculus of advancement through the ranks of the organization felonies are "worth" more than misdemeanors. In a meeting with the victim advocates, Sam told the advocates that a "big challenge was attorneys who don't want to try misdos," attributing this to "ego, status, and the hierarchy."

And trials take more time than resolving cases in the SCR; even in the SCR, time is of the essence. Sam requested that the SCR advocate keep her presentations (written forms that summarize the advocate's assessment of the victim's credibility and willingness to cooperate with prosecution) as brief as possible. "The problem is the number of cases," he said. "We're trying to get them done and out as soon as possible—it's literally a race." He went on to explain that in the SCR, they had reached a "comfortable place where the facts are the same—90 percent [of these cases] are the equivalent of 'you've got dope in your pocket.'" When one advocate questioned whether this was fair to victims, and Eliza Nash asked if the deputies were concerned with threat assessment and lethality factors, Sam responded that the "fact pattern" meant that "it's still going to resolve as a misdo down the line," and "some cases I'm just going to blow [the victim advocate] off. It's just case load. So many cases, so little time." To which Donna D'Amato responded sardonically, "Well, we got out in record time [this morning]."

Sam's comments reveal much about the DVU and the SCR as part of what has been called the "courtroom work group," in which "shared understandings about seriousness [of offenses] facilitates rapid dispositions of a high volume of cases" and there is a "going rate" establishing what particular offenses are "worth" (Walker 1994:31). Like the public defenders who typify "normal crimes" (Sudnow 1979) that meet their expectations, prosecutors categorize cases in order to dispense with them efficiently and quickly. In my summary of what occurred in the meeting between Sam and the victim advocates, I noted that Sam used the language of economics when he talked about cases: "This is what you owe me, you owe me thirty days," he says he tells defendants.

That resolving high numbers of cases influences the progress of deputies through the ranks was revealed by what happened to Carla Thompson, the third deputy district attorney to handle stalking cases during the time I conducted research. Unlike Eric Xenelis and Maggie Hunt, both of whom held the position less than a year before moving upward in rank to Major Crimes and Homicide, respectively, Carla was moved out of the DVU into Misdemeanors. Although she became a lead attorney, the move was seen as a lateral move rather than a promotion. In Donna D'Amato's phrasing, Carla was "devastated" by her treatment, which "all has to do with statistics and how many cases are being processed." According to Donna, the supervisors did not realize how labor intensive the stalking cases were, and attributed the late hours Carla worked to being slow, rather than conscientious. Interestingly, and tellingly, the case files I read that were compiled by Carla were far thicker and had much more investigation and other detail than those compiled by her predecessors, who tended to create extensive documentation for only the most high profile and serious of offenders. Carla treated virtually all of the stalking cases as if they were that serious, which endeared her to victims and to advocates, but appears to have cost her organizationally.

Caught in the Middle: Advocacy for Whom?

Victim advocates face a different but related set of problems in their own efforts to meet the sometimes conflicting requirements of their jobs. Funding for the advocates in the DVU initially came from the state and federally sponsored Victim-Witness Program that provided advocacy and services for victims of all of the kinds of crimes prosecuted in the district attorney's office. When the DVU became part of the Domestic Violence Home Court project, additional funding for advocates became available and the DVU advocates became organizationally distinct from the other advocates. Not only were the DVU advocates upstairs in the relocated DVU, but they held separate staff meetings from the Victim-Witness advocates and complained about the expectation that they continue to attend those staff meetings as well. Frank J. Weed (1995) describes four types of victim services organizations: rape crisis centers, women's shelters, victim advocacy groups, and victim-witness programs. Each of these, Weed argues, defines victims differently according to the needs of the organization, and this shapes the approach of advocates. The purpose of programs such as the one in the DVU is to increase conviction rates by enlisting the cooperation of victims in prosecution. These organizations see a central problem, according to Weed, as

> the tendency of victims to be unwilling, fearful, or disinterested in being a witness against the offender. They are seen as resisting the idea of cooperating with the prosecutor to gain a criminal conviction. The organization's role is to assist the victim to the extent that their cooperation in prosecution of the accused can be assured . . . the victim serves in the role of the witness. (1995: 106)

While other types of organizations are more oriented toward alleviating the harm done to individual victims or to advocate for social change, Weed (1995) says the approaches can overlap, and this appeared to be the case in the DVU. Consider the "Role of the D.A. Domestic Violence Unit Advocate," as described in a handout given to the victim advocate interns:

1. Early and continuing victim contact.
2. Referral system to/from prosecutor, law enforcement agencies, community agencies serving domestic violence victims and other advocates. (note: Full disclosure to prosecutor.)
3. Training is different from other advocates—specific for unique issues present in domestic violence cases

    4. Serve the needs of the victim, however, team approach with prosecu-
tors and investigators.

This last "role" suggests, by using the term "however," that expectations
may conflict.

The handout then lists the services advocates provide. These include
safety planning; crisis counseling and referral for long-term services; explanation and "demystification" of the criminal justice system; the roles of
prosecutors, defense, and victims; court processes, court accompaniment;
providing information on the victim's options; how to report new incidents; how to get defendant release dates; and assisting with housing and
obtaining state victim compensation benefits. Also, and perhaps most importantly, there are the requirements that the advocate "Be a support system for the victim (help to reduce DA phone calls)" and "Communicate
victim concerns to prosecutor." Clearly, advocates are expected to mediate
between victims and attorneys, but to keep the "team approach" in mind.
This means, as Eliza explained to me early on, that victims are told that
they will be working as a team with advocates and prosecutors to prosecute the case, and they have to agree to waive the confidentiality that other
kinds of client/therapist relationships have.

    In the time that I spent in the district attorney's office, the closest rela-
tionships I established were with the victim advocates Eliza Nash and
Donna D'amato. In the course of time, I became privy to "back-stage" conversations (Goffman 1959) on many occasions, during which I learned a
great deal about tensions accruing to the victim advocate role. The dilemma that advocates face is a feature of their position within the criminal
justice system. They are social workers and therapists[10] in a legal and political institution unused to providing victim services, and the actual job
they do is sometimes belied by their title. That is, victim advocates' responsibility toward their supervisors, who are prosecutors, sometimes
places the advocates in the uncomfortable position of being able to do little
in the way of advocacy. Their role is similar to that of the public defender
described by Sudnow (1979), who mediates between prosecutor and defendant in the negotiation of a guilty plea, and conducts what Sudnow
ironically terms a "defense" by selling his client on the virtues of the bargain. Victim advocates sometimes conduct their "advocacy," it seems, by
convincing victims to cooperate with prosecutors, and by consoling them
when prosecutors fail to advocate in turn.

    I began to get a sense of the distress this causes some advocates very
early in the research, when I asked Donna if she would participate in a
taped interview. She and I were alone at the time, in the coffee shop across
the street from the office, and she said that she would need to check first
with Eliza. Then she expressed the concern that at that moment her "per-

spective" was very negative, that she was angry and was going to talk to Laura Lennox about the cause of her anger. I didn't learn what the problem was that day, but Donna dropped a few hints. She started to tell me about a woman whose case had not been prosecuted very aggressively by the stalking prosecutor handling it, Eric Xenelis. According to Donna, Eric had overlooked important evidence and the defendant received a minimal sentence as a consequence.

Donna also brought up a "grassroots" group being started by some "very political" victims who wanted to work with her specifically to address issues having to do with victims' anger and frustration at the lack of support they were getting. When I asked, "From prosecutors? Law enforcement?" she responded, "All of the above," and talked about cases not being treated as important, and women being treated as "hysterical," and not "validated," by law enforcers. Later, in the same conversation, when I read out loud a portion of a *New Yorker* article on stalking to Donna and Eliza, who had joined us by then, the two advocates exchanged knowing glances when I quoted a mention of the "few clear cut cases worth going to the cops about." Donna then said, "Maggie Hunt, that's just like Maggie Hunt." As I was to find out later, the advocates perceived Maggie, the deputy who assumed the stalking case load after Eric left, as similarly career- rather than victim-oriented.

Then, as our conversation was winding to a close, I asked offhandedly about "problems" with the deputy district attorneys. Eliza said that the district attorney's office was very political, and that they did not currently have prosecutors who were very excited about working with domestic violence cases. The attorneys in the DVU were overworked, she said, and— here she made a gagging gesture, with her tongue extended out far, signifying her disgust with these attitudes—domestic violence work was just a stepping stone to the top of the hierarchy, which was Homicide. I said, "Well, stalking is a homicide in progress, right?" (a phrase I had recently encountered) and Donna responded: "That's our motto!"[11]

The preceding account suggests some of the conflict advocates experience in their relationship with prosecutors. It is important to look at the role requirements of each because we will see that these tensions have important consequences for victims. The definitional work in which the advocates engage plays a critical part in the experience stalking victims have of the criminal justice system, as they in turn learn to advocate for themselves. As the conversation described above suggests, however, these varying forms of advocacy take place in an environment in which typifications of victimization can be problematic and contested. Advocates, on a daily basis, do what Holstein and Miller call "social problems work" (1997). That is, they actively categorize and typify the women whom they encounter as women of a particular sort—"domestic violence victims" or "stalking victims"—and thus as exemplars of the "problem" of domestic violence or stalking. In particular, the reality of victimization is "accomplished" (Holstein and Miller 1997:ix) through conversations advocates have with one another and with prosecutors, the very same communications the training handout indicates must occur.

This matters most because prosecutors often need convincing that a case is worthy of their efforts, especially when the "facts of the case" are ambiguous or the victim's credibility is questionable. Advocates are part of the same preparation processes Konradi describes for the prosecution of the rape cases she examined, in which

> patterns of preparation reflect the commingling of factors related to prosecutors' efforts to efficiently allocate their personal resources in the context of their organization positions. Prosecutors' resources include their emotional energy as well as their time. (1997:36–37)

While stalking cases, like most cases in the DVU, resolve as the result of negotiated plea bargains, stalking victims are particularly concerned with the length of time an offender spends in jail or on probation, the conditions of probation, and whether or not the plea is to felony or misdemeanor charges. And in the rare event of a trial, it is often the advocate who convinces the prosecutor that the victim is "good enough" to make this relatively risky endeavor worth pursuing. In sum, the advocate serves as an eligibility worker, determining which victims deserve the services the DVU provides, and then as a crucial constructor of the reality of the problem of victimization and of its seriousness. In this way, advocates are also "sympathy brokers" or "sympathy entrepreneurs" (Clark 1997). They act as intermediaries as they ascertain the moral worth of individual victims— an enterprise "which can translate into material boundaries distinguishing the provided-for from the passed-over when help, connection, and reprieve are meted out" (Ibid.: 125). At the same time, they work to keep these victims connected to and involved with extended and often extremely frustrating legal processes even as they buffer the prosecutors from victims' distress and "(help to reduce DA phone calls)."

Domestic Violence Stalking Victims and Cases

Who are these victims? Before introducing the stalking victims whom I came to know best and interviewed at length, I will briefly summarize a few characteristics of the cases and victims in the prosecutors' files. About one-third of the cases were resolved in each of the years 1995, 1996, and 1997, with the most (35 percent) resolved in 1997. Eighty-three of the cases (about two-thirds) were prosecuted by the three stalking deputies (Eric Xenelis, Maggie Hunt, and Carla Thompson) who held the position during these years. Donna D'Amato was the victim advocate in over half the cases (57 percent) for which advocate information existed, and Eliza Nash was the advocate for one-fifth of them. The cases were resolved as follows: in most (60 percent), the defendant pled *nolo contendre* (no contest) to at least one charge—usually not stalking. Another quarter of the defendants pled guilty to at least one charge. One case went to trial and the defendant was found guilty. The remainder of the cases (15 percent) were rejected or dismissed. Less than one-third (29 percent) of the defendants pled *nolo contendre* to a stalking charge and only 13 percent pled guilty. Given that a felony stalking conviction can result in from two to four years in prison in this state, sentences were relatively light. The average jail term for the 57 percent of the defendants who served time was 122 days, and the median sentence was 90 days. About one-fifth of the defendants did go to prison. The average prison sentence was 4.5 years, although this is skewed by a couple of long sentences; both the median and modal prison terms were 2.6 years.

Victims in Case Files

The stalking victims in this study were all women.[12] They ranged in age from 16 to 73, with the average age being 31 years. Based on a wealth code that provided the median household income for neighborhoods in the county, these victims were relatively poor. One third came from neighborhoods where the median household income was less than $35,000 a year and three-quarters from neighborhoods where the median household income was under $52,300.[13] African-American women were overrepresented in the sample; they are one quarter of the victims but only 9 percent of the population in the county. Hispanic women were only slightly overrepresented (14 percent of the victims and 12 percent of the population), while white women were underrepresented (55 percent of the victims and 67 percent of the population). There were no Asian-American victims, although Asian-Americans represent almost 9 percent of the population of the county.[14]

Most of the time, victims knew their stalkers intimately, even though the cases included those handled outside of the DVU as well as those prosecuted in the Unit. In over half the cases (57 percent) the stalker was the victim's former boyfriend, and over one-third of the time he was a former or current husband (14 percent and 22 percent, respectively). Acquaintances and friends accounted for the remaining cases; in no case was the stalker a stranger. Victims had known or been involved with their stalkers for periods of time ranging from one month to thirty years, with the median length of the relationship prior to separation being three years and the modal length two years. Over 84 percent of the women had known the defendant for more than a year. Victims reported a history of domestic violence in two-thirds of the cases; this figure was corroborated by the defendants' "Rap" sheets (criminal histories) in which 71 percent of the defendants had prior arrests for violent crimes, and over half of the total arrests (56 percent) were for clearly domestic violence related offenses.[15] Victims had children with their stalkers in 45 percent of the cases; this is important to note because custody orders often conflict with orders of protection, and shared children complicate women's and their advocates' ability to prevent and control stalking.

In sum, the women whose cases I studied claimed to be stalked by men they knew well, often men to whom they had been married and whose children they had borne. Their relationships with these men were long term and violent, for the most part, and their attempts to leave these relationships were made difficult not only by the actions of their former partners, but by the intimacy and history of these partnerships. As the victim narratives in the crime reports, and the testimony of these women indicate, exiting is a complex process confounded by complicated human relationships the criminal justice system is often not prepared to deal with effectively. This is even more apparent in the interviews and observations I conducted, and it is the victims I spoke with who are introduced next.

Valley City "Survivors" of Stalking

The stalking victims interviewed, both formally and informally, were mostly women who were introduced by Donna D'Amato or Eliza Nash. The first woman I interviewed was the victim featured in the magazine article that alerted me to the stalking prosecution taking place in the DVU, the woman I call "Nadine Peterson." Nadine was 32 years old at the time of our first interview and had been stalked by an former boyfriend in a case that had generated some publicity, in part because Nadine was proactive, articulate, and telegenic, because her case had some dramatic elements, and because Nadine enjoyed her role as a spokeswoman for stalking victims. Nadine is white, considers herself "educated" despite the lack of a college degree, and was working in the restaurant business when I interviewed her. The man who stalked Nadine was convicted of stalking and sent to prison; during the course of the research he was granted an appeal but was reconvicted in a second trial. Nadine presented herself as something of an expert on stalking, emphasizing the talks on stalking that she had given and the television appearances she had made, as well as owning a "complete reference library" on stalking, when I first discussed interviewing her.[16]

The second woman I interviewed was "Caity Ingalls." Where Nadine exuded confidence and a willingness to make her case publicly, Caity was edgy and clearly unhappy about the prosecution of her case. The man who stalked Caity, according to her story and data in the case file, was a former police officer with many connections in Valley City and an apparently almost flawless presentation of self who instilled a reasonable doubt in the judge about Caity's own complicity in the case. As a consequence, and with the help of a good defense attorney, he pled guilty to a misdemeanor charge and was put on probation. Caity had received what she believed were subtle indications that he was still stalking her, and was very fearful even as our interview took place. Caity also filed a lawsuit against the Valley City Police Department for negligence in their hiring of the defendant, which she alleged placed her in danger. Caity was white, had been to college but not graduated, and was self-employed as a legal consultant. She was 35 years old and lived alone with her young daughter.

The next woman I formally interviewed was "Melinda Sanchez." Melinda was a college student in her mid-20s from one of the worst neighborhoods in Valley City. Melinda had not been able to convince anyone to pursue arrest or prosecution of the man she claimed was stalking her, but Donna D'Amato overheard her pleading her case to a receptionist in the lobby one afternoon, and had been counseling her in a somewhat unofficial capacity for several months. At the time of our interview, Donna described Melinda as someone who had "burned her bridges" with law enforcement, making her one of Donna's "toughest clients." Melinda's interactions with her former boyfriend and with law enforcement, we will see, exemplify many of the problems victims' own behaviors create for them and for those who would help them.

I then met the three founders of the Valley City Stalking Survivors' support group, "Kathy Felson," "Ellen Nichols," and "Carolina Garcia." All three were middle-aged divorced women with children who worked as claims adjusters for the same large insurance company and had been put in touch with each other through the auspices of the security personnel where they worked. Kathy's former husband had no criminal history and had received probation, causing Kathy a great deal of bitterness towards the criminal justice system—especially as she believed that important evidence in the case had been overlooked due to the negligence of the prosecutor. She was the single parent of a young daughter and lived near her own parents, who provided her with a great deal of emotional support and assistance with childcare. Ellen's former husband was convicted of spousal rape rather than stalking, and was serving a prison sentence. She was raising their three very young children by herself. Carolina Garcia was Hispanic and the mother of two teen-aged boys. When we met, at a meeting of the VCSS group, she agreed to be interviewed, but before the interview took place she disappeared under extremely suspicious circumstances. Both a former husband and a former boyfriend were suspects in the case. Her case gained national publicity as a suspected homicide that was never solved, and resulted in a number of interviews and speaking engagements by Kathy and Ellen.

Another member of the group, "Vanessa Ames," was white, a 27-year-old medical assistant with a toddler son and an former husband with whom she shared custody and was on good terms. She said that she was being stalked by a coworker with whom she had become friends, and she had obtained a restraining order, but the man had not been arrested and the case had not been referred for prosecution. "Lee Ann Yamamoto" was one of the undergraduate college women I interviewed about dating relationships. She was a 22-year-old Japanese-American woman, and in the course of our interview revealed that her former boyfriend had attempted to murder her, and the case had been prosecuted in an adjoining county. The other woman whose case plays a particularly important part in this report is "Winnie Newton," a working class African-American woman in her early thirties who lived alone and in whose case I served as a quasi-advocate, when Donna could not accompany her to court and asked me to fill in. The man who admitted to numerous violations of the restraining order and threats to Winnie was acquitted of stalking in a jury trial; as we will see, her case also reveals a great deal about the interplay between victims, stalkers, and law enforcement and the consequences thereof.

CONCLUSION: A ROCK AND A HARD PLACE

Thus far, I have set the stage for the account that follows by showing how stalking has come to be defined as a crime and, moreover, as a form of domestic violence. The women whose stories appear here seek to use new legislation as a resource for managing violent and unwanted continuing interaction with men they are trying to leave. To do so, they must convince criminal justice system actors at varying levels of the fact of their victimization. That is, they must "accomplish" victimization (Holstein and Miller 1990) through complicated processes of identity work. However, they encounter their crucial and critical audiences not simply as potential stalking victims, but as women and as victims of domestic violence, two further identities that shape interpretive frameworks. In order to make their claims heard and to be believed, women who are being stalked must prove that they are truly victims of a crime and that they play no part in its initiation or reoccurrence. This requires much of them; every move they make will be scrutinized and there is almost nothing they do that is not subject to multiple interpretations, many of them unfavorable. It is like walking a tightrope held at one end by an enemy, over an abyss, toward a destination presenting worse yet hazards.

In chapter 2 I show how women who have been legally defined as "stalking victims," or who define themselves as such, interpret the behavior of their former intimates. I use the "victim narratives" from crime reports, interview data, testimony in court, and participant observation in the Valley City Survivors of Stalking support group to explore these women's perceptions and understandings of their experience. I discuss how courtship, surveillance, the threat of violence, and actual violence appear to shape the definition of stalking situations from victims' perspectives. I then delineate some of the actions taken by these women, on the basis of the meanings they confer. I examine how these women describe their attempts to manage the emotions of their former partners, while simultaneously dealing with their own sometimes conflicted feelings. I conclude this chapter by examining some complexities of this confusion and the compliance (or resistance) these mixed emotions may engender. Sometimes women will not open the door a crack no matter how hard a pounding it takes, but sometimes, the door is flung wide and the "enemy" invited within. This perplexes or astonishes the outside observer, but may make perfect sense from the other side of that door, and this chapter places the reader in the role of the victim to illuminate her decision making.

Some of the perplexed observers' attributions of meaning and responsibility directly affect the lives of victims. In chapter 3 I examine how women become "victims" in the criminal justice system. The ways in which victims respond to stalking shape the course of prosecution. Police officers responding to the scene of a "crime," victim advocates, and prosecutors all serve as "eligibility workers" determining who is, or who is not, worthy of attention and aid. I look at how the actions victims take in response to the threat they perceive are interpreted by some of these significant actors. In order to successfully claim the "victim" identity that is the prerequisite for gaining the assistance of law enforcement, women must display the emotion *fear* in ways that conform to culturally derived "feeling rules" (Hochschild 1979, 1983). When stalking victims violate standards for emotion display, in their interactions with either their pursuers or their would-be saviors, they may not get the help they seek. Thus, sometimes, women's continued interaction with both stalkers and law enforcement actors affects their ability to create and sustain credible victim identities. Almost any action a victim takes or presentation she makes has the potential for inducing negative identity attributions; it seems the "tightrope," or identity dilemma, is inherent in the stalking situation.

Chapter 4 takes leave, temporarily, from the Domestic Violence Unit and explores the cultural underpinnings of intimate stalking victimization. It is based upon sorority women and other coeds' interpretations of relatively innocuous unwanted attention, or "forcible interaction," primarily in hypothetical scenarios presented in a self-administered questionnaire. These are young women encountering attentions clearly described as undesired, and that are thus forcible, that is, against their will. Nevertheless, the data from this survey indicate a great deal of mixed emotions engendered by the scenarios and by the actual experiences of these women—an ambivalence particularly true of attentions associated with romance and courtship. When women discussed their interpretations of these behaviors, their accounts suggested that these behaviors confuse and cloud the issue of the violation of the boundaries they have set, in some cases leading them to permit forcible interaction to continue despite their annoyance or fear. This is all the more likely an outcome when the relationship is more intimate than casual. An exploration of the symbolic environment within which these women operate (in the form of a cultural analysis of romantic images in fairy tales, old and new) places intimate stalking in its context in the culture of courtship and romance. I conclude with a discussion of the ambivalence and acquiescence that I argue emerges from this definitional framework—and their implications for the victimization processes occurring in the DVU.

In sum, by examining how the experience of stalking shapes a victim's decisions, and how the choices she makes affect her experience of prosecution, we can learn more about the role she may play in her own downfall. We can do this if we conceive of victimization as a process of claiming and maintaining victim identities over a period of time that includes the crimes that occur *and* their legal resolution. By exploring the meanings attached to the actions women take, we can trace some relationships between attributions of responsibility and victim blaming, in cases where ambiguity is more the norm than the exception. We can see what it takes to establish credibility under the most difficult of circumstances, or if this is even possible. We can illuminate some of the consequences of being discredited. Finally, an analysis of the articulation of victims' identity work, criminal justice organizations, and the larger culture can reveal how human actors struggle to create themselves within the constraints of powerful social forces arrayed against them. In the fifth and concluding chapter, I focus on the question of "what makes a victim?" Here I review the victimization, and "revictimization" processes, described so far, revisiting the themes of victim precipitation and victim blaming and showing how these are all interactive and interwoven processes. After articulating the contribution of this work to victimology, I examine what it reveals about emotion work, identity management, and social problems construction. I explore some possibilities for further locating stalking victim's experiences within their historical, cultural, and hierarchical contexts. I conclude with a discussion of the policy implications for victim advocacy that emerge from this analysis.

NOTES

1. Verbatim transcript from interviews, hearings, and trials has been edited for clarity, as have excerpts from case files. Ellipses indicate material that has

been deleted. I have been as careful as I can not to alter meaning through this selective process.

2. One victim had a restraining order in her purse at the time of her death, a fact portrayed in the media as a poignant indication of the inadequacy of civil remedies (Beck 1992).

3. Numerous law review articles discuss fears that antistalking legislation is too narrow or vague to enforce, or unconstitutionally broad. The laws either fail to provide adequate protection for stalking victims or they criminalize protected behavior, or both, in these interpretations (e.g., Bradburn 1992; Bradfield 1998; Diacovo 1995; Faulkner and Hsiao 1994; Morin 1993; Morville 1993).

4. All the names used are pseudonyms.

5. Intensive interviewing is a technique designed to elicit the experiences and inner lives of interviewees in their own words, through a guided conversation with the interviewer (Charmaz 1991; Lofland and Lofland 1995). As I explained to Donna, the interviewing I proposed to conduct was entirely open-ended and guided to a great extent by the victim herself, making it much easier to obviate her distress and discuss only the topics with which she was comfortable. I assured Donna that the emotional well-being of the informant was of far more importance to me than any data I might collect, and I think this reassured her.

6. I was not able to enter the remaining seven cases into my quantitative database before leaving the field. However, I was able to transcribe some of their contents, and thus I include them in the total number of cases read.

7. While I cannot speak for employees, my own experience of entrance to the building was that of belonging to a somewhat exclusive club—once I was given the code!—and of separation from the often motley public who came to the office for less lofty reasons, and it seems likely that other "members" felt similarly set apart, consciously or not. This distance is exacerbated by the typically vast differences in social class between those who gain entrance to the interior and those who do not, that is, "street people" and the occasional person who is trying to gain access to information about a case or the ear of an advocate or prosecutor.

8. The Domestic Violence Home Court was a specialized court in which all domestic violence cases were vertically prosecuted, that is, handled by a single attorney from filing through resolution. Project goals were to "address the problem of a scattered and uneven criminal justice system response to domestic violence" and "retain as close to possible as 100% of the Domestic Violence cases for vertical prosecution, victim advocacy & specialized investigative staff support" (from a DVU data collection document). In addition to the two prosecutors assigned to the Home Court, there was a specialized unit in the public defender's office for representation of offenders, a specialized probation officer, and cases were all heard before a single judge "trained to appropriately manage the litigants" and "knowledgeable in the dynamics of Domestic Violence" (from a DVU data collection document).

9. The apparent discrepancy in numbers of stalking cases results from cases resolved in 1997 in which charges were initially brought in previous years.

10. Approximately half of the advocates had MFCC (Marriage and Family Counseling) credentials, and half had LCSW (Licensed Clinical Social Worker) degrees. Laura Lennox had both.

11. I think it was at this point that Donna and Eliza began to develop some confidence that I took their concerns seriously, even if the deputies were somewhat less interested.

12. While national statistics indicate that males are also victims of stalking, only two of the felony cases generated by the DVU computer analysts involved a female stalker and a male victim, and for one of them, I was unable to locate the file. It is likely that female stalkers are less violent than males, and that male victims are less likely to seek the help of law enforcement. This could account for their underrepresentation in this sample. Because these cases are such a minority in my sample, they are not part of this analysis.

13. These median income household incomes need some contextualizing; in this county, the median home price was over $200,000 at the time of the study.

14. The overrepresentation of some racial and ethnic groups and underrepresentation of others is consistent with statistics gathered for all the cases handled in the Domestic Violence Unit. These differences likely to be related to reporting patterns rather than actual rates of occurrence in these populations. For example, in an analysis of all DVU cases handled between July and November in 1999 (Kingsnorth 1999) there were significant differences in the willingness of Asian-American women to report domestic violence, to seek medical attention, and to cooperate with prosecution over time; these victims were much less likely to do any of these things. Thus it is possible that their absence from the stalking cases I examined has to do with these kinds of factors.

15. When the charge is "assault" or "battery" it is not always apparent whether this is domestic violence, even if it may in fact be an assault on a cohabitant or former spouse or partner.

16. Nadine used the jargon of some of the current research on stalking in our first conversation, and mentioned how much time she had spent "prepping" for a talk on stalking, prompting me to note to myself that the "trick" with interviewing her would be to somehow "get past the public performance of stalking victim to the more private self" that could more candidly reveal her experience. Later, I realized that the performance of an interview is significantly altered when the person who is being interviewed has gone through their stories many times already, as victims in criminal cases have. There is an element of guardedness and a rehearsed quality to what is disclosed, as a consequence of repeated questions and attacks upon credibility.

2

I'll Be Watching You:
The Lived Experience of Intimate Stalking

In this chapter I ask: How does a stalking situation appear to those women who ultimately seek the help of the criminal justice system, and how do they feel about what is going on? As we will see, how a woman defines the behaviors of her former partner influences how she feels about those actions on his part, and her emotions, in turn, shape her responses. And it is the actions a woman takes in response to stalking and the emotions she manages and expresses, perhaps even more than the behaviors in which the stalker engages, that influence her ability to claim and to convince others that she is really a stalking victim.

In later chapters I will theorize about the ways in which women's thinking, feeling and acting are shaped by the social forces and cultural frameworks within which stalking and prosecution take place. I will also consider, in chapter 4, instances in which stalking occurs as an attempt to *establish* relationships, rather than to prevent exit from them. Emerson, Ferris, and Gardner (1998), for example, illuminate the ambiguities of "relational" stalking that largely involve the former, and that so eerily reflect normal courtship—albeit in a distorted fashion. For now, however, I seek simply to paint the most vivid possible portrait of the felony stalking victims' immediate reality and the ways in which they cope with it, making sense of it from *their* perspective. These women, almost entirely, are attempting to leave men with whom they have been partnered. The intimate lens through which they view their experience both colors and sometimes also blurs it, and is shaped by a somewhat different set of ambiguities.

INTIMATION AND INTIMIDATION:
THE INVENTIVENESS OF STALKERS

When Patricia Tjaden and Nancy Thoennes asked the women who responded to their National Violence Against Women Survey about stalking, they asked if anyone, other than bill collectors, telemarketers, or other sales people, had ever done any of the following: "Followed or spied on you? Sent you unsolicited letters or written correspondence? Made unsolicited phone calls to you? Stood outside your home, school, or workplace? Showed up at places you were at even though he or she had no business being there? Left unwanted items for you to find? Tried to communicate in other ways against your will? Vandalized your property or destroyed something you loved?" (1998a:17). If the woman reported that any of these had occurred on more than one occasion, and that they were very frightened or feared that they or someone close to them would come to serious harm, they met the survey definition of "stalking victim."

All of these, and many more, are behaviors reported in the data I examined. When these things start happening to a woman, her first task is to interpret her experience and decide what, if anything, to do about it. Here, "victims" are the women who claimed this identity for themselves by making the initial police reports that began every stalking prosecution, and whose stories then became part of case files. As suggested above, in addition to reading their files, I met some of these women, and talked to them about what was happening to them. On a few occasions I accompanied them to court or attended Valley City Survivors of Stalking meetings with them. In the course of observing, participating, interviewing, transcribing tapes of the interviews, and reviewing the case files, I found that victims reported a wide range of behaviors directed toward them by former husbands, former boyfriends, and other intimates, seemingly limited only by the imagination of the stalker.

It is useful to group the behaviors into several broad categories for the purposes of analysis, and thus I have arranged data as follows: "courtship behaviors," "surveillance behaviors," "threatening behaviors," and "violent behaviors." I will examine each of these in turn. Note, however, that in victims' descriptions of their experiences, there is much overlap between categories (e.g., leaving cards or gifts for the victim, which may be a romantic or threatening tactic contingent upon the content of the message and the context of the interaction). This can make it difficult to decide which category a behavior falls into, as there are multiple possible interpretations of the things that stalkers do—and a single interaction may induce a complex series of sometimes nearly simultaneous responses from a victim, some of which also fall into more than one category. These are complexities to which we need attend as we proceed.

Furthermore, as these reports are primarily from the perspective of victims, we can only infer the intentions of the defendant, in much the same way judges and juries determine criminal "intent," based on the evidence presented to them. My goal here is not to explain why stalkers do what they do, but to suggest why women might respond to stalkers in the ways indicated in their accounts. Stalking is an interactive process, however, in which a dialogue of sorts, or a dance, takes place; the moves each actor makes are predicated on the lines of action taken by the other. Thus, I ask readers to place themselves in the victim's role to assess how she might be influenced by behaviors that appear to be designed to sway her emotions. We cannot read the mind of the stalker, but as he draws upon cultural understandings we share with him and his victim, we can imagine that he courts her to induce her to return to him, spies on her both to monitor her behavior and to frighten her, threatens her to instill fear and compliance with his demands, and inflicts violence both to express his rage and to frighten and control her. As we will see, her responses bear out these interpretations, and these imaginations help us to make sense out of what she does.

Courtship

Table 2.1 lists the forms of stalking and other forcible interaction reported by victims and the percentage of women in the case files who reported each behavior.

The first set of behaviors I want to consider is those that fall into the "courtship behaviors" category. Although the National Violence Against Women Survey data do not include enough detail to determine the form unwanted communications take, these kinds of "romantic" communications and interactions are reported by stalking victims, who consider them part of their stalking experience. As the table indicates, in about one-third of the cases examined, the victim said that her former partner told her he loved her, and roughly the same number of women reported their former partners begging them to return to the relationship. Often these behaviors take precisely the form they do in nonviolent relationships; stalkers leave flowers, cards, and gifts, or entreaties on message machines, or declare their feelings in face-to-face interactions. For one who is not experiencing stalking, these communications per se may seem innocuous. What makes them especially important to consider are the ways in which, because they mimic culturally appropriate romantic interaction, they sometimes confound interpretations of behavior as stalking (Emerson, Ferris, and Gardner 1998). In some cases, they confuse women and make it more difficult for the latter to decide what to do, or to determine whether or not it is time to seek help.

Lenore Walker, in much-cited research (1979) on what she frames as a cyclical process in violent relationships, writes of a "honeymoon phase" in which a contrite batterer showers his partner with gifts and protestations of love. Women who are leaving violent relationships are also susceptible to these kinds of tactics. Because the men they are leaving are men with

Table 2.1. Defendant Behaviors Reported in Stalking "Victim Narratives"

Courtship	
professing love	36%
begging victim to return	35%
Surveillance	
following	53%
drive by victim's home/work	26%
spying/watching	26%
tapping phones, listening in	07%
Threats	
threatening to kill victim	75%
breaking in/vandalizing victim's car/home	62%
entering victim's home w/o permission	66%
verbally abusing victim	56%
threatening to hurt victim	46%
threatening victim with a weapon	30%
threatening suicide	30%
Violence	
physical assault	52%
preventing victim from leaving some place	32%
sexually assaulting victim	10%
preventing victim from calling for help	25%
Other Behaviors*	
showing up at victim's home	85%
repeated telephoning	77%
showing up at victim's work	38%
contacting victim's family	36%
leaving written messages	36%

*These are behaviors that can fall into any of the categories, depending upon the content of the interaction. For example, cards and letters could be romantic or threatening, falling into courtship or expressive violence categories.

whom they have been intimate and about whom they often still care deeply, even unwanted attention, when it fits within cultural constructions of love, can be interpreted as flattering or romantic. This can occur even when avowals of love are intermingled with surveillance, threats and violence.

Winnie Newton, who filed thirteen police reports before her former boyfriend was arrested, described the phenomenon succinctly in her testimony in a preliminary hearing. On being asked what the defendant said to her on one of the many occasions when he was alleged to have shown up on her doorstep, unwanted and uninvited, Winnie said:

A: I couldn't recall what he said. Probably same thing he always was saying.
Q: Which was?
A: He loves me. He wants to be together. We could work things out.

In the prosecutors' case files examined, there are numerous reports of such efforts by the defendents. Often, the attention takes the form of letters to victims, such as in the following excerpt:

St. Patricks Day 1997
Dear Jane, My Love My Life
You can call the police, [various relatives and friends of hers], the National Guard whoever but I am not going to give up or stop loving you. I was your best friend and we had so many wonderful times together. My love for you is something I have never experienced in my life. I love you and I know you still love me, honey. You're my inspiration my reason for living. You've changed my life. I love you with all my heart. I love you so. I think about your beautiful face the smell of your hair. Your beautiful little hands and feet the way you smile everything. And it breaks my heart. My goal and purpose in life is to make you the happiest most content woman in the world. Think about us at [a fancy hotel] in the lounge by the fireplace kind of dancing and saying how much we loved each other . . . Your [sic] my life my Angel. I love you and always will. Please forgive me and please believe what I'm saying to you. I'm so lonely for you. I feel like I'm dead inside. My best friend my love and my life isn't with me. I'm so sorry. I love you with all my heart and always will[,]
John

Here, the defendant begged for forgiveness for the violence that he had inflicted on the victim, even as he indicated that he would persist in his pursuit of the victim no matter who she called—because he loved her so much. In her notes on another case, a victim advocate wrote:

Since the V [victim] broke off desired contact with D, [defendant] approx. 2 months after their actual separation, the D has repeatedly called, followed, contacted by writing, threatened and assaulted V. On 11/3/94, which was V & D's 11th anniversary, he sent a dozen roses to V at her work place. He sent flowers on other occasions. The D also left cards and notes on V's front door and her car door or window. The D has also begged her to return to the relationship. He has told her that "I was just beginning to show you what a good husband I can be" and that if "you come back and live with me, I'll show you."

An interview with a victim by a prosecutor's investigator told a similar story:

Johnson stated that when Peters would make contact with her, he would always want to talk to her about getting back together, telling her she had

promised to always love him; that he loved her and didn't want the relationship to end. She always responded telling Peters the relationship was
over, to stay away. She has received many letters and notes. Most of them are
love letters/notes, some are threatening letters/notes. The note reads, "I
won't be without you, so now I have to do what to talk to you?" Then it is
signed, "I love you."

The following are a series of messages left on the message machine of a
woman I call "Mary," illustrating the persistent, romantic, pleading, and
apologetic character of many of these attempts at interaction:

You know—only God knows how much I hurt—only God knows how I care
about you—how much I love you—everybody else knows—I love you with
all my soul, with all my mind—with all my heart—I love you to death and
I will always be there for you Mary—If I had the chance to be with you
again—I will do anything—anything—for you—and I mean that—and I
will always mean it.

Mary—I got something special for you Mary—and I got some presents for
you from for the Christmas—and—please Mary—be my friend—that's all I
want from you—I want nothing—I don't want the world. I just want your
friendship—it's all I want—I love you Mary—till the day I die I will always
love you and I hope you believe it.

Baby—this is me—look—maybe it's easier for you to forget about me but
it's not easy for me to forget about you—I love, never loved anybody more
than I have loved you—and I beg you, Mary give me another chance—just
be my friend—you don't have to be my girlfriend or nothing—just be my
friend—Mary, I'll promise you—and I promise to God I will never hurt you
or use you or lay my hand on you as long as I live.

Remember, Mary, nobody is ever going to love you like the way I do—you
don't know how much I suffer—all I ever do is think about you—I love
you—whenever you need me I'll be there for you—no matter what happens—I love you with all my soul, Mary.

Hi, baby, I just called to say that I love you—that my heart is always with
you—and I will always be there for you no matter what happens—even if
you are the last girl on the earth—I will always be there for you—and I will
always forgive you—I love you with all my soul—with all my heart—and I
pray to God to bring us back together one day—and I know its never too late
if you only give me the chance I would make you the happiest girl in the
world—if only—

I love you with all my soul—with all my heart—whoever you're with—
wherever you go—I will always be there for you and I pray to God that one

day you start believing me and trusting me—so we can have a happy life together—that we can move somewhere far with each other—I love you
baby—I hope you always keep that in your mind—bye.

Sometimes the stalker would remind the victim of the nature of their previous relationship, especially when the two had been married. Thus, a letter to a victim began:

Better or worse
Richer or poorer
Sickness and in health
Remember those
Hi I love you

and went on to say, "Baby please think about us and our son and everything the past 16 years and please take me back I love you God knows I
love you and you know I love you." Another defendant referred both to
the past and discussed a future, happier relationship:

Darlene, my love, please carefully read this, and take into consideration the
time we have invested into our family and each other and most of all
please—please believe my words. You are a wonderful person Darlene I am
too. I have a plan, a new condo, I'm not working nights, and we'd have 1,300
dollars more a month than you and the kids have now. I'll watch them during the day like old times. And continualy [sic] look for that good day job
while we have a happy family. We sleep at night-It feels good when I can.
With my life complete agin [sic] I could every night you could too!

Stalkers, their friends, and their relatives often used the language of
courtship and romance to explain the stalkers' violent as well as nonviolent behavior; hence it serves as a "vocabulary of motive" (Mills 1940) that
can justify stalking behavior. For example, an employer of a man convicted
of setting his former wife's house on fire, in an interview with an investigator, had this to say in explanation:

Ya well I mean it's ya know he, he really loved her and ya know when things
got tough ya know and he lost his job on top of all the other shit ya know it
was kinda like she just kinda bailed on him ya know cause he wasn't working and

Similarly, an acquaintance of a defendant told a police officer the defendant was "very much in love with Anne. He is obsessed with her. He continues to believe that she will change her mind and they will begin their
relationship again." In another case, a defendant told a probation officer
that "he acted in all instances incorrectly, as he was so completely in love

with the victim that it prevented him from thinking clearly." Similarly, in a police report, a friend of the victim described repeated phone calls by the defendant. "He was looking for Lisa," the friend said, and quoted the defendant: "He said, 'All I did was love Lisa.'" In an tape-recorded interview, a defendant responded to a query about why he'd vandalized clothing belonging to the victim:

A: Wouldn't you, if she was going out with somebody?
Q: Why don't you find somebody else?
A: When you love somebody, you love somebody. She won't even come out of the house and talk.

In one case, a young defendant was expelled from his high school after assaulting the victim. He then used intermediaries to send gifts and flowers to her before coming to campus one day and stabbing her repeatedly (after seeing "hickies" on her neck). The boy's father said to an investigator,

My son is a very serious young man. He loved this young girl too much, I think, and he had a very difficult time understanding that he had to go on with his life. My son has always been a very tranquil, peaceful boy. He is just very intense and very serious, and he loved this girl too much.

A friend of the defendant said, "It was obvious Miguel was madly in love with Chelsea and would have done anything for her." The defendant himself explained the stabbing in terms of love:

She was my girlfriend and I still love her. I was mad and jealous. I told her, is it okay to give me another chance? And you know, sometimes she told me yeah, and sometimes she tell me nah. She didn't want to talk nice to me. I went all the way inside her class. And I gave her some candies, and a rose. And I said here, to see if it would make her a little happier. I got mad since I saw the hickies, 'cause she told me that she didn't have a boyfriend. She made fun of me 'cause I would talk to her on the phone and she would make fun of me. 'Cause me, I loved her a lot, I always gave her presents. I gave her little hearts and many things, roses and all that. And she would say sometimes, how could I say, sometimes she would say yes, sometimes she would talk nice with me and sometimes she wouldn't, and that would make me get mad, because what she did to me felt bad and that's why, when I saw the hickies, I got mad, mad 'cause I love her a lot, well, I loved her, I still love her.

This excerpt is illustrative of several elements of courtship in stalking cases. The defendant described repeatedly seeking to win back the victim's affections in time-honored ways, and cited his love as the motivating force for his violent attempt on her life. And when he said that "sometimes she would say yes, sometimes she would talk nice with me and sometimes she wouldn't," his words begin to suggest that his tactics were affecting her responses.

Courtship behaviors can exert a powerful influence upon these women's decisionmaking. One of the variables I coded for in the case files was whether victims had tried to leave their partners before the break up that initiated the behaviors resulting in stalking charges. Almost one-third of the stalking victims in this study reported making repeated attempts to leave some time prior to the prosecution of their case, and at least eight women who had left defendants (and then reported being stalked) resumed living with them even as their cases were being prosecuted. Nadine Peterson reported returning to the relationship a day after Victor Kinkaid violently "ended" it. Victor gave Nadine a card and flowers and said, according to her:

> "Oh my God I just had a really stressful day. I missed you. I can't believe I broke up with you. You know how much I love you. I would never do anything to hurt you, and please understand that I didn't mean to rip your phone out of the wall. I'll come and replace it and repair it and fix it, and I'll do everything I can."

"You know," she explained, "so to me I'm thinking, okay, everybody has a bad day right?" She then said that after "fifteen, twenty" phone calls in which Victor kept insisting "I want to be with you. I want to be with you," she gave in and went on a trip with him.

This is how Melinda Sanchez described a pattern of returning to a relationship in which she claimed there was extensive violence, prior to the stalking that occurred when she finally left.

> At first I was able to pack my things and leave, but I'd always get like cards, and letters, and you know, he'd call me and say that his mother died and left him a bunch of money, and he and I are gonna go on a trip and stuff, and I'd go running back . . . he'd always have a way of getting me back. And as long as I was hooked, met him some place in a restaurant to talk to him, that was that, I would be back in his house.

When I asked her what she meant by "hooked," Melinda cleared her throat and paused a minute. Then she said, "I loved him, the day I met him, I love him to this day. Um, I was not strong enough to be able to stay away from him." Although this might seem surprising in light of the extent of the violence Melinda had experienced, her ambivalence was not uncommon.

In the arson/stalking case described above, the defendant wrote a letter at one point in which he said:

and still my heart cries every day for my sweetheart. I knew I was looseing
[sic] you, my wife, my friend, my world and there was nothing I could do to
stop it and all the things I did, I did for you and because I loved you. You've
done me wrong and no matter what
    I will always love you.
    Your husband,
          Steve
P.S. Please believe that I always wanted to just come home. Just be home with
my family, home.

In the arson case during a preliminary hearing, the victim was asked by
the defense attorney about times she had met with the defendant after
their separation. Given the tone of the letter above, her responses seem
reasonable:

> A: There were a couple of times that we met at a restaurant before the re-
> straining order . . . we would talk, have a cup of coffee. I tried to make
> things as peaceful as possible, but I noticed the times that I would get to-
> gether with him, that I felt uncomfortable, thought it would be in my best
> interest not to have contact with Jason.
> Q. Did you and Mr. Jackson discuss reconciling your marriage after the sep-
> aration happened?
> A. After the separation we had, like I said, got together over coffee. We tried
> talking. And at that time, I thought if—it would have been nice, I would
> have liked to have gotten together if things would have worked out.

Here is a terse victim narrative in an application for a restraining order,
in the same case in which I quoted the letter beginning "Better or worse,"
above. It reveals how romantic tactics work even when the violence is very
recent:

> 11/23/96—afternoon—beat me, put gun to my head & threatened to kill
> me—husb. calmed down enough to let me go get pack of cigarettes—es-
> caped—went to friend's home—not there—checked into Howard Johnson's
> & got a room—husband called motels and got lucky—found out room # and
> came there—was calm—had bottle of champagne so let him in.

In a case in which the defendant left flowers on the victim's car, candles
on her floor, notes and a cardboard heart on her walls, and a heart-shaped
pillow on her bed, a police officer summarized an interview with the victim thus:

> 08/03 or 08/04, approximately 9:45 a.m., suspect called her at her residence.
> Suspect told her he loved her, was going to kill himself, and wanted to say
> goodbye. Suspect was crying. suspect told her he wanted to see her. Suspect

also told her if he could not have her, he didn't want to live. The morning after the call . . . she went up to the door to say goodbye to the suspect. Suspect was nice to her. In the residence, she and suspect started talking and praying. Suspect asked her for sex. She consented. She was not scared. Suspect did not force her. There was no fear.

It is interesting that the victim reported being unafraid of the defendant, given that in addition to inundating her with romantic messages and symbols, he had assaulted her while they were together. When she left, he had beaten her dog nearly to death.

Not all women are so easily swayed, however. One victim said of her former boyfriend's protestations of love, "I feel he was messing with my mind." Kathy Felson—who claimed to love her former husband Nick very much prior to his drug addiction and subsequent abuse and stalking of her—refused to interpret his offerings in the way he presumably intended. Here she described his efforts to define the relationship to their friends:

And of course the line to them was, you know, "I love her so much, I want her and [our daughter] to come home, and I'm trying to do everything I can to get them to do that," and you know, "I don't know why Kathy won't come home, I love her so much, she's gotta know that." So there was this sort of um, very subtle thing that was happening with friends, it was sort of like, "I ran into Nick, and he misses you so much." Sort of like, "You should go back to him." They never said that, and of course the people that I was very close to knew at that point, you know, I had begun "telling my tale," um, but the casual acquaintances would be like, you know, "He just, he seems so much in pain, Kathy." Yeah, 'cause he's having to take care of himself, maybe?

In this example, there is both the suggestion that relationships, and separations, occur in social contexts rather than in vacuums and the hint that Kathy has come to redefine Nick's behavior as more instrumental than expressive. Kathy also related how her former husband would leave gifts and flowers for her at her workplace, and she told me that she threw them in the garbage. She had earlier described herself as flattered by the attentions her husband had paid her while they were together, despite ongoing abuse, but added,

You know, maybe a few months before that it would have been, "Well he hits me and abuses me emotionally but isn't that sweet." Where by that point it was, it was just like, "Stop. Don't do this anymore." I mean, even giving me that: "If you just come home, you can make it all better." You know, 'cause "You have that kind of influence over me," giving me that was not flattering. It was just like, unh unh [grunting negatively]. No. We're not going to play this.

Despite being temporarily lulled into compliance by Victor's entreaties, Nadine Peterson left the relationship following the next violent interaction, and began the process of resisting romantic, and later, threatening tactics on Victor's part:

> N: So um, the next day I decided that that I wasn't going to take this. He had bruised my arms. The bruises were worse on my arms. I was totally in hysterics. Um something had to be done because, the phone calls were coming. "You will talk to me. You're gonna talk to me. Why won't you talk to me? Don't you know I love you?" I'm talking ten, fifteen, twenty, twenty five, thirty, and they just increased in number of phone calls.
>
> I: Were you picking up?
>
> N: Um sometimes yes, sometimes no. You know it got to the point where finally I would pick up and say, "Would you please just quit calling!" "I love you. Talk to me." Click. The phone would ring again. Finally we turned off all the ringers and unplugged all the phones. And then the next morning, which was Sunday morning, I called the sheriff's department and a sheriff came out with my mom and dad.

As soon as it was clear that his gestures of romance were not having the desired effect on Nadine, Victor began stalking her in non-romantic ways.

The shift in the definition of the situation can be dramatic; as one woman reported to a police officer:

> I have been separated from my husband for about a year and a half. This morning I was walking to my car in the parking lot at my apartments; I was going to go downtown. I saw Richard putting a rose on my car. I asked him what he was doing there and he said he wanted to get back together. I said I didn't want to and tried to get into my car. He then said I ruined his life. He asked me if I wanted to go out to dinner. I said "No, fuck off, get away from me and get out of my life." He said he didn't know why I wouldn't go out with him. That is when he hit me.

In sum, many of the victims' narratives in the case files, and several of the victims I interviewed, described attempts by former partners to convince them to return to the relationship, using the imagery and language of romantic love and pursuit. Some of the time, these communications apparently have the desired affect, but even when the victim stays away, she may be influenced by them—a point I argue further in the discussion of victims' responses to stalking that follows this examination of stalking behaviors. First, however, I turn to experiences of stalking that clearly diverge from cultural norms governing courtship and romance, even as they sometimes are commingled—as in the following greeting card. An iris graced the cover, and the text inside read:

In the rush of daily living,
there are endless things to do,
And I just don't write the letters
that I keep intending to,
But I hope this special greeting
in some way will help to show
That I think about you often—
lots more often than you know!

The sender added, "I love you woman[,] This card says it all[.]" Only the victim, perhaps, understood the threat implied by the words "I think about you often," in the context of repeated following, showing up, breaking into her house, and threats to kill her and kidnap their children. Below, I describe less ambiguous experiences, of surveillance, threat, and violence— but we will see that even these are subject to multiple interpretations.

Surveillance

Many of the stalking victims in this sample reported feeling as if they were under surveillance by their former partners. Thus while showing up at a victim's home and repeatedly telephoning her are the most frequently reported behaviors, following the victim is also high on the list of favored tactics and was reported by over half (53 percent) of the victims in the case files. One quarter of them said that their pursuer spied on them or sat somewhere, simply watching. One woman told a police officer:

> Ever since we separated, it's been getting really bad. It got to the point where I was forced to get a restraining order because he has been constantly following me, spying on me, calling at my place of employment, and giving me a lot of problems. Even after I obtained the restraining order, when I go home from work, I find him near my house watching me. When I get up in the morning, I see him right across from my house in his pickup. He calls me at my work and follows me everywhere I go.

Another woman described the following "spooky" observation: "He sits across the street in the park. He knows the park really well—he grew up here. He has a way of hiding in the shadows [and] sometimes I catch him at my window, looking in."

Other surveillance behaviors include contacting the victim's family or employer in an attempt to find her, driving by her home, and sometimes even tapping her phone or videotaping her. Nadine Peterson told me how Victor Kinkaid had used materials that are readily available at Radio Shack and that are relatively simple to assemble. He then placed the contraption in the "box" holding lines at the exterior of her home, to listen to her phone conversations despite her repeatedly changing her unlisted phone number. She added that he had admitted as much in the preliminary hearing:

> When Victor got up on the stand and testified, he told about everything! He admitted—I have his whole transcription—"oh, I used a 3/8 inch wrench when I went to bolt the wire to her phone, and then I got stuck because I didn't have a part, so I drove to Walmart in [a suburb of Valley City] because it's open 24 hours to get this part, and I needed this, and I had the equipment in the abandoned house next door, and every time she picked up the phone I could record it, and I did this and this and this," and he got all excited when he talked about it.

Another woman reported that the defendant:

> calls me right when I walk in the door sometimes, and tells me he knows where I am at, and that I cannot get away from him. He has told me that if he can't have [me], no one can . . . I am really afraid of him. I want to get away from him but he seems to always know where I am and what I am doing. I just want him to leave me alone.

Kathy Felson's former husband, Nick, tried to monitor her whereabouts by attaching a homemade tracking device to her car, described in the probation report as:

> a white shampoo bottle attached with duct tape to the underside of the estranged wife's vehicle. The bottle had a string attached like a wick in the neck of the bottle, and was leaking paintlike substance. The defendant stated "I left something on the back of her car so I could follow the drops, so when she drove off it would drip, drip, drip all the way to her boyfriend's house."

Many victims report that their stalkers take care to let them know they have been observed. One woman, a flagger on a road crew, described the following incident in a police report. "He ran through my flag," she is said to have stated, "and slowed down to make sure I could see it was him. He waved at me while he drove by. He had a smug look on his face as if to say, 'I showed you. I can find you anywhere.'" Nadine, who moved in with her parents for a period of time while she was being stalked, told me about the following unsettling experience and its aftermath:

> I was getting out of the shower or whatever, I [had] taken a shower in their back bedroom and it runs along of the side of their house. And I was sitting on the, the toilet and as I stood up there's a window there and the windows were open. It was a beautiful day. We leave the windows open and their alarm is still on. You know they have it to where they can just deactivate one

or two things and I looked up and Victor was sitting on his motorcycle outside the bathroom window watching. And chills just—I ducked down and I remember running to the front and saying, "Mom he's out there. Oh my God." [Shortly afterward] he calls, um, and leaves a message. He calls from the pay phone and said, "Gosh, Nadine, I mean you could have at least waved to me through the bathroom window."

Nadine's story illustrates not only the tactics Victor resorted to in order to watch her after she left her home, but also the way in which surveillance itself can become a means of communication. Simply being ever present sends a powerful message to the victims in this study. Here are two messages left by a defendant on a victim's answering machine that illustrate the articulation of surveillance and threat:

You know, I never cheated on you since the day I met you—and I never stopped loving you and caring about you since the day I met you—I've always loved you and I told you I will always be there for you—I know . . . is coming, Susan, but be careful where you go and who you go with—'cause believe me—I have somebody watching you—'cause I love you—nobody— I'm not going to let nobody have you—all I want is your friendship—you can—you can have the phone off the hook all you want—that doesn't mean there is no other way—

This was followed by:

All I ever wanted from you was your trust and your love and never had that—who—if I ever find you with anyone I will stop you—anywhere you are—whoever you are with I will stop you—I promise that—I know tomorrow's Friday—I know where you cash your check and I know where you shop and I know how you go to work—what time you come—what time you leave—believe me I will be every step you make—I will be there—because I love you and I will let nobody have you—only me—

As might be expected, women find surveillance unnerving if not terrifying. One victim reported that her husband would call her at work and ask her why she had returned home so late the previous Friday night, and refer specifically to something she had left in her car. He also called her at her mother's house and asked her why she had curlers in her hair. She then told the police officer:

I am terrified of my husband. This man knows exactly how to play the game. He stalks me constantly. There is many a morning I come out of my apartment to go to work and he is sitting in his car inside my apartment complex watching me. This man is desperate. Every time I turn around he is stalking

me, so he has lost his job. He has absolutely no regard for the restraining order. I need to stop this madness. Whatever it takes, I need to stop him from
destroying my life.

Kathy Felson said, in a letter to Nick's probation officer:

> I look over my shoulder wherever I go. I am in a constant state of hypervig-
> ilance . . . The only time we feel marginally safe is when Nick is in custody.
> A ringing phone causes us to jump, still sometimes I wonder if I will ever
> have a real life again. Will I ever have anything that approaches a "normal"
> life? People take for granted so many of the mundane day-to-day activities
> that take on gigantic proportions for me. Walking to the mailbox can be filled
> with anxiety.

Surveillance, then, appears to create levels of anxiety that expand to fill and
occupy much of victims' daily lives. Thoughts of the stalker intrude upon
ordinary tasks and interactions, profoundly altering their form and texture.

Threats

Threats consist of behaviors a victim experiences that she believes communicate to her the intent or capability of the defendant to do her harm.
They can be verbal or nonverbal. The most common verbalizations reported by victims are death threats, name calling, threats to hurt the victim or her family, threatening suicide, and (less commonly) threatening to
kidnap, kill, or hurt her children. I include threatening suicide in this category because it conveys the capacity of the pursuer to engage in extreme
violence. Physical violence directed toward inanimate objects similarly
signifies rage and the possibility of like treatment of the victim. Breaking
into a woman's home, vandalizing her home or car, and stealing her property are forms of symbolic violence easily construed as threatening. As
Table 2.1 indicates, these experiences are perhaps the defining feature of
cases that are referred for prosecution and meet legal standards of stalking. Three-quarters of victims in case files reported death threats and almost half (46 percent) reported that the defendant threatened to injure
them in some way. Almost one-third (30 percent) claimed that they were
threatened with a weapon, and the same number reported that their former partners threatened to kill themselves. In about two-thirds of cases,
the victims' homes or cars were entered without their permission and vandalism or thefts occurred.

Threats take other forms as well, and victims find them equally frightening. Sometimes they are messages left for the victim to find when she returns to her home. In one case a victim reported coming home to find her
house "trashed" and the words "your [sic] dead" on her bedroom wall. An-

other woman told an investigator that her husband had left a note written on a piece of cardboard on her front porch. The note said "Bad girl, waiting for you in hell." One investigator reported finding a playing card with the word "Death" in pasted letters on the back, and a black silk rosebud, on the windshield of a car belonging to a man the victim was dating. In another police report, the same victim was summarized by a police officer as saying:

> I was in bed when he came over this morning. He started throwing rocks at the bedroom window. Then, he went around to the front door and started ringing the doorbell. He left one of his trademark candy wrappers on the doormat. He does that every time that he comes over. I don't know what the red stuff on the door is. Maybe it is supposed to look like blood.

In another case, a probation officer reported that a defendant left an unsigned note "constructed of letters cut out of magazines and newspapers" on the victim's car, communicating that he would "keep his promise" of the day before, when he had threatened to kill the victim in a violent incident at her apartment. Of this incident and the note, the victim had this to say in an application for a restraining order:

> The most recent incident was on Sunday Oct. 16 when he told me he was going to fuck me up and kill me. He had a hammer in his hand beating things. He came towards me. I called my son and I told him to call the police. He said fuck the police I'll [unclear] on them. [He] continued making a scene as he went down the stairs to [the] complex screaming yelling and calling me names, bitches and whores and I'm going to fuck you up bitch. And as he was going down the stairs he was beating on the handrail . . . Tom has told me numerous times that if he wanted to kill me a restraining order would not stop him. His statements and reactions have frightened me a lot. Tom has said on several occasions that if he didn't kill me he would have someone else kill me. This is frightening. On Monday, Oct. 17 Tom put a note on my car at work. A note that he cut out [of] newspaper or magazine letters. I feel that this is sinister and premeditated. I feel that the Court should know about this. Even though he was smart enough not to have signed it. I know and he knows that he did it. A copy is enclosed. Both of us work at [the same place]. This fact is very unnerving [sic].

Defendants threatened to kill victims and family members of victims in a variety of ways. One victim's former husband told her he had discussed her with members of the gang to which he belonged, and that they were going to kill her and "cut me in pieces." She went on to say that, according to him , the gang members "also talked about how they were going to undress my 15 year-old daughter and hang her." Another victim reported the

defendant coming to the window of her home and showing her an am-
munition magazine, saying, "This is for you and the kids." In a police report, one victim said that her husband and she had an encounter in which
"He said he didn't know why I wouldn't go out with him. That is when he
hit me. He stated he was going to kill me and chop me into little pieces and
throw me in the dump. " In another case, the victim was staying with her
mother, who told this story to a prosecutor's investigator:

> Alice is my daughter. I was visiting [her]. It was sometime in the afternoon
> when Mike came by the residence. The previous two or three days Mike had
> been constantly calling the residence, ranting and raving at Alice when he
> came over. He came up to the front window and he had a quart bottle of beer
> in his hand. He was yelling and screaming at Alice again. At one point he ran
> around to the back of the house and cut what appeared to be telephone wires
> so that we would not be able to communicate with anyone. Fortunately, he
> cut the wrong wire and the main telephone was still in service. We called 911
> at that time. It took twenty minutes for the sheriff's department to get there.
> While Mike was outside the residence he was yelling and screaming and at
> one point he said that "if I get in there they're going to have to carry every-
> body out in body bags, including your mom. I'm going to bury all of you and
> I'm going to bury your mom next to you."

One woman claimed to have experienced the following range of communications from her former boyfriend over a two-week period:

> He calls up and threatens me on my answering machine with different mes-
> sages that he is going to beat me up, or he is going to take my kids away, and
> he is going to beat up anybody who is seen with me. Tonight, he came over
> here pounding on the door, but we wouldn't open it. He called up on the
> phone just a little while before [the police] got here and told me, "I'm going
> to come over there and slash your throat and slash your little friend's throat
> and anybody I find over there hanging around with you."

Modern technology, perhaps in conjunction with popular new "real
life" television media that introduce civilians to specialized terminologies,
provides new avenues for the making of threats that are timeless. Said one
woman, "He has called my pager and put the numbers '187' on it. To me,
187 means murder, because I believe that is the Penal Code for murder."
Another pursuer made certain the recipient knew for whom the message
was intended, and from whom it was sent:

> [My children's father] has broken the windows of my house and my car, and
> got my address through the post office. He also calls me at my mother's
> house and he pages me over 30 times a day. When he pages me through the
> pager he puts down 187, the number 1 (for me), my drivers license number,

my social security number, and my date of birth. I know it's him because he knows my personal information.

Telephone answering machines, especially prior to the advent of the common use of caller identification technologies, become instruments of torture. Consider the following series of messages: "Don't be home tonight, bitch." "Hope you got plenty of tape, bitch." "Don't worry, you'll hear me knocking." "I'm getting closer, bitch." In another series of messages, the threat is a little harder to discern, but still present:

> When I, when I, when I see you driving or when you go to work or when you leave the house—and I'm going to find out who you're with—because if I can't have you I'm not going to let nobody have you, because I love you—I love you with all my soul.

> Lois—this is [defendant]—I just called to tell you that I do love you—I always did and I will always love you—no matter what you do to me—I will never hurt you, Lois—and I will never pay you back—that God will punish you not me—I will not punish you . . .

> I want to talk to you—not because I want to hurt you—I will never hurt you—God will punish you not me—I'm not going to punish you 'cause I love you too much—and I will always be there for you—just be careful— okay?

Even while making threats the defendant in this case couches them in the language of love so that the message is mixed, and presumably, so may be the emotions it engenders. Moreover, when the caller above says "I'm not going to let nobody have you," he is repeating a common theme. Winnie Nelson testified to the following:

Q: Now, during these periods of 1996 and 1997, did Mr. Daly ever threaten you in any way?
A: Yep. When he's in angry moods, stuff like that, he's ready to die for this numerous times back in '96, [I] remember when he was telling me he could take me somewhere and nobody will find me.
Q: What exactly did he say?
A: He said that—that he could take me somewhere way out far out and nobody would be finding me, nobody could find me. He said he's ready to die for this. He said that numerous times. If he can't have me, nobody else can.

Some messages are exquisitely specific and explicit. Caity Ingalls was "terrorized" by a former policeman whose advances she rejected following a long period of friendship and a brief, regretted, period of sexual intimacy. She wrote the following in a "victim-impact statement":[1]

> On [a particular date], the defendant began a course of conduct which would forever change my life. His actions and his threats included, but were not limited to threatening to see that I lost custody of my little girl; describing in extraordinary detail, at times chemical by chemical, how he could construct an explosive device and place it under my vehicle while I was grocery shopping at Safeway that he could detonate from 50 feet away by using the remote control from a child's toy, the substance of which would be completely untraceable to anyone in the police department; threatening to have me raped by using his contacts from his ten years of patrolling in [inner-city neighborhood]; destroying my business; creating scenes at speaking engagements and numerous fundraisers which I was chairing; and on and on. The defendant made the following statement while standing outside and looking straight at me through the window on the side of my front door: "I own you, I'm going to destroy you, and I'm not going to stop until I can piss on your grave."

When I interviewed her, Caity appeared to believe these threats. She was not always the articulate person, the speaker at engagements, that her letter conveys, but sometimes she was almost incoherent, especially when she talked about what she presented as the most salient thing in her life—her fear. I asked her what advice she would give to someone in a situation similar to hers, and she responded,

> There's no advice I could give a person on how to deal with fear. How do you, you know, there's nothing I could say that's gonna make, especially when you have a child, I mean I, the nights I had to put the knife under her bed, the nights when, what am I gonna do? 'Cause if he was coming in, he had to get through me, to get to her. I mean, totally, I bet you, 70 or 80 nights like that, when he was coming over. And there's nothing, there's no advice I could ever give a person to deal with, there is no way to deal with it. It's the most powerful that there is. I'd never felt that kind of fear before. The only fear I'd ever felt was the kind you feel when a person jumps out in front of you and you almost like, hit him, that roller coaster kind of fear, but walking around with that feeling that you get right at that moment, if you can imagine that feeling again, where you almost hit someone, never leaving. If you could imagine walking around that way, for months after months after months and it never leaving, the fear, whatever that thing that has made you afraid doesn't leave.

By the time she gave this interview, Caity had almost certainly come to understand that getting help from law enforcement depended to a great extent on an effective presentation of fear, and she could have seen me as a potential ally. However, her performance here held no false notes, and was convincingly supported by her gaunt and hollow-eyed, almost frantic demeanor, and the hypervigilance with which she observed everything around us. She was never still, ever watchful, and being in her presence was a nerve-wracking experience that confirmed the awesome effect on her of the manner in which her pursuer had chosen to convey his threats.

Violence

About half of the victims in the case files reported being physically assaulted by their former partners after leaving the relationship. This figure is consistent with the large number of domestic violence restraining orders obtained (only about one-fifth of the women in the sample did not obtain at least temporary orders) and with the number of women—about two-thirds of the sample—who described a history of physical violence in the relationship prior to their separation. These behaviors take many forms, and I include preventing the victim from leaving a place or calling for help, threatening her with a weapon, sexually assaulting her, kidnapping her or her children, hurting her or others, hurting himself, and hurting or killing animals in the category of physically violent behaviors.

Each of the behaviors described can be thought of as having expressive as well as instrumental effects, and physical violence, even when directed toward someone or something other than the victim, is subject to multiple interpretations. Sometimes the violence seems to be a simple venting of rage or frustration, as in the following victim narratives in crime reports:

> Leroy has been bothering me for some time. Tonight, Leroy saw me in my car and chased me to a friend's apartment. He chased me into apartment #195. He grabbed me by the hair and knocked to the floor, while on the floor he attempted to hit me about the face. I blocked most of the blows with my hands and arms. When he saw that he could not hit me very well with his hands, he kicked me very hard on the left thigh.

And:

> I had come home today about 5:00 p.m. and I drove into my driveway. As soon as I got out of my vehicle Sonny was right there behind me. I got out of my car and started to walk towards the front door of my home and that's when he got out of his truck. I started yelling at him that he is not to be here and that he should leave. He then started to walk up to my door alone with me as I continued to demand that he leave. He walked into the house ahead of me and he was saying something about getting a message off of my message machine. He walked straight into my bedroom and he played the message machine. I had been demanding him to leave, in addition to my daughter who had been pleading with him to leave also. I told him to leave the house and

he then went to my answering machine and he started to call me a slut and he was also saying the same things about my mother. He took the tape out of the tape machine and that's when he hit me with his open hand upside my head. He caused me to fly onto my bed. At this point I was trying to call 911. I had tried to go for the phone and that's when he unplugged the cord from the back of the phone. He then grabbed me from behind and lifted me up and then carried me into the living room.

These kinds of incidents were very common, and were reported in over half the cases. Also common were preventing the victim from calling for help (reported in 25 percent of the cases) and from escaping the forced interaction (in almost one-third of the cases). The following are illustrative of these, from a probation officer's report and from a crime report:

When the victim told him to leave her alone he reportedly got mad and grabbed her by the arm and wouldn't let go. [A month later] when she went inside she found the defendant in her bedroom. The victim and the defendant began to argue and when the victim went to use the phone, to call the police, the defendant reportedly pulled the phone out of the wall. Reportedly the defendant told the victim "If I wanted to kill you, I could kill you right now. I'll snap your neck." The defendant reportedly had both hands on either side of the victim's face. The defendant was in the apartment for approximately one half hour and took off running when he heard the police officer's radio.

Similarly, in a crime report, the victim was summarized as saying:

About five minutes passed when I heard the door open. I was in my bedroom at this time when I looked up and in the doorway of my bedroom was Howard. [He] said, "What's the deal with this guy [a male friend of the victim's] anyway? Is his dick bigger than mine, or what? You know I'll kill you both. You know I can, and I will if I want to." I told him to just get out because he was making things worse and he was going to get in a lot of trouble. He told me, "If I catch you with that guy again I'll kill both of you." I tried to leave because he had left the front door open, but he had stepped in front of the door and would not let me out. I tried to go around him, but every time I started to walk out he would slap my hand and push me back. I went back to my bedroom and picked up the phone to dial 911, but I was only able to dial the 9 before he grabbed the phone, twisted my wrist and slammed the phone down. He told me that I wasn't going to call anybody.

In a little over nine percent of the cases I reviewed, the unwanted interaction between the defendant and the victim was sexualized. In some cases, as in the "imprisonment" cases described above, this was seemingly a further attempt by the defendant to control the actions of the victim. This can be interpreted as instrumental, and also symbolic, in that he kept her involved in the interaction, conveyed his ability to dominate her, and maintained or instilled fear. One defendant broke into the victim's house, forced her to drink beer with him, poured beer on her, beat her, and made her take all her clothes off. In another case, the victim reported:

> I have been divorced from my husband for approximately four years. I have been having a terrible time with Robert. He will not accept the fact that I am divorced from him and no longer want him in my life. Today, I allowed him to come over to talk one last time. When I told him that I did not wish to get back with him anymore, he got a knife from the kitchen and slashed the pads on my couch, picked up a glass bowl off the living room coffee table and threw it against the screen of my television, shattering the bowl. He also cracked the mirrored table top of my coffee table. Then he grabbed me around the throat and choked me. He also pulled down my pants while yelling that he needed sex from me. Then he pulled down my underpants and put his hand in my pubic area.

Another example is the more complex experience of Ellen Nichols, a mother of three young children, who planned her escape from her marriage for two years, getting on a waiting list for subsidized childcare, getting a promotion, and finally leaving when her children became eligible for care. Three days after she left, Ellen's husband found her, she says, and she told me this:

> When he found me, he said "When our marriage ends, it's up to me, and you know, you have no right to do this. These are my children, and you are my wife, and I can do and say whatever I please and you have no right to go anywhere without my knowledge." And that's when it really, when I really started experiencing the trauma, I think.

The trauma Ellen refers to was a series of violent sexual assaults, most often following a move to a new apartment, in which she was repeatedly tied up, raped, sodomized, and beaten in what she described as "the punishment for leaving." When I asked Ellen how she felt during this time, (prior to her former husband's arrest and conviction) she didn't describe fear, or guilt, instead,

> It made me nauseous because I knew that it was going to happen again, and I would just look at him and think, you know, don't even tell me you're sorry, don't say you don't like what happens unless you walk out the door and go get some treatment. Because I don't want to hear it. And that was my reaction to it. I didn't feel sorry for him and I didn't buy it. And it just made me angry, too.

In three of the cases I reviewed, the defendant was charged with attempted murder, in addition to stalking. In one of the cases, the 15-year-old stabbing victim (described earlier in the section on courtship) told of breaking up with her 18-year-old boyfriend because of his jealousy and battering. After the boy was expelled from the high school they attended, she said:

> I had been receiving gifts from him such as flowers and candy. On yesterday when this thing happened he showed up at a couple of my classes in between periods, and at some point he noticed that I had hickies on my neck. I was afraid to tell him [that she had been necking with someone at a party] because I'm afraid of him. That's why I broke up with him. He kept telling me that I had to go with him, and when I said "No," and to leave me alone, he started to stab me in the stomach. He just kept telling me that I had to go with him, and then he would continue to stab me. He told me that he hated me and that he was going to kill me.

Another woman described the following incident in a "history of abuse" she compiled in support of an application for a restraining order:

> While driving down Main Street, Nathan jumped in my car while stopped at a sign. I began driving again and he started shouting extremely loud, he sounded like a savage animal! I was terrified. Then again he strangled me while I was driving a moving vehicle. I lost consciousness, and according to him, I was having convultions [sic] for several minutes later.

And in a case that was perhaps unsurpassed for the sheer viciousness of the defendant's actions, the victim was choked into unconsciousness and woke to find herself naked from the waist down with her own feces in her mouth and hair, placed there by her former husband when she involuntarily defecated from the strangulation. He then kept her captive for three days. During the process of harassing her in the next few years, the defendant sent the victim photographs of his penis and pornographic pictures of women with her face pasted on them, and made numerous death threats that she recorded, including telling their son that "next time [I'll] do it right like O.J. did." Importantly, even this defendant was not unambiguously vile in his interactions with the victim; when she regained consciousness he took her to the bathroom and helped her clean herself, and she told an investigator that he would "threaten her at times and then be very affectionate and caring at other times [during her captivity]."

One final set of violent behaviors reported by victims, although rare in the sample, is worth describing. These are the cases in which the defendant inflicts violence on the pet or pets of the victim. Here, the violence hurts the victim indirectly by causing her grief, and sends a clear indication of what the defendant is capable. It seems likely that a woman whose animal is maimed or killed must imagine the same happening to herself. Earlier I described a case in which a dog was beaten to near death. In another case a dead cat bearing a strong resemblance to the victim's cat was thrown through her bathroom window, where her young son discovered it upon arriving home from school. In a similar case, two dead and mutilated cats were left in the front yard of the victim's parents' home. One defendant poisoned fish, but claimed that they were his. Here are two officers' observations of the victim's residence in another case. The first officer that responded described the following scene:

> Walking in to the apartment I could see that there was a small decapitated blue and white parakeet bird on the floor and feathers all over the carpet. There was vandalism all over the walls in crayon and paint with obscenities such as, "Fuck you, bitch," "Fuck you, cunt," "See what an ass-hole I really can be." There was a cut-up dildo laying across some chairs with a note that said, "You left your dildo, cunt." There was broken glass on the ground from a cup and a torn up note written by the suspect to the victim left on the table by the front door.

The second officer on the scene described the victim's responses during a search the two conducted for the head of the bird:

> When I brought her into the kitchen area and showed her the cutting board she became very upset. I could hear her gasp for breath and she started to cry. When I quickly showed her that there was no blood or any feathers, she calmed down. I then, unfortunately, told her that I did observe some feathers in the china cabinet and stated that possible the bird may have flown there. The victim looked in that area where the feathers were and closely examined the surrounding plates. She immediately became hysterical, gasping for air, and screaming. Her body was shaking and her arms were extended forward and trembling. Instinctively I asked her what was wrong and she could not say anything. I moved the plates around and found the parakeet's head in the corner.

Interpreting their former partner's actions is not always a simple task for stalking victims. First they report a wide range of experiences that seem clearly intended to influence their feelings and their decisions to end relationships. These are in addition to the sometimes ambiguous interactions (repeated telephoning, leaving of written messages, and showing up at victims' home and workplace) that are so commonly reported as characteristic of stalking cases. The content and context of the latter determines whether they fall into one or more of the categories I have defined. Thus, a defendant may show up on a victim's doorstep pleading with her to return and telling her how much he loves her, or he may scream obscenities or threats. If he has been violent in the past, his mere presence, like surveillance, can create fear. Some victims reported thousands of phone calls and messages left on answering machines; this is another kind of omnipresence that informs the victim she cannot get away. Third, more than one kind of message can be conveyed in a single communication, as in the card described at the beginning of this section that professes love and alludes to surveillance. Last, sometimes victims are not only inundated with communications from defendants, but must deal with their former partners over a long period of time, during which stalkers' behaviors can vacillate wildly. The length of time between initial separation and prosecution on stalking charges averaged nine months, and took over a year in 26 percent of the cases I reviewed—in one case, a lapse of 6.5 years. Some stalkers are both persistent and inconsistent, continuing to court *and* harass victims even while in custody.

In sum, the victims whose experiences are summarized in the files and who shared their stories with me face a situation in which their former partners may beg them to return, tell them they are needed and loved, tell them that every move they make is being watched, threaten them, make good on their threats, or all of the above—seemingly incessantly. How do these women respond under these circumstances? Below are some of the most common and significant strategies these women used.

"KEEPING HIM COOL": THREAT MANAGEMENT AS EMOTION MANAGEMENT

As might be expected, the actions women take and the strategies they employ in their efforts to deal with unwanted, coercive, and violent interaction with intimates, are diverse and socially complicated. Depending upon how they feel about what is happening, they may try to hide, try to get help, "give in," or fight back. Much of what victims do is directed toward preventing violence by assuaging the feelings of former partners. This, as well as other choices women make, can have unexpected and unfortunate consequences.

For analytical purposes I have grouped victim strategies into the following categories: "avoidance," "help-seeking," "compliance," and "resistance." However, there is often overlap and usually a blend of strategies or shifting from one to another, sometimes in rapid succession. Table 2.2 presents the strategies, each of which is described below, and the percentages of victims reporting each strategy.

In the remainder of this chapter I detail ways in which women attempt to cope with stalking, before turning, in chapter 3, to the ramifications of

Table 2.2. Victim Responses Reported in Stalking "Victim Narratives"

Avoidance	
screening phone calls	40%
leaving the scene	40%
staying w/family/friends	37%
hiding	32%
changing phone number	24%
moving	22%
Help-Seeking	
calling police	92%
insisting on prosecution	37%
insisting on arrest	30%
getting an escort	19%
screaming	11%
Compliance	
accepting phone calls	61%
trying to reason/interact	38%
returning prior to case	28%
opening the door to talk	27%
not reporting	27%
requesting no jail/lesser term	19%
letting defendant in home	18%
requesting case dismissal	16%
requesting report only	14%
initiating contact	10%
meeting defendant somewhere	09%
recanting police report	08%
returning during case	07%
going somewhere with defendant	07%
having sex with defendant	04%
visiting defendant in jail	03%
writing to defendant	03%
Resistance	
stating boundary	70%
not letting defendant in home	40%
threatening to call police	27%
fighting/struggling	25%
hanging up	23%
arguing with defendant	19%
yelling/swearing at defendant	19%

their decisions for establishing and maintaining "victim" identities in the criminal justice system.

Avoidance: Hiding Out and Desperate Inattention

Victims report using many avoidance strategies. Most commonly cited are screening phone calls, leaving the scene of forcible interaction, leaving home to stay with relatives or friends, and hiding from the pursuer or otherwise avoiding contact. Less frequent but still common are changing phone numbers, moving to a new location within the area, and attempting to ignore the pursuer—sometimes by muting the telephone or putting on headphones. Some victims also take extensive security measures. A few of the victims in this sample moved out of the area or changed jobs in order to minimize or end unwanted contact. Most use more than one tactic; one victim reported moving to a new apartment, staying with friends, not going to work, and staying in motels. As she explained to the prosecutor in the preliminary hearing, when her former husband would call and threaten her, "[I] would just get my things together for work the next day, pack my bag, and I went to a motel." Another woman, in a detailed chronology of her experience, described missing work, changing her shift at work, adding call screening/blocking to her telephone service, changing locks, and installing floodlights and a video system. Here is one victim's account of measures she took:

> I gathered my bag and my dog and the police led me to my friend['s] house where I spent the night. The next day I stayed home from work. I called the phone company and ordered a new unlisted number. I looked in the yellow pages for a law firm close to me as I was afraid to leave the house for very long. I found a firm within a block of my house and called them. I continued to keep my trips outside to must [do's] only. I changed where I did my monthly grocery shopping. I changed where I had my dog groomed. I changed my schedule for my monthly [hair] appointment. I found a new way to get to work. I won't say in this document of my whereabouts as I do not want to put this dear couple who have taken me in any danger. My telephone at work is not accepting messages at this time and is forwarded to a "must answer line" which appears on everyone in my department's phone.

In a poignant commentary on being in hiding, this victim added,

> I love [the state I left], I have many friends there that I will miss so very much. I love my job, and the people I work with there are a surrogate family to me. To move alone to a place where noone [sic] knows you is not easy.

In Kathy Felson's "victim impact" statement, she wrote how she tried to avoid her former husband:

> I have spent the last four years looking over my shoulder. I can no longer use my own address on my driver's license or vehicle registration or bank checks. I must put any real property I own in the name of a trust. I am forced to have expensive security systems for my home. My daughter and I both wear body alarms. I must never be without my cell phone. I must be aware of my surroundings at all times. I live hypervigilantly.

It appears to be difficult to avoid forcible interaction for long, in any event, at least from the perspective of victims whose cases eventually were prosecuted in the Domestic Violence Unit. "Every time I move, he finds me," is a common refrain, and as described earlier, some pursuers appear to delight in their ability to subvert avoidance strategies, treating stalking as a game and even referring to it as such. In a meeting of Valley City Survivors of Stalking, Kathy was asked why she didn't move—women who choose to remain where they are sometimes are criticized by friends and law enforcement, in much the same way as are women who choose to stay in violent relationships. Kathy told the people present about an experiment in which a police officer friend (whose personal information was thought to be protected) gave her permission to use his name in an internet search that Kathy paid $125 to a private agency to conduct. "We can find anyone," Kathy said their advertisement read, and the agency easily found the home phone number and address of the officer, within 24 hours of Kathy's request. Kathy's interpretation of this finding was that "if someone really wants to find you, there is no place to hide—so what's the point in moving?"

Seeking Help: The Presentation of Fear

The ineffectiveness of early avoidance strategies may lead, eventually, to seeking help. As we will see, help-seeking too has hazards, costs, and attendant frustrations. Almost all of the women in the case files, and all of the stalking victims I interviewed, sought legal assistance at some point during their experience. Indeed, in order for a case to be included in the sample, it had to have been referred for prosecution by police or, in some cases, by a victim advocate who encountered a victim who appeared to be in significant danger in the daily restraining order workshop (or, later in the study, in the Superior Court Review). Other help-seeking strategies are: getting an escort, asking employers or coworkers for assistance, and screaming or yelling for help, especially in public places. Some strategies are extensions of seeking legal protection: asking or insisting that a report or an arrest be made, a case be referred for prosecution and prosecuted, or requesting jail or a lengthy sentence.

Other victims take "case management" into their own hands, perhaps following the realization that help from law enforcement is limited. These women log every violation of the protective order and every interaction with police and prosecutors, take self-defense courses, and arm themselves. Victims also make the victim impact statements described earlier, write letters to prosecutors, the media, and judges, and form groups to lobby for more resources and for legislation devoted to antistalking measures.

Nadine Peterson appeared to have used a variety of help-seeking strategies, and her case represents one of the few (for reasons I will discuss later) in which her efforts were met with relatively unqualified success. At one point, she enlisted the aid of security guards at a mall where she was working a table at a bridal fair. She described the guards telling her they would do "anything we can to help you out" as she devised a system for signaling them if Victor Kinkaid were to show up at a booth she was tending. Here is how she described the process of obtaining a restraining order:

> It is gonna end here, and I'll do whatever I can to get the son of a bitch away from me. 'Cause this is not right. And this was on a Sunday. Monday morning I went down and filed a restraining order. I went down with a friend. I knew nothing about how to do anything. I had no clue what I was doing. Went down to the court house. They pointed me to this room, it turned out to be that room. They gave me a stack of papers this thick. Said fill this out. Put this in file. Do this. Do that. Do this and when you're done bring me back this copy. Copy to the sheriff's department, a copy to the police department, the original copy to the courts, and you'll be all done. Well, it's not quite that easy. I sat out in the courthouse with a friend of mine, looking in both directions to see if Victor was gonna come in at any time. And I'm writing as fast as I can, and you can tell if you look at it. I mean it's sloppy as heck, because I'm just trying. It's just totally illegible and I'm scared to death. So um, I filed the restraining order. Well, now I have a choice. I can either have the Valley City sheriff serve him for free and they will make three attempts, or I can hire someone to do it myself. Ya know whatever, but they can't be my friend or they can't be my immediate family. So I said great, free sheriff's department. Let's do it. Well, because he lives in [a suburb of Valley City) which is Mountain county; he can not be served in Mountain county unless I get a restraining order from Mountain county. He has to be served in Valley City County. Well he works in Valley City County. Okay, let's try the job thing. Well the sheriff's department makes three attempts, but do they call me and tell me that they're unable to serve him? No. I have to call them day and night and finally drive by to find out that "Sorry we weren't able to get him."

Nadine told me about a friend who served Victor with the papers, but who was late getting them to the sheriff's substation—at which point a particularly helpful staff person at the substation intervened, waiting until Nadine's friend finally arrived with the proof of service required to file the restraining order. I asked Nadine if she had known the staff person, and she replied,

> No. No. He was just a volunteer there. Who I met and clung on to. He was a great help to me. Helped save my life. So [the friend who served Victor with the restraining order] got there at ten after six. Well they closed at 5:30. This man waited for me—'til this woman pulled in. Stamped it. Documented it. Faxed it to the intaker of the DAs office. It became official.

Nadine was able to have Victor arrested several times before he was prosecuted for stalking her, and eventually she was able to have his bail increased as well, by making a direct appeal to the judge at a bail hearing. But even Nadine, who was described by the deputy district attorney who prosecuted her case as "the perfect victim," and by the jury as "the most credible victim" they had ever seen, was not completely satisfied with the law enforcement response to her situation. Much of the language she used when she described the process of getting the restraining order and having Victor arrested for violating it suggested she felt little support. "You can call," Nadine said,

> but it does you no good. I mean you'll find that out over a pattern of three days. I found that out. If you call 911—'What's your emergency? Is he right then and there?' No, of course not. He's gone by now. It does me no good. Ya know I figured this whole thing out."

In fact, the most detailed descriptions of help-seeking come from women who find this process the most problematic. Melinda Sanchez, for example, was never successful in her attempts to have her former boyfriend arrested or prosecuted. She was anxious to be interviewed, if only to have someone give her claims the credence implicit in listening to her full account of what happened to her. Melinda told me about calling the police and having a "macho young cop" act as if "because I hadn't been beaten up there was no problem." Melinda called the police when a rock was thrown through a window at a house in which she was staying. When the police officer arrived (some time after the departure of Tim, Melinda's former boyfriend), Melinda said:

> He was kind of like doing this with his eyes [she rolled hers to demonstrate] you know, like, [I was] another woman, just you know, overreacting, and [said], "Did he threaten you?" And I'm "No." And he said, "Well, there's nothing I can do, he's not here now." And I'm like, "Yeah, but this guy's been bothering me," you know, "sneaking around the yard"—"Well, has he ever hit you, has he threatened you?" "Well no, but he's always around." He's like, "Well, what do you want me to do?" And I'm like, "I don't know, what are you guys supposed to do, I don't know!" And he's like, "Are you sure that the dog's nose didn't hit the window?"

Melinda had a great deal of difficulty convincing people that she was in fact a victim of stalking. When she commented in the excerpt above that the police officer was dismissing her claims as "overreacting," an emotional display Melinda believes the officer attributes to her gender, she suggested the importance of an effective presentation of victimization—in this case, one that is not too histrionic. It appears that the success of help-seeking strategies (like all interactional strategies) depends to a great extent on the personal and behavioral characteristics of the help-seeker. Cultural constructions of gender and associated "feeling rules" (Hochschild 1979), among other things, may influence law enforcement definitions of stalking victimization. This is a central point, to which I will return in the chapter that follows.

Like Melinda, Ellen Nichols called police repeatedly without being able to effect an arrest, and was not able to get police to come to her home when her former husband would show up, until one final, last-ditch effort on her part. After making many calls and getting no response, Ellen decided to drive to the sheriff's department and ask for help in person; if this didn't work she planned to go somewhere to kill herself, so that her children wouldn't see her killed by their father.

The perception that law enforcement is unable or unwilling to help came through clearly in the following letter, written by a victim's sister, addressed to the judge, and copied to a prosecutor, two detectives, and a probation officer involved in the case. The sister wrote that the victim was in danger of "falling between the cracks" like a recently murdered woman who had been in the news. "This is intolerable," the sister said, and explained that her sibling:

> has filed reports on all [the stalker's] activity, she has talked with the District Attorney, with detectives in both the Metro Division and the Police Department. She has done everything she [is] supposed to do to enable the system to protect her.

Another victim's letter illustrates that help-seeking is a process in which initial efforts must often be followed up with further, persistent attempts to get continued help in the face of ongoing stalking, and suggests frustration:

> I was told that I had to get a restraining order in order for the Deputies to act on my behalf, and I did exactly that I have reported and reported and reported, each and every event, pressed charges, and still, no arrest has been made and he as of today is still stalking me.

Victims learn that there is a hierarchy of people who can aid them, that they must determine who can help and when to go over someone's head, and that they must tread cautiously if they want to succeed.

In another letter, this same woman apologized for "bothering" a sheriff's deputy by requesting to file another report, and thanked him for his help. She expressed her "respect and admiration" for the deputy, offering to "repay" him by washing and waxing patrol cars "or whatever." She also mentioned that she had been approached by a journalist who wanted to write a story about her case, perhaps thinking this would make the deputy take her more seriously.

Here is another excerpt, this one from the letter written by the victim quoted earlier who had left the state:

> [After seeing the defendant in her driveway, in violation of a restraining order] This was about six thirty p.m. on a Sunday. I called my lawyer the next morning and she told me to call the police. I called and was asked if I had asked him over. I told the policeman, "No! why would I have a restraining order and ask him over?" I was told it happens. Was I sure I didn't ask him over? Again I said absolutely not! He said that it would be Anthony's word against mine and would take three months to go to court and it would probably just make him mad. He told me that the next time I should call right away. I knew why I hadn't called the police sooner. This is what happens.

Many of the pleas for help that I read alluded to ways in which the victim's own responses to the stalking might have interfered with effective help-seeking. This same victim wrote a letter to a prosecutor in which she thanked the prosecutor for being "the first person outside friends and family to show any concern for what has happened to [her]" and continued: "It bothers me terribly that the first question out of every official's mouth has been 'did you know him?' and 'did you date him?'" The victim who offered to wash patrol cars said, in the same letter, "I am ashamed that I couldn't see what Mike was a lot sooner. I don't know what I would have done if anything had happened to any of the Deputies that helped me." A close reading of the case reveals that this woman returned to the relationship at least once after law enforcement became involved—prompting a prosecutor to write, in a note to the probation officer, that the victim was "very cooperative but often far too passive to her detriment, taking defendant back."

Another victim described "going through policeman [sic] legal papers, domestic violence counselors, and now the D.A. [for five years]," adding, "I admit there have been times I couldn't win, and therefore gave in. At least he was civil for a short while and that meant I was safe." This brief excerpt (and the prosecutor's comment cited above) is an example of a common, if not the most common, response I found to intimate stalking: the set of behaviors I call "compliance." In the course of trying to obtain legal assistance, in this case over an extended period of time, this woman sometimes faltered in her resolution and resumed interacting with her former partner. Moreover, she clearly defined this as instrumental; she managed his emotions to keep him "civil" and thus, herself "safe." Below, I explore the uses of this coping strategy in greater depth.

Compliance: Soothing the Savage and Salvaging the Suitor

Almost all of the women in the study chose to comply in some form, at some point, with their former partners' demands for continued interaction. Often, this was a type of emotion management the women referred to as "keeping him cool." Compliance is a strategy that takes many forms and appears in different degrees. These include: accepting phone calls from a former partner or continuing to interact face-to-face with him (especially trying to reason with him or calm him); opening the door to him or letting him in the house; meeting him somewhere or going somewhere with him; visiting him in jail or writing him; deciding not to call police or to report a violation; asking that a report but not an arrest be made; requesting that the case be dismissed; continuing to have sex; returning to the relationship (both prior to and during prosecution); and recanting the statements made to police.

The following victim narrative excerpts from crime reports are typical of simply continuing to interact, strategically:

> He was trying to break in. Finally, I spoke with him. On 11/15/96, he showed up at my work. He was a little calm. I didn't want him to make a scene, so I spoke with him for 10 minutes.

> V [victim] stated D [defendant] was yelling at her at this time. She recalls telling him to calm down. [D threatens to slash her tires with a scissors he has, and starts walking towards her car] as he did so she started walking towards J's house hoping to get D to follow her. D stopped and followed her. As she was walking towards the house, with D following [she sees the cops arriving and she] told D the police were coming to get him. She was scared. She did not know what D would do. She recalls talking to him to calm him down.

> D would drive by her residence daily numerous times, drive by her place of employment daily and drive by her bank while she is banking. Numerous times D has approached her in her employer's parking lot, held on to her arm when she attempted to walk away he forced her to speak with him. Sometimes V would go with D to talk or have coffee. When D frightened her or was "mean" she would not. V was questioned why she went with D. She replied, "It was easier than all the fighting, I thought maybe if I talked to him I could get him to leave me alone."

In each of these cases, victims interact with former partners to fend off violence, in the last case not only in the immediate situation, but in the hopes of avoiding future violence. A police officer put it succinctly in one case, noting first that the defendant had been to the victim's house uninvited on several occasions and then commenting that the victim had been "civil and cooperative with [the defendant]" to avoid a confrontation. One woman reports: "It took [the police] a while to arrive and I couldn't take his yelling anymore. I finally opened my door so he wouldn't break it down." Said another: "I decided to talk to Sam so he wouldn't hurt me."

Or this woman, who told the responding officer:

> Kurt was outside banging on my door and yelling. I was scared. He started kicking my door again. I called the police. He broke the door just after I got it fixed. I was afraid he would come in and hurt me, so I went to the window and talked to him. He said, "I won't hurt you if you would just talk to me." I kept talking to him until the police got there.

Another woman was asked in court why she wrote to her former husband in jail. "I was just trying to smooth out communication with him," she replied, a few moments later explaining that she was "trying to tone— to have him focus on himself and try to quit writing me, and basically leave me alone. Just mellow things out for him and to have him focus on himself instead of me."

Importantly, women make these decisions in a context within which stalking often continues despite their help-seeking and avoidance efforts. In a police report, the "civil and cooperative" victim in the case cited above described her situation thus,

> The restraining order hasn't worked. He won't leave me alone. He has already been arrested for stalking me. He refuses to stay away from us. I moved six times in one year in trying to get away from him, but he just keeps moving wherever I am. I have moved at least ten times trying to get away from him. Nothing seems to work. The restraining order doesn't seem to matter. All the officers tell me that I just have to keep calling whenever he violates the order, but it doesn't matter. Whenever he gets arrested, he goes into jail and he comes back and makes my life more miserable. The piece of paper just won't stop him. He doesn't care. He has told me he doesn't care. When he comes around, I try to just keep the peace so he doesn't go off into a rage. I don't know what to do anymore. The system doesn't work for me. I don't want it to come to physical violence. I want him to stay away from me. I am so frustrated with everything I don't know what to do. I don't know if I want him arrested because when he gets out, and he will get out soon, he will just make my life hell again, and it will be a lot worse

This victim, like most, tried a variety of tactics to evade and protect herself from continued interaction with her former husband, but to no avail, according to her. It is this combination of factors, of fear and frustration and even resignation, that appears to make many women comply. Some women just seem to get worn down by the combination of threat and persistence they perceive in their pursuers. Caity said of her former lover, who would threaten to call her friends and convince them that she was crazy, "He could get me. Some days it might take twenty-five calls but he could ultimately get me to pick up the phone."

Another woman told a police officer of nearly ultimate compliance with her estranged husband, to whom she had been married seventeen years:

> He drove up to the house where I am now living. [My husband] was outside the house and was yelling at me to come out. He told me: "Come out here and let me kill you." I was standing at the entry to the front door which was open. I am tired of dealing with him so I started to go outside.

Fortunately for this woman and her five children, a roommate prevented her from acceding to her husband's wishes.

Sometimes victims do more than simply continue to interact. In some cases they will resume a relationship with their former partner, and police reports only hint at the complexity of their reasons for doing so. Under "Relationship History" in an investigative report, a prosecutor's investigator said the victim had

> initiated contact with the defendant on a limited basis to deliver or arrange pick up for his mail, forward messages, assist him with his father's death, and to do favors as requested. [She] has gone to visit the defendant in jail since his arrest on this offense.

The victim told the investigator that she visited the defendant because he wanted to apologize to her, and had maintained contact "to convey to the defendant she did not wish to be enemies but was not going to be involved in a relationship." Another woman received a call from her former husband after two deaths in his family, "and for the first time in a long time I talked to him as a friend. We ended up friends, but I did not lift the restraining order." Despite this claim, this victim did admit to having "intimate relations" with her former husband during this time.

In another case, Donna D'Amato, the stalking victim advocate, described a discussion of the consequences of voluntarily meeting with the defendant with a victim, who "appeared stunned" to discover that the case was "contaminated" by this action on her part. Donna felt that the victim was "still in love" with the defendant, and ultimately the case was dismissed for "insufficient evidence" when the victim destroyed tapes of the defendant threatening her, had the restraining order removed, and (according to the prosecutor) "they got back together."

While it is not possible to determine this woman's reasons for returning to the relationship, in reports she had made to police, she said that she had tried to break up with the defendant, but was afraid of what he would do to her or her car. The defendant had thrown something through her windshield while she was driving (shattering it), had cut her off in traffic, had scratched the words "fucking slut" into her car hood, and had left numerous messages on her answering machine, including the following:

> You do not know what you've done. You do not know what you have done to yourself. I did not want it to have to come to this.

> As long as I feel I've been gotten to, I got to get even and I won't stop. I am not going to give up. I have to get even.

> If your car gets stolen, the insurance will only pay blue book value. I'm going to show you how fucking stupid you are. You have no idea. I want to see you crawling.

> You had some car problems. What are you going to do without a car? I'm having fun.

Another woman requested that the case against the defendant be dropped by prosecutors, reporting that she and the defendant had "since made up," that he had repaid her for damages to her apartment, and that she was six months pregnant with his child. She did this, even though she had earlier told police of a long history of trying to get away from the defendant. "But he won't leave me alone," she said, "he says that he's going to kill me, he knows my every move, and that he would get me before the police came."

In some cases, victims quite explicitly link their compliance to intimidation and fear. A probation officer reports that a victim tried to separate from the defendant, but "due to his threats against her, she reunited shortly thereafter because he continuously stalked her at her place of employment." In one case, family members and others explained why the victim returned several times to a relationship in which she claimed the defendant had tried to choke her, threatened to kill her and her family, dragged her down the street by her hair, threatened her with a firearm, left numerous harassing and threatening messages at her work and home, shown up at her work, run her off the road in her car, rammed the back of her car, disabled her car, attacked her with a Rottweiler, stalked her family and friends, and left mutilated cat corpses in her yard. Early in the process of trying to leave, her mother reported to police that the victim "has had problems with Austin and states he controls her mentally. She is extremely afraid of him and is having trouble leaving him." In a petition for a harassment injunction, her father described how the defendant threatened the victim's 16-year-old sister, and the consequences:

> Fearing that a tragedy may occur if she does not do Austin's bidding, she succumbs to the emotional blackmail, and leaves without our knowledge to return to him so that he will "leave her sister alone." She calls to let us know that she has returned to him to keep her sister safe. What she relates to us as the reason for this forced acquiescence is a series of threats from Austin to the effect that he will harm any of us, her belief that he is certainly capable of following through on his threats, and from her understanding that Austin has ways of "making certain things happen, and no-one [sic] could ever trace the responsibility to [him]." She is in terror of these statements, and the possible harm that could come to our family members, if she does not do what he says, and essentially, she "enslaves" herself to Austin by returning to his home. [quotations in original].

While this case appears to be a relatively straightforward example of the coercive effects of stalking, others are less so. In an interview conducted with the victim of an arson that destroyed all of her belongings, an investigator had great difficulty getting the victim to discuss her relationship with the defendant. After describing an incident in which the defendant came over to the house where the victim was living with her new boyfriend and assaulted him, the victim said "Uh, after that I stay with Larry for a while, he wanted another chance and so I decided to give him a chance." When the victim mentioned that the defendant "beat [her] up big time," the investigator discussed why the victim should make a complaint, and her need to protect herself. Then the investigator asked the victim if she had been afraid for her safety when she returned to the relationship. "That's why I stayed with him for so long," replied the victim,"because I was afraid, I used to have nightmares about it."

This victim refused to go into details about the physical violence the defendant had inflicted upon her, except to say that in addition to beating her up, he had kept food away her, kidnapped her, and "done all kinds of shit to [her]" that she was trying to "block out." She said, "I always did basically know I would go back with Larry even though I didn't want to, just so things wouldn't happen." Later, after expressing her fear that the defendant was getting "more annoyed" because of the arrest and investigation, she said, "I tried and tried, before I was always scared that's why I always stayed with him, but I was always, I always ran away from him, but three and a half years of him finding me." When the investigator interviewed the new boyfriend, he explained the victim's actions thus:

> [W]hen Larry got out [of prison], you know, she's really kind hearted to her [sic] fault, she was letting him use her car and stuff and he, when she would go over there he'd, he'd keep the keys away from her and just the old ownership game and uh, finally convinced her to uh, stay away from me, you know she'd take off at night and she wouldn't come back until the next day and said she was just staying over to friends or whatever and uh, come to find out that she had moved back in with him, because he threaten [sic] to blow us both up if she didn't leave me alone and she just scared to death of him. She didn't want him to hurt me, because of her and everything so she gave in to, you know, to, you know, his wishes.

In this case, as in several others, it appears likely that the victim's compliance arose out of her fear of the defendant, but this would have been hard to determine if not for the persistent questioning of the investigator.

Resistance: The Instrumentality of Anger

Last among the range of strategies victims choose to discuss are what I call "resistant" strategies. These fall along a continuum, beginning with the verbal statement of an interactional boundary—a request or insistence that the relationship and all further contact end. By definition, this is never sufficient in cases of stalking that end up in the district attorney's office. In these cases, and in others in which the forcible interaction is interpreted as dangerous enough to warrant it, the verbal boundary is usually followed by the obtaining of a restraining order. This is a help-seeking tactic that can also be interpreted as a form of resistance. Like saying "no," this action failed to deter intimate stalking in most of the cases in the sample: only 22 percent of the victims did not have restraining orders in effect at the time the stalking occurred. Once the order is obtained, it is incumbent upon the woman to enforce it. She demonstrates her continued resistance by hanging up on him when he calls—a resistant strategy that sometimes follows the compliant strategy of picking up the phone in the first place, and other times occurs when the victim is tricked into speaking with her former partner—and by refusing to allow him entry into her home when he shows up. Resistant victims also threaten to call the police, argue with their pursuers, use sarcasm, yell and swear at them, or physically struggle and fight. As Table 2.2 indicates, almost three quarters of the police reports in case files mentioned the setting of a verbal boundary, and approximately one quarter of victims engage in one or more methods of "fighting back" at some point during the stalking.

The following police report is typical of victim resistance. After telling the police officer that her former boyfriend was "acting all messed up" following their break-up, "following me around, and calling me on the phone, at home and at work, calling me a bitch and telling me he is going to kill me," the victim described two encounters with him:

> About the middle of July, Calvin came to my apartment and started yelling and calling me names. He was saying that he knew I was sleeping with someone and that he was going to kill both of us. I kept yelling at him to just go away. He was pounding and kicking the front door, but I would not open the door. I called 911 and told them what he was doing. Today [when I got home] as soon as I pulled into the parking lot, Calvin was here. He started yelling at me and calling me a bitch. I yelled at him to stop and to just leave me alone. I ran into the apartment and closed the door. He ran up and started pounding and kicking on the door and yelling at me. I yelled through the door that I was going to call the Sheriff.

Setting a verbal boundary is not always as easy as one might think. The following is excerpted from a transcription of a tape recorded conversation between a victim, "Christina," and a defendant "Mark," who is calling in violation of the restraining order:

V: I'm simply telling you that it's over.
D: You think it's over.
V: It is over.
D: I guarantee I'll be with you, I bet you within two weeks.
V: Nope.
D: You don't think so?
V: Nope.
D: I bet you won't move [from] your house for two weeks 'cause I will sit at that mother fucking corner and wait. You want to play psycho chase games again?
V: No.
D: Ha! That's what you're asking for, 'cause my heart rate is already goin'.
V: Well, I'm not trying to get you goin', I'm tryin' to tell you that it's over.
D: Christina.
V: Please leave me alone.
D: Please, you better get over here.
V: Please don't call here any more.
D: You want to make a bet?
V: Okay, it's over.
D: I'm on my way over there right now.
V: Please, no.

Later in the conversation, Mark became verbally abusive, and told Christina, "Don't fuck with me." She responded, "I'm not. I'm not going to sit here and be yelled at." When she reiterated that the relationship was over, Mark insisted that it wasn't over until "when I say it is over and you say it is over." Finally, Christina said, "Haven't you got it through your head yet that I'm not going to see you any more?" and eventually she hung up on Mark.

Kathy Felson described a transition from compliance to resistance. She had agreed to meet Nick to discuss their marriage, and when he confessed his addiction to methamphetamine, promised to get into treatment, and begged her to come back to him, she declined to do so. When Nick began yelling and calling her names, Kathy said that for the first time, she was able to walk away. "Before," she said,

> I would engage, and I would try to calm him down, you know, I'd try to deny, "No, I'm not a bitch, and a cunt, and a whore, and a tramp." I recognized that if I did truly care about this person, that I had to say, "No, these are the limits." I started looking at my responsibility in this dance that we were doing. And I realized that if I elected not to dance, then he couldn't either. You know, I mean, he could dance, but he'd be dancing with himself. Um, and that was a big, that incident was a big turning point for me, I mean a really big turning point. Um, I can remember driving away and being really shaky and teary, and, but at the same time, having this kind of like, "I can do this. I can say no to him." And I just continued to say no.

Kathy's feelings were still conflicted, by her account, and this part of her story illustrates how women are sometimes torn by the investment in their relationships that still remains. Nevertheless, Kathy, like many victims, holds herself accountable in this excerpt, and in so doing, suggests that she is not powerless in this situation.

Nadine Peterson and I discussed her move back into her home after staying with her parents for a while, in an attempt to evade Victor. I asked her how she came to the decision to return, and she related a conversation with her mother in which she told her mother she had a telephone, locks, and a baseball bat, and was as prepared as she could be.

She then described her own transition, from a state of relative helplessness to the following, more proactive stance:

N: I was pissed that I let this happen to me, ya know I was so mad at me.
I: Why were you mad at you?
N: Because I got involved with this person. That was where my feelings were. How could I do this? How could you be so stupid? Now you've got to deal with it. Get your—no more pity party. Don't cry about it; be effective and aggressive.

By "aggressive," Nadine meant that she would actively pursue prosecution of her case. Sometimes, victims act aggressively toward their former partners. After the second time a defendant went to the victim's day care provider's house, the victim became angry. "I went off, really," she said, in a crime report, telling the defendant "Get the fuck out of here. I don't want anything to do with you. Leave me alone, or I'll call the cops."

Another victim, in a letter to a judge, said that she told the defendant, who was trying to force entry into her house, "I'm sick of going through this with you, get the hell out of my house. We were at the front door and he would not get his foot out of the doorway. So I could shut the door, I pushed him." A victim who caught her former husband putting a rose on her car related the following interaction to a police officer:

> I asked him what he was doing there and he said he wanted to get back to-gether. I said I didn't want to and tried to get into my car. He then said I ru-ined his life. He asked me if I wanted to go out to dinner. I said, "No, fuck off, get away from me and get out of my life."

Nadine herself was involved in an altercation with Victor, after Victor assaulted her aging father:

> And I was crying and I was hysterical. And I was calling him every name in the book. And I was like I don't understand how you could do that. I can't believe what you've done to my father. And just screaming and yelling. All this kind of stuff, "Just move your arms and let me go!" Raging blood must have been coming out of my nostrils (laugh).

In a crime report, a victim was portrayed as extremely resistant. When her former husband showed up at the daycare center where she was pick-ing up their children, she told him "to just leave and to leave [her] alone." Then, in the presence of witnesses, the defendant pointed a gun at the vic-tim and tried to force his way into the victim's car. According to the victim, the defendant "told me to slide over because he was getting in. He said 'Bitch, I'm going to kill you right here.' I told him that he was just going to have to take me out right here in front of all these people. Another victim, in a plea for help in her application for a restraining order, threatened to "take the law into my hands" because she was "at rope end" [sic].

CONFUSION, COMPLIANCE, AND OTHER COMPLICATIONS

In the preceding pages, I have used the accounts of stalking victims to cre-ate a sense of what being stalked is like, so that the reader might begin to understand something of what these women experience and how the mean-ings they attribute shape their responses. I have tried to show that none of this is simple or straightforward. Rather, stalking victimization is highly variable and so are the ways in which women attempt to cope with it. Nevertheless, there are patterns discernable here, and these commonalities suggest that when faced with similar circumstances, women are likely to respond in fairly predictable ways, even if their reactions seem strange to others. In the chapter that follows, I will explore some of the consequences for prosecution of stalking cases that arise from victims' decisions. I will also begin to place these women's actions within larger social contexts of gender and culture, and examine how the reproduction of structural inequalities plays out in the interactions I have described. For now, however, I simply want the reader to envision stalking from the perspective of victims and begin to mull over some of the complexities and patterns that have emerged.

For example, although stalking and the threats associated with it may seem far removed from ordinary courtship, the language and imagery of romantic love appears frequently in victims' accounts, and even women who are very frightened and trying very hard to separate themselves from violent relationships are susceptible to its siren song. They may be so because they are confused, or they lower their guard, or they believe that the situation has changed. In the same way that the "honeymooon phase" documented by Walker (1979) induces women to stay in abusive relationships, the same tactics employed in this phase sometimes lead women to return even after leaving. As reported above, almost one-third (30 percent) of the stalking victims had left their partners repeatedly prior to prosecution for stalking, and 7.6 percent of victims resumed a relationship with the defendant *during* prosecution—leading to dismissal of charges for "insufficient evidence."

While the latter group is very small, six of the nine women who returned during prosecution reported the defendant professing his love, and over half of the 36 women who had returned previously (19 women or 53 percent) reported this behavior in the current stalking case, compared to one-third (32.9 percent) of the women who had simply left (Chi Square = .04). All but one of the six women who had sex with the defendant during prosecution reported romantic verbalizations or imagery. Less dramatic capitulations are also involved: over half the women who went somewhere with the defendant (often in violation of the restraining order) reported love talk, compared to a little over one-third of the women who did not accede in this way.

Of course, if courtship were all that was occurring here these would not be stalking cases. While professing love is frequent, being followed, threatened, and assaulted are more likely experiences. Even so, well over half of the women (61 percent) accepted phone calls from defendants, and over one-third of them (38 percent) tried to reason and continued to interact with their former partners. Over one-quarter (27 percent) opened the doors being pounded upon and 18 percent of the victims allowed the defendant into their home. In some cases, there may be alternations of romantic and threatening overtures that account for some of these decisions. But here we must probably consider primarily what it is like to know that one is being watched, and by someone who wishes one ill. Here now enters fear upon the heels of love. The former partner makes his presence omnipresence; he is everywhere the victim turns and he makes certain she is aware of this. He follows her wherever she goes, he appears at her home and her work, his note is under the windshield wiper of her car, his letter is in her mailbox, and his voice appears insistently on the machine in her home, that most private of realms. Sometimes he whispers and cajoles, more often he is muttering murderously and raging obscenely, leaving the evidence of his obsession and ire behind or, more frightening still, appearing in all his anger before the now terrified victim. She tries to hide, but he finds her wherever she goes.

She tries to get help; this is not as easy as it might seem. She knows what he is capable of. In two-thirds of the cases victims reported a history of violence in the relationship and 71 percent of the defendants had violent criminal histories. Despite this, others are not convinced. Victims struggle to get police officers to come out to their homes, especially if there is no restraining order or if the stalker has left the scene. Then they must sometimes insist that a report be made. One police report is not enough in most cases; over one-quarter of the victims reported four or more calls to police before the case was referred for prosecution. It may then take a while before prosecution occurs, as we have seen.

Meanwhile, the stalker persists. The phone calls continue, the tires are slashed again, he's at the doorstep yet again. Sometimes, the victim holds her ground. She insists that she be left alone (in 70 percent of the cases I reviewed). Forty percent of the time she does not let the defendant in her home, and she starts keeping track of what he does to her (in 19 percent of the cases). But she also continues to interact with him, complying with his demands to pick up the phone, to answer the door, to please just meet him somewhere safe, Denny's maybe, for a cup of coffee, he promises he won't hurt her, he just wants to talk. She is tired of repairing the door, changing the locks, calling the police, appearing in court, waiting for things to change. Sometimes her anger and frustration overwhelm her and she lashes out at her tormentor.

While she waits, she tries everything she can think of to get the stalking to stop. She uses varied strategies that are situation- and context-specific, and that may well be linked to wildly shifting emotions. Thus few of the victims to whom I spoke, and whose accounts I read in the case files, could be characterized as solely compliant or resistant. For most of these women, no single type of response was predominant. Rather, they employed many different strategies over the course of their experience.

Importantly, the vast majority of victims (89.5 percent) used at least one compliant strategy during the course of the stalking. Fifty-eight percent of them used three or more of the compliant strategies I recorded, and about 12 percent used six or more of these means of coping. In sum, while women are not compliant as a matter of course, virtually all of them succumb to the demands of their former intimates at some point during the course of the stalking—and these are only the cases that are documented, and in which the victims have good reason, we shall find, not to reveal their compliance.

Resistant strategies are less common, but not unusual. About nine percent of victims reported no resistance as I defined it, and about one quarter of them reported only one resistant strategy. However, almost half the victims used three or more resistant strategies. About one fifth (19 percent) of the victim narratives in the case files revealed instances of victims arguing with defendants, and the same proportion of victims yelled or swore. One-quarter of the victims physically struggled or fought their pursuers.

The problem with all of this is that even a response as common as talking with the stalker or as little-used as physically struggling with him can backfire, and none of these strategies are without risk and complications. "Avoidance" strategies are ways of subverting unwanted interaction by making it more difficult to accomplish, but may have the unintended effect of making the stalker angry and escalating the stalking. They may also be ineffective, overall. "Help-seeking" strategies involve law enforcement in the intimate stalking situation, but are time-consuming, arduous, and can alienate important potential advocates if done "inappropriately," as we will see.

Most importantly, perhaps, the choices these women make are part of what law enforcement actors take into account when assessing victim credibility, and thus these are consequential decisions—even if victims do not realize it at the time. "Compliant" strategies are especially problematic. The pressures to comply may be tremendous, arising out of ambivalence, love, fear and frustration, and these choices may come into play when law enforcement aid is absent or when such assistance is slow in coming. Nevertheless, they can make the help of law enforcement all the more difficult to enlist. Finally, "resistant" strategies involve "fighting back." Like compliant strategies, they emerge in the course of ongoing stalking processes and can be similarly counterproductive when held up to the harsh light of criminal justice system critics.

As Kennedy and Sacco (1998) note, victimization does not take place in a vacuum, and the "aftermath" of victimization—particularly the involvement of the criminal justice system—is as necessary to our understanding of the phenomenon as everything that precedes it. Next, through examining how the strategies women use appear to shape their ability to enlist the help they need, I explore a complex interrelationship between "stalking victims" and law enforcement. Women draw upon a wide range of possible responses to stalking, and it seems that not all of the choices that they make are equally useful in accomplishing their aims. Some decisions make things worse, and ultimately determine whether victims are able to successfully establish that they are, in fact, truly victims of crimes and therefore deserving of sympathy and help. The ways in which victims manage, or fail to manage to do this, are the subject of the next chapter.

NOTES

1. The law in the state where the research took place provides crime victims the opportunity to make a statement in front of the judge presiding over sentencing.

3

Innocence Lost:
Accomplishing Victimization in the Domestic Violence Unit

In this chapter, I examine how women negotiate "victim" identities while still immersed in coping with stalking itself. The continuation of stalking and the cultural ambiguities associated with this newly and sometimes ill-defined crime tremendously complicate matters for victims, as they make, shift, and, of necessity, change their identity claims. How do women become "stalking victims" in the criminal justice system? In exploring some complexities of achieving and maintaining a "victim" identity, I look at the "emotion work" (Hochschild 1979, 1983) that the women do as part of their self-presentation as terrorized victims. The women whose stories appear here must manage their feelings of confusion, fear, distress and anger to convince actors in the criminal justice system that they are afraid, and for good reason. Consider the following excerpt from an interview with Nadine Peterson who described seeking help from the criminal justice system to end stalking by Victor Kinkaid, her former boyfriend.

> I had been before the same judge, Judge Smith, it was over at the jail, where we had appeared. I think this was like, my third time. His bail was like, $20,000 and they increased it to $50,000, you know, blah blah blah, he bailed out each and every time and every time he got out he came after me. Finally, the last time, I stood up in court and said, "Judge Smith, he doesn't get it, okay? If you don't put this person on no bail, he's gonna kill me, okay? That's all I have to say. And I'm sorry I've spoken out, but I needed you to know."

Here Nadine reiterated that she had made repeated attempts to get the judge to understand her situation. She insisted that she was still being stalked, and she posed the possibility of even worse victimization if the judge would not believe her claims and intervene. Nadine's apology, moreover, suggests that she took care to remain deferential in an interaction in which the judge held the rank and the power to confirm or discredit the identity she proffered.

As we have seen, stalking victims also work to manage the emotions of their stalkers, while simultaneously claiming to be stalking victims. Yet because their attempts can discredit them in the eyes of legal authorities; "stalking victim" can be a difficult identity to maintain. Sometimes these women's continued interactions with both stalkers and law enforcement actors affect their ability to create and sustain credible victim identities. Almost any action a victim takes or presentation she makes has the potential for inducing negative identity attributions. Therefore, the stalking situation poses inherent identity dilemmas. For example, the identity that these women struggle to socially construct, in complex and often adversarial processes, is one that carries stigma. Ironically, some of the "victims" ultimately choose not to be defined by the label they have won at such cost. Instead, they assert with great bravado that they are, in fact, "survivors."

CONTEXTUALIZING THE CREDIBLE VICTIM: BLAME, CLAIMS, AND EMOTIONAL DEVIANCE

In chapter one, I argue that identities socially constructed in face-to-face interaction are fluid, and consequential (Altheide 2000; Blumer 1969; Goffman 1963; Holstein and Miller 1997), and that stalking victimization is an identity-conferring process. A review of literature on victims' experience of the prosecution of rape suggested that the role victims play or are perceived to play in their own victimization affects their credibility and, subsequently, whether they are treated as "true" victims. Furthermore, the rape literature argued that this process is influenced by tensions between the organizational constraints faced by prosecutors and victims' needs and interests, and shaped by normative expectations of gender and victim roles.

Stalking victimization similarly illustrates that "victim" is a problematic identity and one that is often contested in legal arenas. As Kennedy and Sacco (1998:206) put it: "The characterization of the victim (credibility, past history, and current demeanor)" can be as important as the actual evidence in deciding whether to investigate or prosecute a crime. The efforts of prosecutors to screen victims attest to the inherent conflict. In their "rethinking" of victimization, Holstein and Miller (1991:114–115) describe victimization as a labeling process in which "victim status is [sometimes] openly negotiated, contested, and even imposed" and note the frequency of such "victim contests" in legal proceedings. At issue are assignations both of "injury and responsibility":

> Calling someone a victim encourages others to see how the labeled person has been harmed by forces beyond his or her control, simultaneously establishing the "fact" of injury and locating responsibility for the damage outside the "victim." (Holstein and Miller 1991:106)

Achieving an identity as a victim absolves women so identified of blame for their predicaments. To successfully claim to be stalking victims, these women had to make themselves believed and believable. To do this they had to present themselves as innocent and therefore blameless.

Candace Clark makes much the same point in her discussion of sympathy and morality, arguing that in order for people to be judged deserving of sympathy, their moral worthiness is assessed by potential sympathizers, making sympathizing itself a "morality-constructing act" (1997:22). One crucial determinant of sympathy is blamelessness—"Is the person at fault or a victim? Does he or she deserve affirmation and reprieve, or not?" (Ibid.: 22)—and Clark goes on to argue that sympathy is directly contingent upon the extent to which a person is deemed "free of responsibility for a problematic situation or deviant act" (1997:207).

The identity work in which victims engage is thus consequential and sometimes costly. Even women who are successful in their efforts to claim victimization can violate normative expectations. They may find themselves devalued in a process Goffman (1963) defines as constituted by the discrepancy between our ideas regarding how victims "ought" to be and who they "actually" are. The "true" or "worthy" victim loses some of her halo if her presentation falters, and there are a number of ways in which this can happen. If it occurs, the consequences range from emotional "distancing" on the part of victim advocates to dismissal of charges by a judge.

One way in which intimate stalking victims become "deviant" is through violation of normative expectations governing the feeling and display of emotions. Hochschild (1979, 1983) argues that people actively seek to manage their emotions to bring them into internal and external conformity with "feeling rules." Following this argument, Konradi (1999) has closely examined the emotion management of rape survivors in courtrooms. She found that rape survivors worked to align their emotions with norms governing appropriate demeanor for both witness and victim identities. Importantly, this emotion management sometimes created dilemmas for survivors:

> The display rules that accompanied these two ideal images were somewhat contradictory with respect to an appropriate emotional intensity, calling for emotional suppression on the one hand (the rational witness) and evocation on the other (the traumatized rape victim). (Konradi 1999:56)

Sometimes, Konradi found, the self-protective achievement of a calm that enabled continued participation in direct and cross-examination violated feeling rules (1997:72). Stalking victims walk similar emotional tightropes as they navigate between personal (Goffman 1963) and legal identities.

In sum, defining someone as a "victim" is a complex interactional process in which social actors make assessments and evaluations of moral worth. Certain victims, particularly when they do not "conform to the ideal" (Kennedy and Sacco 1998:14) are presumed to be causally, as well as morally, culpable for their victimization (Felson 1991). The identity of "victim" is always contingent. Victims must meet cultural stereotypes (Stanko 1981, 1982), and successful claims rest upon the ability of the claimant to establish blamelessness (Clark 1997; Holstein and Miller 1997). Victims may do emotion work as part of identity management (Hochschild 1983, 1979; Konradi 1999). However, because victim identities, like all identities, are emergent and situationally fluctuating (Altheide 2000), there is always the possibility for redefinition and discrediting (Goffman 1963).

The experience of intimate stalking and prosecution, like other crimes in which women claim victimization by intimates, involves complex processes of gaining, losing, and regaining moral ground in high stakes identity contests. In them, a loss of innocence occurs in the very process of establishing such. The accounts that follow illustrate these arguments, and I discuss their implications.

ACCOMPLISHING "VICTIM" IDENTITIES: INTIMATE STALKING AND FINITE POSSIBILITIES

There are similarities in law enforcement responses to sexual assault, especially acquaintance rape, and intimate stalking. Stalking, like rape, is a crime in which men are disproportionately represented among the defendants and women among the complainants, and most stalking occurs in formerly intimate relationships (Tjaden and Thoennes 1998a; Zona, Sharma, and Lane 1993). This means that the ways in which women respond to perpetrators and the ways in which others evaluate these responses differ from cases of violations committed by strangers. An element of ambiguity enters; women's motives are more easily called into question (Bohmer 1991; Estrich 1987; LaFree 1989; Schulhofer 1998).

There are striking similarities in the manner in which significant others, friends, law enforcement, defense attorneys, and other legal actors treat stalking victims and rape victims. Both are likely to be blamed for their predicament. This tendency is further complicated by the necessity, in the state in which I conducted this research, for a "credible threat" to be present for the behavior to meet the legal definition of stalking. As a consequence, in order for a woman to be successful in her claim to stalking victimization, she must show that she is afraid, *and* that she is blameless. These requirements are not easy to fulfill. Victims must simultaneously manage their own emotions and the emotions of stalkers.

"She's a Participant": Everyday Understandings of Victims' "Compliance"

Intimate stalking has only recently been defined as a crime (Lowney and Best 1995). How do women convey their experience of intimate stalking to law enforcement? How do women who are victims of this newly defined crime enlist the aid of these important "third parties" (Kennedy and Sacco 1998)? What identity claims must they make, and what happens to women when the identity, "stalking victim," is attributed to them? How is this process of attribution influenced by the powerful and sometimes contradictory emotions women feel and choose to express, and by the tactics women choose to temper the violent emotions of their ex-partners?

More often than not, the victims I interviewed or whose cases are analyzed here attempted to manage the emotions of intimate stalkers by continuing to engage in unwanted interaction to some degree—the strategy I characterize as "compliance." Ninety percent of these women engaged in at least one compliant strategy during the course of the stalking, and in over half the cases I recorded three or more compliant responses. In the case of intimate stalking, these choices can diminish women's ability to protect themselves. Such decisions also compromise their chances of successfully enlisting the aid of law enforcement personnel, who may take continued interaction as evidence of victim "complicity."

Furthermore, women who cannot effectively present a "victim" self may have difficulty managing their own emotions in gender- and victim-appropriate ways, further reducing their credibility and decreasing their likelihood of obtaining aid. How are victim strategies interpreted by agents of the criminal justice system? What are some of the consequences of prosecutors' and judges' evaluations and attributions? Like Lorber's "good patients" and "problem patients," stalking victims face the evaluative assessments of criminal justice "practitioners" as they negotiate their way through the system.

Compliance is problematic because women who report stalking have left or are attempting to leave their violent relationships; however, they still bear the stigma of "battered women" by association. Police officers, the general public, and prosecutors often typify women who choose to stay with abusive partners as suffering from some pathology:

> Police standards of harm, responsibility, and victimization [make] officers generally unsympathetic toward women who express ambivalence about their relationships and pressing criminal charges. [T]he most common stereotype of battered women is that they will not follow through with prosecution (Ferraro 1993:167, 170).

The legal scholar Martha Mahoney (1991, 1994), in her analyses of legal and popular images of battered women, makes a similar point. Mahoney (1991:39) argues that cultural stereotypes influence legal proceedings by shaping understandings of battered women as "utterly dysfunctional women," whose learned helplessness keeps them passive and unable to effectively resist their own victimization. Moreover, according to Mahoney (1994), agency is equated only with leaving the relationship.

These typifications spill over into characterizations of stalking victims. Several of the victims I interviewed reported being asked by friends and family what they had done to encourage their former partners' attentions. Caity Ingalls told me that her family had not been "terribly supportive"—

C: . . . My family has a difficult time with the concept that a person could behave this way for absolutely no reason.
I: So they think that—
C: I did something to cause it.
I: Uh huh.
C: [long pause] 'Cause people don't react that way for no reason.
I: That sounds like a hard thing to deal with.
C: It's um, the most painful part of all. My father's reaction was, well, when [my daughter] and I, when he was finally arrested and [my daughter] and I were placed under protection for two weeks and we moved out of our house, and my father said, "I have lived sixty-two years, and I have never known anyone that this has ever happened to, and I could live probably another sixty-two, and not know anyone that this has happened to. What the hell did you do, Caity? What did you do?" And, you know, the most painful part, is, there's been a lot of fallout, that's the worst part, and that's the most difficult part for me to deal with, the most painful part. It was difficult, to, you know, think that a jury's going to believe you, when your parents don't.

Victims themselves suggest that women will get little help from law enforcement until they obtain a restraining order, which lends symbolic weight to their separation from their partners. For example, in a discussion of restraining orders that occurred in a VCSS meeting, Kathy Felson commented that "The restraining order doesn't protect us, we protect ourselves, but what are [law enforcement personnel] going to do for us if we don't have it?" Ellen Nichols replied, "Yeah, it will make things worse, but they will get worse anyway." In this exchange the women recognize that a restraining order is required before a woman can claim victim status, even if the restraining order causes violence to escalate. Importantly, any compliance with the defendant is seen as permission to violate the restraining order and violates the expectation of other key actors that women break off all contact with defendants.

Kathy was aware of typifications of domestic violence victims and of the problems victim compliance can create, an awareness the following example suggests was acquired at some cost. Here, in an interview, Kathy described a friend who obtained a restraining order and who then agreed to meet the restrained former husband to discuss the relationship. Kathy had done this herself, before obtaining her own order. Kathy said that she told her friend that the meeting encouraged violation of the husband's order. Kathy said of her friend:

> And she goes, "Well yeah, but," and I said. "No. What will happen, is if later on something comes up, that's going to be brought up, that obviously you felt okay about being with him, because you met him, and you allowed him to violate the restraining order." See, that's what I know. I mean, having been through this, that's what I know will happen. So, whether you want to talk to him or not, um, you don't do yourself any good, meeting with him, talking to him, seeing him, because then the restraining order is worthless. In the eyes of the Court you have to be consistent in what it is you want.

Based on her own experience, Kathy recognized that unintended consequences arise from victims' actions. She then alluded to how victims are generally perceived. "Needless to say, they moved back in together this weekend, after a year of this kinda, [blowing out through her lips to make an exasperated sound] fairly typical I would think, domestic violence kind of situation." By using the phrases "needless to say" and "fairly typical," Kathy indicated the generic features of her friend's behavior—that is, the cultural understandings she shared with prosecutors and potential jurors. Battered women return to their batterers, in this representation, after failing to set clear boundaries delimiting acceptable and unacceptable behavior.

Interestingly, when women do continue to interact, this response is often attributed to the woman's desire, conscious or not, to remain involved with her former partner on some level. As one prosecutor put it in a discussion we had about stalking victims, "Some of these women just seem to want to stay connected, they just seem to put out an energy that draws these men back to them." In one case a victim testified in a preliminary hearing that she allowed the defendant to come to her house because he had automobile registration paperwork that she needed "badly," and when, after she let him in the house, he attempted to rape her she fought him and finally told him "Go ahead, have your way with me. Fine. Get it over with." When asked why she did not report this to police, the victim said that she was "hoping that [she] could just have this go away, that [the defendant] would come to his senses, that it would end." She also pointed out that the defendant was threatening to plaster her workplace with copies of police reports regarding her past criminal history. The defense questioned the victim extensively about times when she talked to the defendant or initiated contact. Then the following interchange took place:

Q: Did you do anything since the restraining order was issued to lead him on?
A: As I told both the detective and Mr. Viceroy [the prosecutor], I was nice to him and I knew that was—now in retrospect I know that was a mistake.

Here, by using the terms "lead him on," the public defender drew on a cultural framework for understanding intimate violence reminiscent of how defense attorneys in rape cases draw on "rape myths" (Burt 1980) to link victim culpability and a teasing female sexuality. Like Amir's (1971) rape victims, stalking victims are thought to initiate their problems.

Previous researchers have found that attributions of victimization are linked to stereotypes. For example, numerous studies have found that actors ranging from schoolchildren to juries believe that women sometimes say "no" when they mean "yes," wear suggestive clothing, send mixed messages, and otherwise precipitate sexual assault (LaFree 1989; Schulhofer 1998; see White and Humphrey 1991 for an extensive review of research on young people's attitudes toward acquaintance rape). The public defender in Winnie Newton's case attempted to define the situation similarly when he told the judge he did not think the dozen or so restraining order violations reported to police "withstand the charge of stalking": "I feel this is a relationship that's been going on. I think, even though she denies it, that she participated, and I think the relationship was there and that this does not come up to stalking." Winnie adamantly denied having a desire for continued interaction of any type with the defendant in her case; nonetheless she was characterized as a "participant" rather than as a victim.

Winnie's case exemplifies the range of strategies and attendant complications I found. When asked by the prosecutor about interactions in which she did not call the police—a question the public defender later attempted to use to portray her as compliant—this is how she explained herself:

I tried to get along with him. I tried to just, as he would say, wean him away from me. I tried to talk to him just to keep him calm. I almost—like me personally, it was like me trying to amuse him just for my benefit. I tried to—I just tried to keep a nice conversation with him and stuff, because I got tired of my stuff being tore up. If I didn't talk to him, something going to happen. If I do talk to him, I end up arguing, something going to happen, didn't matter what I did try to wean him off of me, whatever, and nothing worked.

Winnie made it clear that her continued interaction with her ex-boyfriend was instrumental emotion management. She was tired of the destruction to her property that followed noncompliance, and she made many calls to police, to no avail, prior to his eventual arrest. And, as she pointed out, compliance was not a good choice in this relationship either. When the public defender questioned her further, she said that she had tried to "work with" the defendant, explaining that she "tried to get along with him, to keep him cool and try to, like he said, let's just be friends, try to be friends, conversate [sic], and I tried to do that with him."

Kathy referred to her own initial compliance as "playing the game." When I asked her what she meant by that, we had the following interchange:

> K: When he showed up at my office, I didn't have to go down to reception. You know, I could have said, "Send him away." But I didn't want to create problems, so I would go down, and see him.
> I: Were you thinking that if you talked to him . . .
> K: That he would leave me alone . . . Other times it would be, he'd want to get into a discussion about, "Let's get back together, I love you, I miss you, I'm sorry," you know . . . I was still speaking to him, where I, I shouldn't have done that at all.

Sometimes women comply with their pursuers because of their perception that resistance is inherently dangerous in violent relationships. One woman was ordered into her car by her former husband. In the structure of the crime report narrative, it appeared that she had to explain this action to the investigating officer, who wrote:

> She agreed to get into the car because [her friend's] children were in the driveway and could see what was happening. The defendant], on getting into the car, immediately put his left arm around her neck and started choking her, yelling at her, calling her names. He choked her to the point she could not breathe at first. She doesn't know why she didn't jump out of the car. She was scared. She may not have jumped out of the car because she was just used to him assaulting her. When he has assaulted her in the past, she does as he says to calm the situation down.

In this example, the officer's evaluative inquiry was implicit. No matter how frightening the situation, he must question the woman's decision not to resist, much like rape victims are sometimes assumed to have given consent if there are no visible signs of a physical struggle inscribed on their bodies. Moreover, the officer clearly implied that this woman used compliant tactics in the past, perhaps successfully.

In the following case, the defense attorney cross-examined the victim and was able to get her to admit to a number of compliant acts, including returning the defendant's telephone calls, going places with him and their son, and having sex with him—all while a restraining order was in effect.

He drew explicitly on an ideology of victim pathology when he argued that:

> We're talking about something different here than somebody doing something against their will. We are talking about a deep psychological problem with somebody being bonded to somebody else and doing something not for their own good, not necessarily criminal conduct on the part of the defendant.

The prosecutor redirected the victim in an attempt to clarify her reasons for compliance. "Why did you tell him [you were his woman]?" she asked, and the victim replied, simply, "Cause I didn't want to be hurt any more." The prosecutor asked the victim what happened when she did not return the defendant's calls, and the victim replied that the defendant would either show up at her home or threaten her family. "Is that the only reason why you return his calls?" the prosecutor asked, and like other victims who report emotion management strategies, the victim said, "Yeah, I try to calm him down." The victim explained that she would take the defendant places because:

> I was afraid for him to hit me. He would—he's—I have almost wrecked driving and stuff 'cause he'll—when I'm driving he'll pull me out the seat. So like if I give him money and he'll say take him to get something to eat and I just go through the drive through.

When she took along their son, she said, it wasn't the "family outing" that the defense attorney portrayed it to be, but an attempt to protect the little boy during his father's visitation, because the defendant told her "he would cut my son's neck to make me suffer the rest of my life."

This is how the defense attorney characterized this victim's compliance with the defendant:

> It defies credulity to believe that since [the restraining order went into effect and the present date] that this victim did not initiate, welcome, or encourage some kind of contact between her and the defendant. I mean, my God, you just simply cannot believe that. She is resuming contact with the defendant. She has had consensual contact with him. We know she did. Furthermore, I think the restraining order is null and void, because we can't believe her that she's—he has initiated contact against her will every single time and how can there be a stalking charge here when she has got the man at her home? She is sleeping with him, picking him up at work, picking him up at the jail, whatever. Where do we draw the line in what is against this woman's will? She admits all the physical particulars. She puts a spin on it. "I didn't want to do any of that. I didn't want to pick him up at work. I didn't want to pick

him up at jail. I didn't want to let him in the house, somehow he had a key. I didn't want to go to the McDonald's. I didn't want to go to the movies." It spins the law on its head, your honor. It is ridiculous. She went to a lot of those places, did a lot of those things with the defendant because she chose to do them. She has to communicate—or actually, what she has to do here is *not* communicate with him. And when she violates his restraining order every time by encouraging contact, communication, phone contact, extending into going to the movies, going to McDonald's, et cetera, et cetera, having sex with him, no, there is no strong suspicion of guilt on that particular count [felony stalking].

Here the defense attorney called upon legal and everyday understandings much like those attached to rape: just as an alleged rape is sometimes actually a consensual act, so might be the alleged stalking. It is something the victim "encouraged," in fact—like a rape victim who "asks for it." Because the victim continued to communicate with the defendant after the restraining order was issued, the defense attorney attributed responsibility for the violation of the law to her. Tellingly, however, the defense attorney initially told the judge "She has to communicate," perhaps implying that the stalking victim is like the rape victim who fails to say "no." He corrected himself, however, because part of his argument was that the victim was continuing to communicate with the defendant when she should not have been. Nonetheless, his argument suggested that this victim was one who said "no" but whose actions belied her words.

One defense attorney asked a victim if she had been "giving [the defendant] mixed signals" by continuing to interact with him after breaking off an intimate relationship. The victim explained that she had continued to see the defendant because "we had broken up on good terms when he moved out [and] it looked like we could continue being friends." Here, it appeared that stalking was not the initial tactic employed by the defendant to induce the victim to return, but even the victim admitted that "doing dinner or casual kinds of things that friends would do could very well be considered mixed signals."

The public, the public defender, and the court may all define the situation differently than do victims, who try to make it clear that they comply out of fear and the need to prevent further violence. This is how the prosecutor elicited an explanation, from the victim above who "encouraged" the actions of her stalker, of the repeated nonconsensual sex acts in which she participated. First, the prosecutor asked the victim, "How come you didn't tell [the defendant] you didn't want to have sex with him?" The victim replied, "If—when I do, um, he just takes off my clothes and he'll hit me. He'll take off my clothes and he'll hold me, hold my hands together or he'll start hitting me. He'll lay on me too like when I can't move." The prosecutor then established that the defendant weighed twice as much as and stood a head taller than the much shorter and smaller victim. She went on to tell the judge:

> [The victim's] experience has been she calls on the violation of restraining orders and if [the defendant] gets arrested he is out in three days and/or nothing happens. So she was feeling a bit hopeless. He has restraining orders, [and] protective order[s] and he has been in constant contact with her from the beginning. These restraining orders mean absolutely nothing to him. She does not initiate contact. She is afraid not to have contact when he demands it, because in the past when she refuses to have sex with him he rapes her. When she refuses to do anything for him like get him food, he beats her up. When she refuses to go to the movies with him, he slams her head into the car and grabs her hair. He is six foot five and 300 pounds. She is 5'6" [and] 150 pounds. She has no control over the situation when he—when he—when he imposes his will on her. She is scared to death of him. The best thing to do is go along with it, or the worst end of it is that she is hurt or killed.

Or consider this victim, who just wanted "peace" in her life:

> I didn't contact him, period. I never called him once. The only contact I had with him is when he called me and when he called—you have to realize I went through hell from the time he decided that—from—when he figured out we weren't going to go back together, which was in October or November when this all started up until he went to jail for being down here, he—I probably had 10, 15, maybe 20 police reports and—of things he had done, being in my back yard. And for the whole month between November and December, I stayed more in a motel than I did in my own house. I had an automatic garage door put in my house. I put it on so I would not be scared of him sitting in the bushes. When he called and said let's be—when he went to jail, they charged him with nothing else. Nothing else happened to him. When he called and said, let's be friends, I was more than willing to be friends. I was tired of living like that, tired of being scared. I'm still tired of it. I just want peace in my life. I just want to be left alone. That's all.

This excerpt illustrates the instrumental character of compliance for this victim. She indicated her hope that being "friends" with her ex-husband would keep him from threatening her, especially since she was not getting the help from the criminal justice system that she had expected. Reporting his violations to the police failed to help this woman. "Nothing" of legal consequence happened to him.

Other victims described similar decisions based on mingled feelings of fear of the defendant, hopelessness that he will give up, and despair of law enforcement help. Caity Ingalls expressed the belief that her former boyfriend would kill her if she went to the police, and said in court that she did not get a restraining order because:

I wasn't certain that they would—the police would help me, and I knew that by doing that, it was going to escalate this to a place even worse than it already was, and I was afraid that if I—I was going to make it worse, and that nobody would help me. If he came to my house and I called 911, nobody would respond. So I—I just didn't feel—I was afraid it was going to make it worse.

Another victim had this to say about why she did not call the police:

A: Um, I made a couple reports before that and, um, they told me that he would have to violate his restraining order like four times before anything would happen.
Q: So?
A: Sometimes I just felt like—I just felt at that time—just wasn't no need.
Q: There wasn't a need?
A: Yeah, I didn't think anything was going to happen to him.

Another victim called police to tell them that the defendant was calling in violation of the restraining order, "and the police said that there is nothing, nothing that, that they could do. He has to violate the hundred yards or, you know." The victim tried to explain that the defendant was describing which cars were currently parked in the driveway, something he could only know if he was at her home. "Did he describe [them] accurately?" asked the prosecutor, and the victim said, "Yes, to the 'T'. And that's what I told the police officers on the phone and they said, 'Well, if you see him over there, then give us a call again.'"

Thus there are numerous forms of compliance that appear to arise from feeling that one's former partner is not only dangerous, but that he will never go away, and that the law cannot really help. The victim quoted above who submitted so many times to sex with her 300-pound former boyfriend called police, as she told the defense attorney in the following interchange, but she did not cooperate with prosecutors:

Q: And do you recall reporting to the police that on [this date] he committed a battery against you and a sexual assault against you?
A: Yes, and nothing happened.
Q: He was arrested for all three of those incidents, wasn't he, ma'am?
A: Not that I—he was arrested one time and he spent a couple of days in jail.
Q: Ma'am, you just testified that you requested the DA to have the rape charge dismissed and that was one of the three incidents I just referred to . . . isn't that correct?
A: I told him that I couldn't go through with it. I couldn't. I don't have the money or means or anything to fight and go through court. And when he has people I don't even know where they stay or anything and they are contacting me and they know where I stay, I cannot, I couldn't go through

with it. And I told them, I did not tell them that those charges were not true, but I told them I couldn't go through with it. I told the prosecutor, I did not tell them that it didn't happen. I told him that, in fact, I didn't talk to him. I talked to a [victim advocate] in the department and I told her that I can't take it. I just cannot take it. And I told her and she tried talking to me and I told her that I couldn't.

And here is a victim explaining why she resumed her relationship with the defendant:

I was scared if I didn't that something would happen to me. I felt like he won't—he won't let me go. He's proven that. He will not leave me alone. He still won't leave me alone. He keeps coming toward—coming for me. He won't—he keeps hitting me. He—he just won't let it go. He won't get the message. I don't want him. He will not leave me alone. He will not get on with his life. It was—it was hard to explain. It's hard to explain. Um, I guess we were together. But the only reason I was with him was because I feared if I didn't then he would hurt me. The police were not protecting me, they didn't get there in time. I felt like that was the only thing I could do to protect myself and my son.

Even though the victim makes the choices she does *because* she is afraid, and *because* the defendant is violent, a difficulty for the State (and thus for her) arises. There are meanings imputed to her behaviors that muddy the representation of fear that is required in stalking cases, as well as the construction of "innocent victims" that is the moral standard in most criminal cases. Attempts to manage the emotions of former partners interfere with victims' ability to present the emotion that is requisite here for establishing victim identities. Compliance is equated with precipitation (Amir 1971), victims become at least partially culpable (Felson 1991; Ryan 1971), and "true" victimization is questioned.

"She Seems Fairly Tough": Resistance and "Mutual Combat"

Compliance is not the only victim strategy that makes prosecution problematic. In a preliminary hearing, Winnie described repeatedly, and unsuccessfully, how she tried to tell her ex-boyfriend to leave her alone. Then the public defender asked her if she had ever accepted gifts from the persistent and violent defendant (this question suggested that the defense attorney was attempting to establish compliance). The ensuing exchange mesmerized me:

A: I got out the car. I go to unlock my gate. He's at the gate. He had these tickets. He said, "I brought my tickets to you." I hit him over the head with the lock. He left.

Q: You hit him?

A: He pisses me off. Yes, I did. He made me so mad that night. I took the lock, and I swung it, hit him on top of the head. Felt good, too, though.

Q: You do have a bad temper, don't you?

A: I don't know [if I] have a bad temper. He brought out things that I didn't know existed. He brought things deep down that I didn't know existed.

Q: Did you ever hit him with a baseball bat?

A: I sure did.

Q: Did you ever use a knife on him?

A: I kept a knife with me. I kept a knife handy just in case he did something to me.

Q: Did you ever stab him?

A: No, I haven't. I threw the knife at him a couple times, I threw it.

Winnie looked fiercely at the smirking defendant as she related the foregoing without the slightest hesitation. Her demeanor suggested to me that she did not want him to know she was afraid of him. Like Konradi's (1999) rape survivors, Winnie repressed emotion while on the stand, if for somewhat different reasons. In this case, because Winnie probably expected to have to continue to interact with the defendant, she reminded him that she put up a fight in the past. After all, Winnie had filed over a dozen police reports of restraining order violations before the case was referred for prosecution, and she may have had little reason to believe that prosecution would change her situation much. She had tried compliant strategies to no avail, and she also resisted mightily, continuing to do so on the witness stand.

Ironically, this emotion management strategy may have kept the defendant at bay during the period when he was out of custody, and Winnie may have been trying to fend off future problems, but it had unintended and unforeseen consequences for her. The defense attorney argued that for the defendant to be guilty of stalking, "you have to show that there was great fear of bodily injury by the victim. I don't think she's expressed that." The judge pointed out that Winnie had made repeated calls to police, "Yet, at the same time, she seems to put up a fairly tough exterior here." In doing so, Winnie violated a normative expectation (Goffman 1963) that victims possess the attribute of meekness. Winnie was required to demonstrate not toughness, but fear, if she was to get legal help. As her story of fighting with her former boyfriend shows, resistance to intimate stalking, like compliance, can affect the credibility of victims. The judge's response to her declaration suggested as much. Not only do women who fight back continue to interact, but they present themselves less as victims than as willing participants in what police officers call "mutual combat" (Ferraro 1993).

Consider the following exchange at a preliminary hearing, when a victim described what she called a "tussle" with the defendant to his attorney:

A: I was trying to leave the room, he was trying to hold me and I pushed him.

Q: Okay. When you talked—used the term "tussle" do you mean kind of mutual pushing or contacting?

A: Yes.

Q: Okay. Had you during the three years leading up to this time when he started this behavior, that is, calling you names, had you ever assaulted him?

A: During that tussle that I'm speaking of.

Q: Okay.

A: That wasn't an assault. That was—he was holding me and I pushed him and he fell through a closet.

Q: Up to that point had you ever hit him?

A: No. One time we were having an argument. It was one morning and he started screaming and hollering and he went into his "I'm going to kill you, no good bitches," and all types of names. So, yes, I did grab him and I tore his—the buttons on his vest and I grabbed him. I said "If you're going to kill me go on and kill me now." And he told me, "I'll kill you when I'm ready to kill you."

Q: Okay. Did you ever call, had you ever verbally called him names?

A: Once.

Q: On one occasion only?

A: Yes. I called him a motherfucker.

When the defense attorney characterized the tussle as "mutual pushing or contacting," he drew upon law enforcement understandings that sometimes victims are, in fact, participants. Winnie described a similar "tussle" in which her former boyfriend grabbed her keys and some money from a table, "and he started to run out the door." Winnie said that she grabbed the keys, and "probably pushed him a few times" trying to get them back.

Winnie's case was one of the few that went to trial, and what happened in that trial seemed to illustrate precisely the problem for prosecution that resistance engenders. After the preliminary hearing described earlier, in which Winnie smiled as she recalled hitting her former boyfriend with a lock, I talked with the prosecutor, Teresa Martini, about what had happened. Teresa felt that the judge did not understand what she called "the cultural piece" at all; Teresa said that working class black women "have to be tough to survive" and that Winnie's responses to the defendant "[made] a lot of sense given the circumstances." Because Donna was out of town, Teresa asked me to call Winnie and discuss her testimony with her. In this conversation, I told Winnie that she should not be afraid to let people know how scared she was of the defendant, and that in fact she would have to if the stalking charge was going to "stick." Winnie said, incredulously, "You mean, I need to be *weaker?*" I replied, "Exactly," but in my field notes I wrote "But that is gonna be hard for her."

I was not at the jury trial, nor was I able to obtain a transcript of the proceedings before leaving the field. Upon returning to the DVU after a brief absence, I was told that Winnie, whom all of the advocates and the prosecutor characterized as "extremely credible," was "destroyed" on the witness stand when she admitted to the defense attorney that on one occasion she had gone over to the defendant's mother's house, screamed for the defendant to come out, and then kicked him in the testicles when he opened the door. Winnie tried to explain that because the defendant was at his mother's house, she felt safer than when he was at her house, and that she was enraged because the keys that he had once again glued in her door locks prevented her from entering her home. However, even though the defendant admitted on the stand to all of the violations of the restraining order with which he had been charged, gluing the locks, breaking out the windows of Winnie's car with a tire iron, and all of the acts of violence of which he had been accused, the jury "walked him," in Donna's words.

Donna was shaken by the verdict, and told me that when it was read, Winnie ran out of the courtroom crying hysterically, after telling the jury "You don't know what you have done!" Donna explained the verdict to me. Teresa had told me that she had picked a "middle-class, middle-aged, white male" jury because she was "going for educated, gentlemanly types who would think a man who beats a woman was scum." Donna felt that this was, in retrospect, a mistake. The jury, Donna said

> simply couldn't understand Winnie's experience, and they couldn't deal with the fact that she's an independent woman living alone, taking care of business, mowing her own lawn, and getting mad enough at her ex-boyfriend locking her out of her own house for the umpteenth time that she went over to where he was living with his mother and kicked him in the nuts.

"They just couldn't prove the fear element," she concluded. Teresa added that even though Winnie kept a baseball bat by the front door, sat up late into the night on her porch watching for the defendant, and carried pepper spray with her wherever she went, the jury thought, "She wanted him there." If Teresa and Donna were right, not only did Winnie's acts of resistance violate normative expectations that victims are passive in their fearfulness, but behaviors framed as "mutual combat" are defined as a kind of complicity.

Again, victims explain their actions differently than do legal actors and the public—as motivated by anger, fear, and sometimes frustration following repeated, ineffectual attempts to get legal protection. Stalkers do not go away, and victims must continue to cope with them over a period of time. As we have seen, these women used many different strategies during a process that lasted months if not years. Unfortunately, the things women choose to do to cope with their pursuers can interfere with their ability to present and maintain an identity as being legitimately afraid, "true" stalking victims, and therefore entitled to legal assistance. In such a "victim contest," a victim should be neither too passive nor too active in her own defense. Judges, prosecutors, advocates, and others attribute responsibility as they confer identity (Holstein and Miller 1991, 1997), and they do so on the basis of a victim's behavior and demeanor (Frohmann 1994; Konradi 1996, 1997; Stanko 1981, 1982).

MAINTAINING "VICTIM" IDENTITIES: "IT'S THAT WOMAN AGAIN"

Stalking victims use emotion work and other identity management strategies in their efforts to present themselves as legitimate victims. Simultaneously, they must sometimes cope with ongoing victimization, which has unintended consequences for self-presentations. Resistance, like compliance, has its pitfalls. Resistant victims typically threaten to call the police, argue with their pursuers, use sarcasm, yell and swear at them, or physically struggle and fight—all of which can raise the question of their own responsibility for their situation.

Other forms of resistance, however, also have interesting implications for identity work in stalking cases. Earlier I said that some stalking victims become very proactive as they take "case management" into their own hands. Like the rape survivors Konradi (1996) observed, they seek to build the case against the defendant by gathering evidence; often they are instructed to do so by their advocates. Some particularly frustrated victims step up the intensity of help-seeking behaviors to the point that their actions toward prosecutors mimic the behaviors of their own pursuers. They telephone constantly and contact anyone who might gain them greater access to the prosecution process. In fact, I suspected some women chose to be interviewed in the hope that I would facilitate prosecution. "Help-seeking" thus intensifies in some resistant victims. This kind of behavior might be expected in cases where crime is a process rather than an event, like compliance and resistance. When stalking continues, victims—for this very reason—are perhaps more likely to experience frustrations in their interactions with law enforcement personnel.

Ironically, this too can create problems, as women struggle to maintain their victim status over the course of time. Victim identities are not created once and for all, but must be negotiated and renegotiated as stalking situations ebb and flow. The aggressive pursuit of assistance, like other forms of resistance and like compliance, can hinder ongoing claims of victimization. A victim who is characterized as a "pain in the ass" may hurt her cause. Prosecutors and other advocates avoid interaction or make attributions of "borderline" personality disorder to victims that justify less interest, and effort, on their part. My field notes contained many ways in which women were characterized: "compliant," "borderline," "histrionic," "combative," "saintly," "grounded," "accountable," "annoying," "demanding," "noncooperative," "credible," "innocent," "proactive," "a survivor," "a 'real' victim," "'still' a victim," "too 'into' being a victim," and even "not a typical victim."

Goffman (1963:3) argues that violating normative expectations leads the audience to "reduce life chances" of the person so discredited. He is writing about the consequences of devaluing identity and conferring stigma on the devalued person. Law enforcers, and the generalized juries to whom they mentally refer (Stanko 1981), expect victims to be "innocent" (to bear no responsibility for their own victimization) yet proactive (take responsibility for their own safety). In addition, victims must not comply with defendants at the same time that they must cooperate with their prosecution. Unfortunately for victims, these constraints are sometimes difficult to adhere to. In their efforts to legitimize victim identities, these women sometimes violate unspoken norms proscribing certain kinds of law enforcement-victim interactions. These interactions can take on a "re-victimizing" character (Kennedy and Sacco 1998) from the perspective of victims in conjunction with the attacks on victim credibility that are a normal feature of preliminary hearings and trials (Frohmann 1994; Holmstrum and Burgess 1983; Kerstetter 1990; Kerstetter and Van Winkle 1990; Konradi 1996, 1997; Madigan and Gamble 1989, Martin and Powell 1994; Rose and Randall 1982; Stanko 1982).[1] Victims negotiate yet another identity dilemma as they learn what they must do to keep the attention of their advocates without overdoing it.

Demanding Women: Constructing the Deviant Victim

Nadine Peterson, a high-profile stalking victim whose story was eventually televised, decided to become, in her words, "effective and aggressive." This included persistent efforts to make herself heard in the district attorney's office:

> Because it was like I was getting nowhere. I'd get, "Well, we'll have him call you back. Yeah, we're on that, we're working on that." But they finally, the DA's office heard me so many times, "Who is this Nadine person, somebody has got to deal with her. Somebody needs to look at her case. She's calling here every day. She's even coming down here."

Nadine attributed her success in having her case prosecuted to her own efforts, in part. Ellen Nichols made a similar point when we were discussing
her future safety. She told me that she was "visible enough with the people within the system," and that she was presently enough of a "credible
person" to get the protection she needed. When I asked her how she had
become credible, she said: "Screaming, fussing, writing letters. Being the
bitch that he [her former husband] told me I was." She described calling
the prosecutor every week:

> And I know it irritated her. But you know, who cares, as long as you're pay-
> ing attention to my case. Just keep bugging people, is the only thing I can say.
> Bug them and bug them and bug them, until they get so sick of you they are
> either going to call you back or do something about it.

When I asked, "And do you bug them in a nice way, or an angry way?" She
replied, "Oh, in a nice way, but with a little bit of a threat behind it." Then
she told this story, laughing a little:

> I know I called Elaina Cross [her victim advocate] one time and I said, "Elaina,
> I haven't heard from Katrina [the prosecutor] in about a month, I know no
> investigation has been done, the trial is in four weeks, and I would like to
> know what your office intends to do as far as investigation. But if you don't
> have an answer for me I'll certainly call Laura Lennox [the lead attorney in
> the DVU] or Karen Thompson [the district attorney for the county, the su-
> pervisor of all of the deputy district attorneys who actually prosecuted cases,
> and an elected official]." I would just put it out there in a nonthreatening
> manner, but at the same time I am not going to tolerate this. I'll tell you what,
> Katrina came to my job the next day and sat down and talked to me for three
> hours after I did that. And all of a sudden an investigator was out in the field.
> I guess I reminded them that a trial was coming up, I don't know, it made me
> angry. There was a lot of evidence lost because they didn't follow up on it.
> End of story. I don't like blaming people, but that's the truth.

Ellen, like Nadine, acted in her own behalf when she felt that her case was
not being actively prosecuted and, like Nadine, was one of the few victims
whose cases actually went before a jury. She indicated her understanding
of the hierarchical organization of the district attorney's office and her willingness to make use of her knowledge to maintain her victim identity—
that she was someone who continued to be deserving of help.

Not everyone speaks quite so positively of the outcomes of this kind of
identity management, however. A highly proactive presentation of self can
contradict expectations that victims ought to be relatively passive and
compliant in their dealings with their advocates. While claiming that "pestering" the district attorney is necessary, it doesn't always seem to "work,"
as Kathy explained when she talked about encounters she expected to have

with the criminal justice system. She began by presenting strategic persistence as a tool: "I feel more able to deal with [prosecution], more able to advocate for myself. You know, I've been through the system a couple of times, I know what buttons to push, I know whose face to get into." She then talked about not wanting other victims to have to go through what she and the other VCSS members had gone through. For example, a member of the group lost her house in an arson fire before her husband was finally arrested. I asked Kathy if she felt that she was not taken seriously by prosecutors. This prompted the following exchange:

> K: Oh, I was not taken seriously. I absolutely was not. Donna [D'Amato, the stalking victim advocate] took me seriously. The second DA that was involved, you know, after Nick violated the first time took me seriously. But the first DA? No . . . No, uh, I mean, it's like, I, I would call Xenelis, and it was (she makes a dismissive sound) "She's on the phone again? What does she want?" I mean, I was treated like a hysterical female.
> I: Were you hysterical?
> K: I was scared, uh, but I mean, you've talked to me. I think I'm reasonably articulate. I didn't, I didn't jump up and down, you know, point my finger in anybody's face, uh, I, I tried to use reason. I tried, but I mean, it's like I had to sell myself over and over and over and over. Donna heard me. And I think had it not been for her intervention, nothing would have happened.
> I: About the violation of probation?
> K: About any of it. About any of it.
> I: You mean you don't think your case would have gotten prosecuted?
> K: No, I don't.
> I: Wow.
> K: I do not.

Kathy went on to describe the deputy district attorney's lack of investigation of her case and the dropping of most of the charges, attributing this to the politics of prosecution: "Because," she said, "they could plead him down, Eric Xenelis gets a little win in his book, and he moves on to bigger and better." When I asked her what she meant by selling herself, she echoed Ellen's words, sighing as she told me:

> You sell yourself by telling your story, supporting your story, selling your witness potential, you know, trying to get people to understand that you have integrity and ethics and the other thing, I, I, I remember telling Xenelis, I will testify, I will do whatever it takes, 'cause I know a lot of DV victims go sideways before trial. I guess, what I mean by selling yourself is just that, you have to keep telling the story over and over and over and over and over and over, to get somebody to listen, you know, to get somebody to say, "Oh. Yeah."

Like Ellen, Kathy showed a sophisticated grasp of the prosecution process, even using the attorneys' term ("going sideways") for uncooperative victims. She indicated that she had to keep at it, even in the face of indifference or resistance. She also seemed to recognize that establishing her identity as a "true" victim depended upon her ability to present herself as a "good" victim, one who has "witness potential" (Stanko 1981, 1982).

However, as Kathy's earlier reference to being treated like a "hysterical female" indicates, persistence does not always pay off and sometimes has the opposite effect. Caity Ingalls, for example, was a victim who appeared to violate the normative expectations of many in the DVU, primarily by being *too* proactive. As an employee of a law firm, Caity may have had the sense early on of the importance of documenting her experience. What is particularly interesting in this case is that Caity chose to document her interactions with law enforcement in as much detail as she paid to her interactions with the man who pled guilty to stalking her. In her case file was a carefully formatted, eleven-page document detailing her experience with these institutions, beginning with her initial police report. The document was written in the third person and began: "Caity Ingalls (hereinafter "Ingalls")," legalistic terminology that was maintained throughout. Police officers were identified by badge number as well as name. It was as if, by using this legalistic style, Caity attempted to present what prosecutors call "the facts of the case,"—the legal equivalent of reality, credibility, and Truth.

The document revealed Caity's desperate effort to make her claims heard, or, ironically, her persistent harassment of the people who tried to help her. The latter understanding hindered rather than helped in presenting herself as a "true" victim. Following her initial report, Caity described being interviewed in an interrogation room, "approx. 3ft. × 4ft." after which she was told by Detective Graham ("hereinafter, 'Graham'") that he would contact her within a week with a report on the status of her case. Nine days later, Caity called to obtain this status report, and subsequently left four voice mail messages in as many days for Graham, requesting return calls each time. Three days later, Caity tried to contact Graham's supervisor and left a message on his voice mail. This call, according to her document, was never returned, and Caity again left a message on Graham's voice mail. Two days later, Caity wrote:

> Graham returned Ingalls' telephone calls and informed her that his investigation was continuing, but this was not his only case and there were only so many hours in a day; that Ingalls needed to let him do his job and if she was unhappy with the way he was handling the case she was welcome to call his boss, Sergeant Schaeffer; and that he would have the matter sent to the DA's office for review by the end of the week.

Four days later, Caity again left voice messages for Graham (three in a week) and received a return call. According to Caity, Graham expressed indignation that she had hired an investigator, "and if she felt he was not doing his job she was welcome to call his boss." In the next couple of weeks, Caity left six voice mail messages for Graham, who unbeknown to her was on vacation, and then one message for Schaeffer. Schaeffer called her back that day and told her that "her case was no more important than any other case and that she needed to learn how to play the waiting game better." At this point Caity appeared to have shifted her attention to the district attorney's office and devoted the rest of the chronology to her interactions with Eric Xenelis, who "walked through" the arrest warrant before turning over her case to Samuel Ennis, the deputy district attorney who eventually prosecuted it.

This carefully constructed account of Caity's experience as a victim suggests the hazards adhering to some proactive strategies. Not only did she appear to use the strategies of "bugging" law enforcement and going up the chain of command ineptly (these strategies were effective for other victims), but in the process she managed to offend the very people she needed most to help her. One attorney told me she did not like Caity because Caity kept "dropping names of all the important people she knew, like she was someone special." The chronology revealed a similar interpretation on the part of the detectives; in Caity's report she told Sergeant Schaeffer her case "ought to take precedence" given the dangerousness of the offender, but the sergeant disagreed emphatically.

An attorney later wrote her own chronology of the investigation (perhaps guessing that Caity would sue the city), in which a joint meeting with Caity, the supervising victim advocate, several prosecutors, and an investigator was reported. Caity was described, parenthetically, as follows: "Ingalls fluctuates from initially cordial, to hostile, tearful, attacking, defensive, hysterical, sarcastic. It is difficult to focus her on the case being investigated rather than on the investigating agencies." This report suggested that Caity had a chance to "make her case" but failed to present herself in a manner that would gain her the sympathy and support of prosecutors. Instead, in a manner similar to how she dealt with police detectives, she alienated her advocates. By trying to present herself as extraordinarily deserving of law enforcement assistance, Caity made herself a less than ideal victim. Her inability to manage her emotions "appropriately" further diminished her ability to avoid a "revictimization" (Kennedy and Sacco 1998) experience she later described eloquently in a victim impact statement:

> I have been on trial for the past year, not the defendant. Every aspect of my life has been invaded, sliced, diced and placed under a microscope. [I]t has been a year of legal hell, unlike the preceding year of illegal hell only in the

sense that I was no longer being verbally threatened with death, rape, etc. by the defendant.

In this case, the emotion work Caity did on herself, rather than on her stalker, called her claims into question. The result is the same, however; Caity lost her balance, and her victim status wavered accordingly.

Further Violations: Being a "Bitch"

Melinda Sanchez had difficulties enlisting help, as I suggested in chapter 2. She described a number of problematic interactions with law enforcement at various levels. When the young police officer asked her if perhaps the dog had broken the window, rather than her former boyfriend, she told me disgustedly, "So I was like, 'Leave. There's the door, get out.'" She also told me about several calls to police:

> I'd call the police and as the police were coming up the patio I'm like, "There he goes!" and I'd see him run around the corner, and they'd just real slowly turn and look, and they're like, "Who?" [she laughed] and I'm like, "You missed him. Leave."

If Melinda was as curt and peremptory in her interaction with police officers as she was in her retelling of these stories, it is not surprising that she was unable to get them to make reports, the crucial first step in the accomplishment of stalking victimization. Melinda said that she "had more anger toward the police department for their lack of action than [she] did toward [her former boyfriend]." Her accounts of interactions suggest that she did not try very hard to conceal her feelings of frustration, anger, and disgust, and it is likely that she paid a price for her inability or unwillingness to be appropriately deferential.

Before I interviewed Melinda, Donna told me that she had "burned her bridges" with law enforcement, and that Maggie Hunt, the stalking prosecutor at the beginning of the study, did not want to file charges against Melinda's former boyfriend because of "counter allegations." Donna herself expressed feeling that Melinda was "manipulative," although she continued to counsel her despite the fact that Melinda was not "officially" a stalking victim. Thus Melinda appeared to have alienated virtually everyone who could possibly help her. In our first conversation, a telephone call I made to arrange an interview, the role of feeling rules and their violation became apparent.

Melinda said that she could not get anyone to take her seriously. A detective told her that restraining orders were for "people who are afraid for their lives, not people who just walk in off the street," and Melinda replied to the officer that she was angry and "had no more tears to cry." She also described telling detectives they had "minds like sieves." She described the following interaction with Vivian Vitale, the police detective in charge of stalking cases:

> And this is when we had the trap on the phone, and we got five crank call matches to his place of employment, I was told that's not evidence, because it was from a public place. She was like—this was with Vitale—telling me, "Well, it could have been anybody doing that." I'm like, "What have I done to you?" [she laughed] You know, "What in the hell have I done to you? Why do you, you know, you know it's him. I know it's him, everybody else knows it's him, why can't you say you know it's him too?" But, "You don't have evidence." You know, "That's not evidence." At least she could have said, you know, "I feel for you, and we understand what you're going through," but there was nothing; it was almost like I was the problem."

Detective Vitale had a reputation in the DVU for being sensitive to victims' needs, but Melinda framed her as the opposite. Vitale may well have been generally sensitive, but the problem for Melinda resided in her inability to effectively present herself as a victim. A "true" victim must have a "victim" demeanor, and Melinda appeared incapable of mustering the requisite emotions and expressions. Not only did she find herself unable to convince another detective (of whom Melinda said, "[H]is face [was] all contorted like this, like I had shit stuck between my teeth") that she was being stalked, but she became so angry that she returned to the police department to complain that important information had been left out of the police report. This is how she described the ensuing interaction with the detectives she spoke to next:

> I saw red, and I flew down there, and I said "I want to talk to the supervisor here." And she said, "Well, what's going on?" And I said, "This fuck blew my case. I've had a problem with this boyfriend, ex-boyfriend, and all the relevant facts were left out." I said, "I have a copy of the report right here. I want to talk to his supervisor." So, I'm waiting there like ten minutes, and all these cops are like coming out looking like, "Who is this here to complain about one of our people?" And here comes this Jones, Detective Jones, and he's like, "Can I help you ma'am?" And I was like, "No, thank you, I'm here to see your supervisor." And he's like, "Well what's going on?" I said, "I'm here to see your supervisor!" He said, "Well, I'm acting sergeant for today. I am the supervisor. What, what seems to be the problem?" And I said, "You know, you blew my case, okay." And we went back and forth. He said, "I did the best that I could do," he said, "with the information you gave me." And I said, "If that's your best, you're either negligent or you're grossly incompetent." And I said, "I want a conviction, I want this investigated," and you know we just went back and forth, and anyway, I said, "You know what," I want to talk to your supervisor. If I don't get anywhere here, I'm going to the

police chief, I'm going to the City Council, I'm going to Internal Affairs," and I said, "I want to involve the media." He picked up a quarter, threw it down on the table that I was sitting at, picked up the pay phone, slammed the receiver down, and he said, "I don't need to take this." He goes, "Do you want—there's the door!" He said, "You want me to leave?" and I'm like "Get on out of here, roly poly!" [she laughed]. I did not ask to talk to you. I came to talk to your supervisor. You roll on out of here." He's like, "I don't have to take this!" and went walking away, and all these cops are standing around, you know, behind the glass, they're looking at me like "You little bitch." You know, and I mean, [they were] really giving me some hard, hard looks.

This is how Melinda "burned her bridges with law enforcement," in a display of emotion that culminated a long series of interactions with various legal actors in which her growing and visible frustration made things worse for her. She chose the wrong tactics and expressed the wrong emotions, and thus never successfully constructed herself as a victim and deserving of help. To be sure, her case was complicated by the same kinds of decisions to be both compliant and resistant that made things difficult for other victims, but to her it appears that it was her interactions with the criminal justice system, more so even than her interactions with her former boyfriend, that prevented her from accomplishing victimization.

Like Caity and Melinda, some of Kathy Felson's identity management experiences illustrate the potential pitfalls of being demanding, of framing one's self as unique, and of violating normative standards for emotional display (Hochschild 1979, 1983; Konradi 1999). When I asked Kathy if *how* the story is told matters, she said:

Absolutely. I think women who walk in to this office who have limited educations, who, because of the situation may be extremely fearful, without the help of people like Donna, and even with their help sometimes, I don't think things bode so well for them. I mean, I work in litigation. I understand what the game is about. The game is about witness potential, it's about who the jury's going to believe, you know, you come into this office as a victim, you're on trial. One of the first questions is "What are we gonna dig up about you?"

Here Kathy distanced herself from more "ordinary" victims even as she asserted her own special competency. Later, she reiterated this point when criticizing what she saw as her secondary victimization and the halfhearted prosecution of her case:

I hate to do this because we rely on this office so much, but you know, my god, there, there's gotta be a better way to approach—and like I said, I understand. And I, I told Eric when I first came in, I said, "I work in civil litigation, I understand the process, you don't have to treat me like somebody who doesn't understand that. Just be straight with me." Um, but the, you know, the first thing out of the chute was, "What are we going to find out about you?" You know, "Is this a child custody issue?" And I understand, they deal with that too. But when you come into this process and you say, "okay, here's this evidence, here's this evidence, here's this evidence, here's this evidence. Please look at it." And the DA chooses to ignore that, not use it.

This type of identity claim may simply put prosecutors on the defensive, rather than force them to pay special heed to a case. The construction of a victim as "difficult" or "demanding" may also make the prosecutor less inclined to take a case to trial, as a trial necessitates continued, extensive dealings with victims. Kathy had similar difficulties with her former husband's probation officer and a police officer with whom she maintained regular contact, as the following story illustrates. She reported receiving a telephone call from the probation officer in which he told her that Nick was "acting really weird. He's up to something. I'm not sure what it is, but be careful." Kathy called the police officer to report this. A few days later, Kathy told me:

> [T]he police officer calls me back and says, "Look, I just talked to Nick's P.O. [probation officer], and he says everything's fine. He says Nick's doing great on his probation." He says, "Kathy, what are you doing?" Excuse me? And I said, "What, what are you accusing me of?" And I said, "I, you know, I got the call from the P.O., to be careful. I didn't make that up, I don't want to make that up. I'd like nothing better than for Nick to do really terrific on his probation, because then, I'm safe." [In a deep voice that mimicked the police officer's] "Well, I don't understand why he'd tell me that everything was fine if it wasn't." "Well, you'll just have to ask him about it."

Here, Kathy suggested implicitly that the police officer was accusing her of overreacting, or of manufacturing danger where none really existed.

Kathy was aware that her actions at a violation of probation (VOP) hearing might have hurt her case. As a litigator, she knew that she would be asked her address when she testified. She extracted a promise from the prosecutor that she would not have to reveal this information—given that the man who was convicted of stalking her would be present in the courtroom. Apparently the judge was not informed. When the public defender asked Kathy where she resided, the judge informed her that she had to answer the question or it could adversely affect the outcome of the hearing and place her in contempt of court. At which point, Kathy told me that she said, "Well, Judge, you can lock my ass up right now, 'cause he doesn't get to know where I live."

After this less than respectful remark to the judge, the prosecutor immediately called a recess, and Kathy chose that occasion to vent her anger
towards the judge on the prosecutor, screaming at him in the hallway of
the courthouse. Of the judge, she said, "I wanted to climb over the bench
and strangle his scrawny neck! And say, 'Get a clue here!'" Then, in an icy
tone that I suspect resembled her emotional expression at the time, Kathy
told me about the victim impact statement at the hearing:

> I told the judge, "Our daughter had to come into this court and testify against
> her own father. Because of him. We're here doing this again, because of him.
> I said 'no' to him and I want the Court to say 'no' to him. I want it to stop. It
> didn't stop the first time, it didn't stop after a jail sentence, it didn't stop af-
> ter probation. Make it stop." So he got nothing, essentially.

Kathy attributed the suspended sentence the judge handed down (against
the recommendation of the district attorney and the probation officer) to a
"system" that "just doesn't take the victim seriously," adding, "And is that
because we're women? I don't know." It may be that Kathy's gender creates role expectations that she somehow violated, rather than made her less
likely to be taken seriously. Rather than be properly deferential in the court
(a highly ritualized venue), Kathy had the temerity to be a "bitch." This
characterization, like Winnie's "tough" demeanor, is at odds with a successful presentation of victimization. This discrepancy reduced her ability
to get the relief she sought (Goffman 1963) and further illustrates how difficult the accomplishment of victimization can be (Holstein and Miller
1991; 1997).

TRANSFORMING "VICTIM" IDENTITIES: "SURVIVING" AND THE COSTS OF SUCCESS

Continued stalking exacerbates processes of identity maintenance. Through
interactions with law enforcement actors, women learn—sometimes the
hard way—about normative expectations of victims in general and stalking victims in particular. In the excerpt quoted in this chapter, Nadine was
"sorry" because she had "spoken out." The following portion of a letter,
written but not sent to law officers, similarly reveals how victims become
sensitized to the effects of their persistent presentations of victimization:

> There has never been any more reports filed with the DA's office since 11/
> 96. I am in amazement! to say the least. I left a message for Sergeant Brown.
> The message was why are the officers not following up on this, why are they
> not returning my phone calls? Why are they not serious about this? You lis-
> ten to the cassette tapes yourself and tell me he is not serious. I am afraid for

my life and they can't even return a home page let alone get the reports up to the DA's office. Please, please help me. I don't want to be afraid. Sam already knows the response time for the sheriffs to get to my home usually between 25 minutes and 2 hours. I wouldn't be bothering you but I don't know what else to do, and would appreciate any help you can give me at all. I know how busy you are and I apologize for any inconvenience this may have caused you. Thank you.

Even in her desperation, this woman is careful to indicate her respect for those who would define her. Some stalking victims became very "savvy" as they continue to negotiate victim identities and the services that attend successful claims. They fended off attempts to redefine them in negative ways, or to discredit them, in Goffman's (1963) terms. In so doing, they appeared to be cognizant of ways in which their identities might be "discrepant" (Goffman 1963:3). They acted purposefully to dispel potential stigmatizing.

"Media Bitches": Victims as Advocates

When I first began sitting in on the VCSS group meetings, it quickly became apparent that the three women who founded the group, Ellen, Kathy, and Carolina Garcia, were actively involved in victim identity management and renegotiation. During one of my first meetings, Ellen and Kathy were telling Donna about the sheriff's briefings they had been invited to attend, a major coup in their eyes. One of the officers they had befriended was at this VCSS meeting, and he praised Ellen for starting out the briefing by "establishing credibility." Kathy affirmed the value of this, telling us that she and Ellen wanted to be seen as "peers and as professional women." She said that as victims, "we are convincing cops that we are human beings, that we are valid," so that the police officers would file the reports that are so important for making a case.

Kathy and Ellen laughed when they told the group about bringing big batches of cookies to the sheriff's briefings, as a deliberate "PR strategy" directed toward "feeding the egos" of cops whom they described as having "hero complexes." This meeting, the women decided, and the VCSS group itself, was "about strategies and counter tactics." As Kathy put it, it was about "the need to be so proactive that sometimes it is exhausting." Kathy and Ellen were very self-reflexive about how they presented themselves and their "cause" to potential allies. Recognizing that victim credibility was the basis for eligibility for services—in this case, a more active enforcement of restraining orders—they took care to present themselves as the middle-class housewives, mothers, sisters, and daughters they were, bringing cookies to emphasize the roles they played.

Later that month, Carolina disappeared from the front yard of her home, leaving behind her purse, her car keys, and her children. This event shocked, terrified, enraged, and galvanized Kathy and Ellen, who found themselves at the center of a media whirlwind. Because Kathy and Ellen cofounded the VCSS group with Carolina, they were obvious choices to speak for Valley City stalking victims and to plead for the public's help in finding Carolina and bringing her home. Beginning with the local news media and moving quickly to national news programs such as "The FBI's Most Wanted," Kathy and Ellen were invited to speak about Carolina and the group. Perhaps in an effort to assuage their own fear and grief and perhaps because these two politically savvy and highly motivated women saw the opportunity for "social problems work" (Holstein and Miller 1997) on a much larger scale than had been possible previously, they entered into their new roles with a vengeance. They began describing themselves to Donna and me as "media bitches," an ironic allusion to their newfound fame and continued testiness and frustration with a system they still characterized as unresponsive.

This dissatisfaction was clear in a telephone conversation I had with Ellen a couple of months after Carolina's disappearance, when the media attention had subsided and Ellen and Kathy's lives had returned to the routines of work, child rearing, and grass-roots activism.[2] Ellen told me about meeting with various law enforcement representatives. She felt that she was "still trying to gain credibility within our own boundaries," and saying, in effect: "Pay attention to me because I am credible, I know what I am talking about and I am not going to go away." She said that she was experiencing "big frustration" trying to alleviate the "fear that we might roll on you, like the victim who goes sideways." Ellen stated, however, that she made "headway" with one of the law enforcement agencies by establishing direct connections with supervisors.

Two weeks later, I had lunch with Ellen and Kathy. I wrote the following in my field notes:

> [They] look like middle-class, slightly overweight, slightly frumpy "media bitches". Ellen is wearing a little bit too much lavender eye shadow, and Kathy is wearing porcelain face makeup, is carefully coifed, has red lipstick and [was wearing] a black velvet dress with a leopard patterned scarf. They both look tired. They are on their way to meet with a judge to talk about conflicting domestic violence and family law court orders. They say they are overwhelmed by all of the attention generated by Carolina's disappearance. "[A local television station] is still calling," Ellen says, and Kathy adds, "but at least they treat us as credible." The trip to Texas (at the invitation of a state agency working with stalking victims) was "great," they tell me, "they ate us up with a spoon."

In this and the other excerpts, we can see how the complex process of victim identity management takes place in the case of the VCSS group. The group itself was composed of a handful of articulate, well-educated, angry, middle-aged, middle-class women determined to be taken seriously. Their own credibility was clearly their salient concern. They were careful about their presentation of self. They drew on their commonsense understanding that their very normality in the face of victimization most likely gained the attention and respect of key players in the criminal justice system. At the same time, they took advantage of tragic, abnormal circumstances to dramatize their situation. In this way they moved from constructing victim identities at the lower echelons of local-level law enforcement to the national stage and from there, with newfound claims for attention, back to higher levels of Valley City legal players. But their very proactivity contradicted norms governing how victims ought to behave.

"Moving On": Victims as Agents

The deviance from victim norms underscores yet another identity dilemma that stalking victims face. As the data throughout this chapter show, defining oneself successfully as innocent, and therefore as a victim, is not easy. Many accomplished and maintained victim identities despite considerable obstacles by negotiating the tensions between compliance, resistance, cooperation and persistent help-seeking adeptly, although through much trial and error. Ironically, however, some of the very women who struggled so desperately to claim victim identities came to discover that victory was double-edged. They gained access to resources initially seen as vital but in the process claimed a status that ultimately devalued them. Caity Ingalls told me how she "just hated being called the 'victim'"; she didn't see herself as a 'victim' and she hated seeing ''victim' after her name on the documents associated with her case. She then emphasized her lack of responsibility for what had happened to her, saying:

> Like it's that walking down the road thing, you know, and someone just walking up and hitting you with a two-by-four. It's like terrorism, you know, where the person is just randomly chosen almost, and that's frightening because you know that if it's random [she laughed] that it could be, that there is nothing you did to bring it on yourself, means that it could happen to anyone.

After describing herself as a "very strong, emotionally strong person [and] stubborn" Ellen Nichols spoke of her irritation with a therapist she saw after her husband was arrested. She said:

> [I]t wasn't a pleasant experience for me. I walked away feeling much more downtrodden than when I walked in, and I think it was because she hit upon my pet peeves. "You must have had a bad relationship with your dad, or you must have something, a part of you that wanted to be abused." And that re-

ally ticks me off because I would almost argue with her and say "Are you not listening to what I'm saying? You're not listening!" It wasn't that I wanted to be, but that I had no day care, my family wasn't there for me, I didn't have that option. I didn't have anybody to turn to and I was afraid to talk to people because I always heard "It's your fault, it's your fault." So, my issues weren't that I loved him and I wanted to stay with him and make it better, my issues were logistically that I couldn't, I couldn't do this, and I didn't know how. I didn't know what resources were available and I wasn't reaching the right people to find that out.

In this excerpt, and the identity claims that preceded it, Ellen specifically disclaimed the pathological attributes associated with everyday understandings of domestic violence victimization, and alluded to the stigma associated with "weakness." By framing her decision to stay in the relationship until she could find child care in terms of "logistics," she redefined herself as an agent who could make choices if they were provided her.

Earlier I argued, following Clark (1997) and Loseke (1999) that the identity of victim is inherently deviant. As Clark (1997:197) puts it:

Because people receive sympathy only when something goes wrong, even the most innocent sympathizees are potentially labelable as "deviants." Sympathizees have experienced losses, illnesses, stigmata, misfortunes, or dilemmas that are not "normal" or "routine". People in plights may slip in others' estimation for the mere fact of undergoing them.

Thus, any stalking victim faces the possibility of being judged and found wanting simply for being a victim in the first place.

Victims worked hard to define themselves as not responsible for their victimization—a claim jeopardized by both compliance with and resistance to stalking—and struggled to maintain victim identities without violating normative expectations that victims be compliant with prosecution and not overly demanding or emotionally deviant. Nonetheless, from the perspective of advocates and victims themselves, victims "ought" to transcend their victimization and become *survivors* in the definitional process Clark (1997:22) refers to as the "morality-constructing act" of sympathizing. Women are required simultaneously to be victims (that is, blameless) and to be agents who take responsibility for their situations.

The women in the stalking support group thus made much of the fact that they were "survivors" rather than "just victims." They realized that they could not rely on protection from the State, in part because of the negative meanings that adhere to victim status. For example, Kathy made the following comment in a VCSS group meeting where a male victim was being counseled to let his neighbors know what was going on. Kathy said this was "hard but necessary," explaining "We take on the shame of what's going on, and we shouldn't. It's the offender's shame. As Donna knows, I had a hard time with that. *You* haven't done anything wrong." Kathy referred to the discrediting of victims by family, friends, and acquaintances. She acknowledged victimization as the acquisition of a deviant identity and implicitly framed asking for help as repudiating claims of competency and independence. In addition, she explicitly recognized that victims are sometimes held accountable for the actions of offenders.

Donna drew on similar cultural understandings and quasitheories about stalking when she described the difficulty victims faced when trying to establish credibility with juries because "stalkers don't treat the general public like they treat their victims—and 'we' think they should have picked up on 'signals.'" To illustrate her point, she cited media accounts of Carolina Garcia's disappearance that focused on the fact that Carolina had restraining orders against two different men, thereby suggesting that Carolina had a predilection for choosing stalkers as lovers—even though, according to Donna, "men don't act like stalkers in the *beginning* of the relationship!" Nadine expressed this morality trenchantly in a presentation to a Valley City Community College classroom, telling her audience that she informs all "her" victims that "no one can do this to you if you don't let them; no one can take your self-esteem if you don't let them." She clearly equated self-esteem with self-efficacy or agency. Perhaps she drew on stereotypes of battered women as suffering from low self-esteem as well as violence (Ferraro 1993; Lamb 1999; Mahoney 1991).

Thus the women of VCSS were instructed by Donna, Ellen, and Kathy to resist victimization, to learn how to rely on themselves rather than the criminal justice system,[3] and to become "survivors." During a meeting Kathy introduced herself as a "survivor" with a firmness and enunciation that was an avowal of pride—the pride of the stigmatized. To be a survivor was to disavow the helpless passivity associated with the victim identity. As Nadine put it, she had to tell herself to "get off your pity pot" and "empower" herself by becoming "effective and aggressive." This focus on victim "empowerment," came up numerous times in VCSS meetings. When Kathy commented "The restraining order doesn't protect us, we protect ourselves," she was saying that women like herself and Ellen *must* act on their own behalf. Ellen responded to a certain resignation in Kathy's framing by telling me that they could not allow themselves to become "depressed or defeated," but need to be proactive. Kathy said, "We need to be empowered," and Ellen explained that VCSS was "born" out of a therapy session dealing with the fatalism engendered by ongoing victimization.

The central dilemma remains, however, even when transcending victimization by "moving on." Here again, victims may sometimes be too active on their own behalf. Nadine had a videotape of a talk she had given at Valley City Community College. In it the woman who introduced Nadine was an advocate from the local rape crisis / battered women program. After casting stalking as a domestic violence-related problem becoming "more and more common," and "affecting more and more people," the spokesperson introduced Nadine by stating she was "someone who went from being a victim to being a survivor." The advocate went on to say how "important" a "transition" this was, how "healthy" it was, and how Nadine decided to "really take charge" because she was not going to "let this [stalking] happen."

Interestingly, the advocates in the DVU looked somewhat askance at Nadine, who embraced the "survivor" role and created a very public persona as the "proactive victim." While both Nadine and Ellen, for example, actively engaged in "social problems work" (Holstein and Miller 1997) with media actors as well as in the District Attorney's office and both "moved" from victim to survivor identities, they were perceived rather differently. Nadine seems to have played her part a little too earnestly. One observer remarked that while her activism might be part of her "healing process" or a way of "dealing," "She really likes the limelight." In the process, Nadine inadvertently appeared to have engendered the judgment of observers that she too fully embraced a "professional victim" role, or as Clark (1997:225) put it, she became a "career sympathizee." To the self-presentational hazards already identified, we can add another possibility. This potential deviance resides in the very character of claiming, maintaining, and ultimately—of necessity—transforming victimization.

VICISSITUDES OF VICTIMIZATION

Sometimes identities are fleeting attributions, yet far-reaching in their effects. Even under the best of circumstances, much is at stake, for no one wants to have called into question her claims about who she *is* and how (therefore) she ought to be treated. The discrediting of a presented self results in a range of consequences from uncomfortable interaction to an unwillingness to grant the most basic of rights and courtesies (Goffman 1963). This examination of stalking victims' identity work illustrates the contingent and consequential character of the social construction of selves (Altheide 2000; Goffman 1963). It also situates these processes within historical, cultural, and organizational contexts. Emergent and sometimes contradictory constructions of what it means to be a victim (Best 1997; Clark 1997; Holstein and Miller 1991; Kennedy and Sacco 1998) shape how women become victims in the DVU. Normative expectations, including those of gender (in this gender-specific crime), enter in to definitional processes (Stanko 1981, 1982) in which credibility is the crucial attribute a victim must possess (Frohmann 1994; Konradi 1996, 1997; Stanko 1981, 1982).

In the case of intimate stalking victimization, such meaning conferral really matters. For women whose former partners threaten their lives, the ability to successfully make their claims that they are legitimate and worthy victims can mean the difference between living in hell and having the opportunity to transcend the dangers and move on. Victims told about managing their emotions and those of furious former partners while interacting with law enforcement. Women faced myriad opportunities to err in their choice of coping strategies and of demeanors to express; the decisions they made were not independent of one another.

A woman who claims to be a stalking victim has to convince law enforcement actors of her fear when that very emotion may cause her to act in ways that cast doubt upon the truth of her claim. If she complies with her former partner, she is thought to be a willing participant in a pathological relationship that deprives her of her agency even as it makes her responsible for her own victimization. If, on the other hand, she chooses to fight back, she no longer possesses the requisite passivity that is the normative expectation for true victimhood. Moreover, she has to carefully negotiate her ongoing victim status as the stalking, and the involvement of law enforcement, continue. Here she needs to heed the dangers of being overly needy, of demanding too much, of allowing her growing frustration, despair, and disgust to show—as all these are ways, again, of violating feeling rules. Then, should this woman navigate these hazards to become and stay a credible victim, she is asked in the end to give up this hard won identity, in favor of yet another, "survivor."

While the accomplishment of survivorhood resolves some of the dilemmas of victimization, it is unclear how well this new identity serves to protect women from the stigma (Goffman 1963) that attaches to being a "victim"—it may be a hollow victory. The women whose experiences of prosecution and its aftermath I read about in the case files and observed in the DVU and the VCSS group cast themselves as ordinary women who faced extraordinary circumstances over which they have no control and thus for which they bore no responsibility. They had to be seen as blameless in order to be defined as victims, for they would get no help unless they were able to so construct themselves.[4] A stalking victim cannot have brought her situation upon herself; no voluntaristic agentic action is involved on her part if she is in fact a victim. The victim cannot, by definition, precipitate stalking.

But there is a cost. It resides in the ideology of victimization that posits "undesirable connotations" attached to the identity "victim" (Best 1997:13).[5] This ideology constitutes understandings shared by victims: they recognized the need to transcend the victim role in favor of a role more consistent with the expectation that social actors control their own destinies. Deviance and absolution go hand in hand, as the women come to realize.

This realization—coupled with an increasing awareness of the inability or unwillingness of law enforcement personnel to effectively intervene in the stalking process itself—led women to begin to take responsibility for their ongoing experience of victimization. That is, they now claim to be not "victims," but "survivors," women who both protect and advocate for themselves because they must.

The final irony is that it is difficult, if not impossible, to be both worthy and blameworthy simultaneously. If the essence of victimization is the claim that one is *not* responsible, then to have responsibility returned to one is in some sense to take on blame. Becoming an agent is the only way to avoid the stigma attached to victimization. Then, however, the women truly lose their innocence: not just the innocence of the blameless, but, worse perhaps, the innocence of the naive. To be a "survivor," then, is to survive not just being a stalking victim but also the process of becoming a "victim" in the eyes of the criminal justice system.

AMBIVALENCE, ACQUIESCENCE AND FURTHER COMPLICATIONS

In this chapter I have focused on compliance as an emotion management strategy borne out of a victim's fear of her former partner and, often, her perception that the stalking will continue despite her efforts to get help from law enforcement actors. As we saw in the previous chapter, however, there are times when compliance arises out of murkier emotions, making the accomplishment of victimization all the more difficult. Stalkers are not invariably threatening. Many of them use courtship and the language of love, either initially or alternating with intimidation and violence. Thus the following kind of exchange will take place in court, when a defense attorney questions a victim:

Q: Were there conversations that you had with [the defendant] that were amicable?
A: Sure.
Q: You never—you didn't feel threatened during some of these conversations?
A: No, not all of them, no.
Q: Did you feel threatened by all of the letters that he wrote to you?
A: No.

Given this kind of interaction, I argued, some women succumb to the entreaties of their former partners to return, as the following woman explained to another defense attorney:

Q: Did you actually fill out paperwork on the restraining order?
A: Yes.
Q: What happened as a result of that?
A: What happened was he kept calling—I did the restraining order, we were supposed to have gone to court. And I was getting ready to go to my class reunion and he kept calling me and I gave in because I loved him.
Q: What do you mean, you gave in?
A: I didn't go to court.

Women also described feeling responsible for the pain their former partners were expressing. One victim told the following story in court:

[My former husband] called me about a week after that and he said he needed a ride because he needed to make some money, nobody would do anything for him and he didn't have anybody. So he asked me if I would give him a ride. So I did. I dropped him off. And about two o'clock in the morning he was knocking on the door. His knuckles were bleeding. It was raining. He said he had got in a fight where I dropped him off at and he didn't have no place to go. He asked could he spend the night. He said he would leave early in the morning. I said "no" for about an hour and a half. Finally, I got tired of his begging. I felt sorry for him, too. I let him in and he slept on the couch.

Even though this victim's former husband had a violent criminal history, had been charged with assault as well as stalking, and (according to her narratives in the case file) had spied on the victim, followed her, driven by her house, shown up at her work, broken in to her home and her car, vandalized her property, kept her from leaving, abused her verbally, threatened to kill himself, threatened to hurt their child, and threatened her with a weapon, he had also left her a romantic card, told her that he loved her, and begged her to return to him. When he begged her to give him a ride and to let him in out of the rain, at that moment, he was more pathetic than frightening. She "felt sorry" for him.

Caity was asked by the attorney defending her former boyfriend to read the text of a letter she had written, after the breakup, into the record of the court proceedings. "Dear Tom, there is nothing left to say other than I am so sorry," she read. "Please believe me. I love you now and always will. You will remain in my heart always. Love, Caity." She paused, and then tried to explain:

You're, you're—you don't understand the context. My meaning is different than the way that you are taking it, and so I really can't—I can't answer that because you're taking that to mean something that it did not mean. He was my best friend. I mean—he was obviously hurt, and I am seeing a person

that I'd never seen, never—I was looking into eyes that I'd never seen . . .
what I was sorry for is that this ever happened—that we have changed from
where we were, but I recognize how you are trying to make that sound . . .
but that is not how it was intended. He was my best friend, and this was very
sad. It's that simple.

Caity had written the letter to a man she claimed had threatened to destroy
her life, yet she felt responsible for him, and tried to salve his wounds.

Another victim came under attack in a preliminary hearing because she
allowed the defendant to attend church with her, when the drug- and
alcohol-abusing defendant claimed that he was going to try to "straighten
up his life." First the defense attorney asked:

Q: During the period of the restraining order, did you ever tell [the defen-
   dant] that you loved him?
A: I told [him] that I cared about him.
Q: My question to you: Did you ever tell [him] you loved him?
A: [He] was trying to get treatment, and I was trying to encourage him.

Then the defense attorney established that when the defendant attended
the victim's church, she had spoken willingly with him, "Even though you
knew the restraining order was in effect?" "I did know that," the victim an-
swered, "but, you know, I felt that if he was going to get the help and—for
his alcohol abuse and get the help, and going to church to me was the best
way you can do that." Did she feel threatened while at the church?

No. Because [he] wasn't drinking at that time. And he wasn't—[he] is a horrible substance abuser. And when he drinks or does drugs, his whole personality changes. And that time he wasn't drinking. He said he was seeking
treatment. He was looking for gainful employment.

The victim then added, tellingly, " I don't hate [the defendant]." And even
Winnie, who came to hate a man whom she said "brought out a side of her
she didn't know existed," became teary when she found out that the case
against him had become a serious felony with the potential for a long
prison term. "Why are you doing this to me?" her former boyfriend asked
in a letter from jail, and Winnie's resolve to pursue prosecution wavered,
albeit briefly.

What these stories illustrate is how resistance can be undermined by
mixed feelings. The stalker in these cases is no stranger, but someone with
whom the victim once shared herself in an intimate relationship and for
whom she may yet feel a sense of obligation. She may be scared out of her
wits, but when her former partner begins his assault on her decision to
leave with symbols of their lost love, or abandons (however momentarily)

his violations in favor of gentler persuasions, her fear may be eclipsed by confusion, care, or guilt. Ambivalence becomes acquiescence. How this is possible, and sometimes even likely, is the topic of the next chapter. In it I turn from the experiences of victims in the Domestic Violence Unit to what at first might appear to be the far different experiences of young women in college. Their stories show that ordinary courtship, forcible interaction, and intimate stalking are sometimes inextricably intertwined through complex vocabularies of emotion and gender role. These add to our understanding of the decisions some stalking victims make.

NOTES

1. One victim, Caity Ingalls, refers to this as "legal stalking."
2. The woman I call "Carolina Garcia" was still missing when my field research and interviewing concluded. Detectives suspected homicide, according to Kathy Felson and Ellen Nichols. They claimed that Carolina's former husband, a suspect in the case, was a security guard on an unused air force base, and knew of the existence of deep underground bunkers where a body might never be found, even using infrared technologies.
3. In the VCSS group meetings, often police officers or security personnel will be the invited guests, informing victims about "options" and describing safety procedures.
4. As Charmaz points out in her analysis of stories of suffering, high moral status is defined by the "involuntary onset" and "blamelessness for condition" that characterizes certain forms of illness (1999:369).
5. Because victims are *not* agents, they have no power. According to Holstein and Miller to "'victimize' someone instructs others to understand the person as a rather *passive*, indeed *helpless*, recipient of injury or injustice. [This] 'disables' a person to the extent that victim status appropriates one's personal identity as a competent efficacious actor." (1991:119)

4

A Romantic Interlude:
Cultural Constructions of Courtship and Compliance

This chapter examines how undergraduate women, mostly sorority women, interpret and respond emotionally to a series of hypothetical and real attempts at forcible interaction in dating and long-term relationships they seek to terminate. I use the term "forcible interaction" rather than "stalking" because these attempts range from what we might define as merely "pestering" to behaviors that begin to emulate the stalking reported by women in the Domestic Violence Unit. I look at interactions that encompass more (and less) than what we have seen thus far. I want to start to sort out what is and is not problematic for women, and at which point they "draw the line." This is important, because stalking does not usually spring full-blown into birth. Rather, as we have observed, women come to see it as developing over time. This means that how women respond in "early stages," if such there be, can affect the course of stalking that does emerge, leading to ongoing processes of definition and redefinition. Most of the data derive from a survey of 267 sorority women, in which I focus on the influence of romantic cultural imagery and the effect of "relational circumstance" (Goffman 1983), or type of relationship, in hypothetical situations and in these women's experiences. These data are supplemented by interviews conducted with twenty undergraduate women about their dating experiences, in this and in an earlier study (Dunn 1998).

In the preceding chapter, we saw that stalking distresses and frightens women who claim to be its victims. However, when the actions taken by stalkers "fit" within romantic cultural repertoires, this significantly complicates these women's interpretations, no matter how "objectively" coercive, intrusive, or violent such behavior might seem to an uninvolved observer. In what follows, I explore how culture (in the form of "vocabularies" of emotion) and social structure (manifested in patriarchal gender role expectations) interpenetrate to shape young college women's responses to similar situations. As appears true for stalking victims, the norms and imagery of heterosexual courtship and romantic love play a

121

part in these women's choosing to continue unwanted interaction and to redefine the relationships from which they are attempting to disengage themselves.

We will also see that "violation" is relative and socially constructed. Rather than being an objective condition in the world, it resides in interpretations of behavior that vary across cultures and over time, and it prescribes some actions and proscribes others. This variability suggests that what women define as unwanted, coercive, or threatening behaviors on the part of others will take many forms, and, moreover, will depend upon the perceived intensity and degree of violation. Consider the case of sexual violation. It can, from some women's perspectives, include such acts as "minor" as "street remarks" made by strangers—the violations of norms prescribing civil inattention in public places (Gardner 1995; Goffman 1983). An increase in the intensity of the experience may lead women to interpret further or similar actions as sexual coercion, ultimately culminating in definitions of behavior as sexual assault. This is not to say that rape is somehow not "real," but that behaviors, interpretations, and responses are all culturally—and historically—specific. What is now defined as "marital rape," for example, was a husband's right until recently in the United States (Russell 1991). Furthermore, the context, the situation, and the relationship of actors to one another in an interaction often lead to tremendous interpretive ambiguity—as in "acquaintance rape" (Bechhofer and Parrot 1991).

Like acquaintance rape, forcible interaction (including stalking) is a similarly graduated and complicated form of perceived violation. Forcible interaction, like the stalking reported by the victims in the DVU, is interaction that takes place against the expressed will of one of the actors involved. The type of forcible interaction that concerns me here is like the stalking we have been examining in that it occurs when one person in a dating or intimate relationship refuses to discontinue ongoing interaction with the other. Such unwanted attention can appear relatively innocuous, be mildly disturbing, or create profound fear and perceptions of danger.

Importantly, such interactions often involve behavior that is acceptable in some "relational circumstances" (Goffman 1983) and unacceptable in others. As Goffman (1983:4) says, what is a "courtesy or mark of affection if we proffer it" is a "presumption if taken from us." The violation resides in taking by force what is not offered freely and in the character of the relationship between profferer and presumer. In this way forcible interaction, like acquaintance rape, involves actions and interpretations that emerge from the same cultural repertoires as interactions that women define as "appropriate" expressions of desire and need. As Emerson, Ferris, and Gardner put it, "The core dynamics in relational stalking—persistence in seeking a relationship in the face of continuing rejection—mirrors in extreme the dogged pursuit of 'true love' idealized in the culture and media" (1998:292).

An additional complexity enters in the form of hierarchical social arrangements. Patriarchy intersects with cultural frameworks to shape understandings of gender-appropriate behavior, emotions, and roles. These normative expectations may make women more vulnerable than men to such violations of spirit and body, of emotional and physical space. Social constructions of courtship, love, and romance may, like cultural myths about rape (Burt 1980), profoundly influence the ways in which men and women define forcible interaction, and through this meaning conferral, the actions they take. One possibility, for example, is that when unwanted suitors or former partners clothe forcible interactions in the language of ardor, women may not perceive these interactions as deviant or problematic. When men and women account for these incursions upon the "territories of the self" (Goffman 1983:4) by employing romantic vocabularies of emotion and gender role, they obscure the hierarchical and instrumental character of these behaviors. Women may, then, become inadvertently complicit in their own invasion.

The interpretive frameworks upon which these women draw shapes their decision making, and through this, their course of conduct in the situation. Exploring the imagery and norms that enter in to this kind of "deviant" and sometimes violent interaction thus illuminates the boundaries of socially acceptable interaction in intimate relationships. It also begins to articulate a complex relationship between the structural, the cultural, and the individual—in situations where actors differ both in their desire for interaction, and, perhaps, in their ability to shape its course.

Some Relevant Research and a Conceptual Framework

Forcible interaction takes many forms. These can be conceived of as falling along an interpretive continuum ranging from perceptions of violation as relatively nonviolent and unobtrusive to definitions of interaction as more explicitly threatening and dangerous. The *undesired* character of the interaction from the perspective of the recipient is what connects quite varied acts. Importantly, it does not necessarily follow from this unwillingness to interact that interpretations will be unequivocal on her part. A brief review of research indicates that some women are significantly disturbed by even the least explicitly "violent" behaviors (Gardner 1995; Sheffield 1989; Spitzberg and Cupach 1996; Stanko 1993). However, research on violent relationships suggests that other women may not interpret even the most dramatic actions as problematic—particularly when it is an intimate who violates. Women not only suffer more at the hands of intimates, but tolerate more (Gelles and Straus 1988; Henton et al. 1983; Jackman 1994). It could be that this "acceptance" of violence is due to cultural norms that permit a fair degree of violence in close relationships, but I will argue that it may be because women sometimes conflate love, passion, and violence in their hearts and minds, muddying the interpretive waters through which they sometimes flounder.

Stalking is an extreme form of forcible interaction. The research cited in chapter one indicates that women are more likely to experience stalking at the hands of intimates than strangers, and when this is the case, the relationship was likely to have been violent (Tjaden and Thoennes 1998a; 1998b). Mahoney (1991) describes a type of forcible interaction, "separation assault," that she argues frequently follows attempts to disengage from violent relationships and consists of

> [an] attack on the woman's body and volition in which her partner seeks to prevent her from leaving, retaliate for the separation, or force her return. It aims at overbearing her will as to where and with whom she will live, and coercing her in order to enforce connection in a relationship. It is an attempt to gain, retain, or regain power in a relationship, or to punish the woman for ending the relationship. It often takes place over time. (Mahoney 1991:65–66)

This is the kind of forcible interaction the stalking victims whose stories appear here describe so vividly. In addition, researchers and policymakers often characterize stalking as an escalating process (National Institute of Justice 1993; Fein and Vossekuil 1994), a characterization that lends weight to my claim that the role victims play in interactions with stalkers is important.

For this reason, and because of the ambiguities that inhere in situations where interactions cannot be reduced to "either/or" situations, stalking is not the only kind of forcible interaction that interests me here. Some researchers examine a broader range of problematic activities, not only in the context of research on stalking (Spitzberg and Cupach 1996), but also in explorations of what researchers term "everyday" violence (Stanko 1993), "public harassment" (Gardner 1995), and "sexual terrorism" (Sheffield 1989). These researchers emphasize the problematic character of various seemingly insignificant forms of forcible interaction, arguing that harassment in public and private is both pervasive and distressing (Gardner 1995; Sheffield 1989; Spitzberg and Cupach 1996; Stanko 1993). For example, Spitzberg and Cupach (1996) assert that almost 40 percent of the college students in their sample experienced even the "more serious forms of intrusion that would ordinarily be called stalking," and caution against the minimizing of "milder" forms of what they call "relational intrusion." Again, for my purposes, it is not the behavior itself that is at issue here, but the interpretations and responses that follow.

Importantly, people who perceive violence as shocking in other interactions do not always perceive it as negative when it occurs in intimate relationships: Henton et al. (1983:474) studied college students' interpretations of abusive behaviors in their dating relationships and discovered that over one-quarter of the victims of violence, and almost a third of the aggressors, interpreted abusive behaviors as meaning "love." Gelles and Straus (1988:51–52), in what is perhaps the most widely cited research on family violence, claim that the notion that "violence and love are incompatible" is a "myth" and that the phenomena "coexist" in families in part because of their structure of intimacy. Jackman makes a similar argument, pointing out that intimacy makes easier the use of violence directed towards subordinates by superordinates, in part because:

> The emotional bond that exists between the individuals in each one-to-one relationship swathes their personal interactions and makes it more acceptable for the individual from the dominant group to express anger and to indulge in physical violence within the confines of that personal relationship. A woman often excuses physical violence if it is perpetrated by the man she loves (and who she believes to love her). Explosions of anger and violence are considered acceptable for a man within the context of an intimate, love relationship with a woman (1994:82–83).

Nor, conversely, does it appear to be the case that even the most dangerous of pursuers restrict themselves to threatening strategies—the stalking cases examined in the previous chapters reveal that over one third of the men charged with stalking reportedly intermingled declarations of love with their threats to commit mayhem. Because the stalking of intimates often involves these "permutations and exaggerations" of ordinary behaviors (Emerson, Ferris, and Gardner 1998:289) "recognition" of stalking is not a given, but a definitional process that can be "highly problematic" (Emerson, Ferris and Gardner 1998:291). This tension, between violent and romantic interpretations of interaction, is the focus here.

From a symbolic interactionist perspective, forcible interaction, like all interaction, is shaped by the meanings actors confer upon it (Blumer 1969; Thomas 1978). Responses to forcible interaction, such as those described in the previous chapters on stalking victimization and further detailed in this chapter, are part of a process. The actions of both men pursuing further interaction and women trying to forestall it are based on their respective definitions of the situation and an ongoing construction of meaning in their interactions with each other.

Further, forcible interaction by definition involves conflictual interactions and thus contested definitions of situations. Goffman (1983) argues that all face-to-face interactions carry with them "enablements and risks" in which, particularly if one is ranked low along some hierarchical dimension of social location such as gender, that actor becomes vulnerable to violations of the normative expectations she brings into interactions. We learn about the normative order when something occurs that calls the meanings actors assign to what is going on into question—what Goffman (1959:13) terms "definitional disruptions." In the case of forcible interaction of the type described here, an insistence on continued interaction is a violation of the expectation that interaction is properly reciprocal rather than coerced. However, women, because of their lower status in patriarchal social arrangements, may not have or recognize grounds for complaint.

Forcible interaction can thus be seen as inherently problematic, but nevertheless quite complicated. Previous research on intimate violence, stalking, and other forms of forcible interaction suggests that these interactions fall along an interpretive continuum of invasiveness, intensity, and violation, and cause great distress in some women but not others. Moreover, there may be contradictory emotional responses to and interpretations of these interactions, shaped in part by norms that dictate "appropriate" responses. My objective in this chapter is to illuminate just such kinds of ambiguities and complexities, and suggest a cultural and structural framework for understanding this range of interpretation.

Surveying the "Sisterhood": Sorority Women, Students, and Research Methods

I approaches these concerns by examining (1) the emotional responses of undergraduate sorority women to hypothetical scenarios depicting a series of attempts at forcible interaction made by unwanted suitors, and (2) these and other undergraduate women's experience of forcible interaction in their own lives. The survey is designed to illuminate the influence of courtship imagery upon young women's interpretations of unwanted attention, especially when romantic tactics are chosen not just by dates, but by men with whom these women have maintained intimate relationships—both hypothetical and real. Some young women were interviewed about coercive dating experiences and others about difficulties they had disengaging from relationships. Of the resulting data, I ask, do the trappings of love easily sway these young women? And if so, are they more or less vulnerable when their pursuer—however unwanted—is someone whom they know well?

I surveyed women (N = 267) in six popular sororities at a large Western State university, using a self-administered questionnaire. I surveyed women because stalkers are predominantly male (Tjaden and Thoennes 1998a) and because in a pretest of the survey, male respondents' perceptions of female pursuers were unambiguously negative, for reasons the cultural explanation proposed here may further illuminate. The women filled out the questionnaire during regular evening meetings. Only two sorority women chose not to complete the questionnaires, and although 5 percent of the sample left one or more questions blank, all of the questionnaires provided usable data. The respondents ranged in age from 18 to 24; most (93 percent) were between 19 and 22 years old. Almost 40 percent were seniors at the time of the survey and only 5 percent were first-year students. About 80 percent of the respondents described themselves as White, 6 percent said they were Black, 8 percent said they were Latina, and the remaining 5.6 percent described themselves as Arabic, East Indian, Filipina, Greek, Native American, or Pakistani. Respondents reported 44 different major fields of study, of which I could categorize 68 percent as humanities and social sciences, and 32 percent as mathematics and other sciences.

Sorority women are a particularly appropriate population in which to study young women's interpretations of courtship and dating behaviors. They are actively involved in dating relationships in part as a function of their membership in these social organizations, and, by virtue of their social location in the Greek system, are frequently brought into contact with fraternity men. Both sororities and fraternities inculcate norms of aggressive male sexuality and acquiescent female sexuality (Boeringer, Shehan, and Akers 1991; Martin and Hummer 1989) that are quintessentially "traditional" representations of culturally appropriate attitudes toward courtship, romance, and love. College campuses are a setting in which romantic interpretive structures link the attention men pay to women to the latter's desirability and thus worth (Dunn 1998; Holland and Eisenhart 1990). This is especially true in sororities. In these organizations, formal and informal rules shape traditional gender-role socialization processes and courtship patterns (Risman 1982) and reinforce both a "culture of romance" (Holland and Eisenhart 1990) and through it, the particular vulnerability of sorority women to sexual commodification, exploitation, and abuse (Stombler 1994, Stombler and Martin 1994).

I designed the questionnaire to elicit women's emotional responses to hypothetical scenarios. In these scenarios she has clearly stated to either a man with whom she has had one date (in one version) or a long-term partner (in another version) that she no longer wishes to have any contact with him. Then the date or former boyfriend engages in a series of increasingly intense attempts to coerce or force interaction ranging from leaving messages on an answering machine (or on e-mail) to threatening to kill or hurt himself. In the questionnaire, the women are instructed to indicate how they thought they might feel if they were to experience each of these attempts. Open-ended probes followed half of the six attempts described, to elucidate why women responded as they did. Also, because hypothetical scenarios are useful for gathering data about hidden behaviors and sensitive subjects, but inherently speculative, additional open-ended

questions in the text asked for respondents' opinions of men who continued to pursue a person who has made it clear that she wishes to be left
alone, whether they had ever been in a situation where someone engaged
in these or similar behaviors, and if so, what happened and how they felt
at the time.

Based on previous research on the relationship between stalking and
domestic violence (Kurt 1995; Tjaden and Thoennes 1997; Williams, Lane,
and Zona 1995), the questionnaire focuses on the perceptions and experiences of women regarding relatively ordinary interactions, rather than the
less frequent attempts at forcible interaction engaged in by strangers. Because women may interpret seemingly abusive behaviors as romantic
(Henton et al. 1983), and because it is suspected that forcible interactions
draw upon cultural constructions of courtship, romance, and love, the
women were asked to indicate whether they perceived these attempts as
flattering or romantic as well as annoying or frightening. In addition, romantic imagery (gifts and flowers) are included in two of the attempts described. Respondents were asked about a series of attempts that vary in
their degree of invasiveness (operationalized as face-to-face contact) and
violence. If forcible interaction is the escalating process that we instruct
women to avoid, and if women fail to perceive early stages of the process
as problematic—interpreting these attempts as appropriate rather than in-
cursive or invasive—they may respond in ways that fail to effectively discourage further forcible interaction, with potentially adverse consequences.

By moving from and between nonromantic and romantic attempts at
forcible interaction, noncontact and contact attempts, and implicitly and
explicitly threatening attempts, I sought to simulate a variety of situations
young women encounter, and especially the escalating or persistent character of these events (Fein 1994; Emerson, Ferris, and Gardner 1998; National Criminal Justice Association 1993). Hypothetical attempts a rejected
suitor might choose thus were varied as follows:

(1) leaving messages (a nonromantic communication not involving face-to-
    face contact),
(2) showing up (nonromantic but involving contact),
(3) leaving a card and a gift (romantic but not with contact),
(4) waiting with flowers (romantic and with contact),
(5) threatening to hurt or kill himself (explicitly threatening but not with
    contact
(6) following in a car (implicitly threatening and involving contact).

Importantly, intimacy may further confound women's interpretations of
abusive behavior (Henton et al. 1983), so half of the respondents were
queried about a hypothetical terminated dating relationship and half were
asked about attempts following the termination of a long-term relation-

ship. Versions of the questionnaire were stacked and distributed in an alternating fashion to approximate random assignment to each condition within each sorority. For each attempt, respondents reported how flattering, romantic, annoying, and frightening it seemed on a scale from "0" to "8", with "0" meaning "not at all" and "8" meaning "extremely".

A pretest of the survey suggested considerable ambivalence in women's responses to forcible interaction, and I anticipated that women would provide explanations of their responses if subjected to an (implicitly) valuative inquiry. Because an emphasis on vocabularies of emotion facilitates a greater understanding of both the expressive and the instrumental features of these interactions, these open-ended questions were coded for mentions of anger, guilt, jealousy, and love. Importantly, as noted above, the women were also asked about their actual experience of forcible interaction. Women's descriptions of how they interpret and respond to the attempts they do in fact encounter in dating and intimate relationships can help to explain their responses to the hypothetical scenarios I presented. For this reason, also included in this analysis are data from some of the seven in-depth interviews conducted with undergraduate women as part of the larger study on stalking victimization, and the twelve undergraduate women interviewed in an earlier study (Dunn 1998) of sexual coercion.

RESPONSES TO FORCIBLE INTERACTION

As explained earlier, the objective was to find out how young women interpret a range of forcible interaction attempts, some of which are characterized by the use of cultural imagery drawn from romantic repertoires and some of which come from intimates rather than mere acquaintances. Are women truly frightened by an unwanted suitor who shows up unannounced, or will they be flattered by this demonstration? What if he shows up with flowers? Will that change how they perceive him? What if he is a former lover? Will she grant him more invasive latitude? In the sections that follow, I examine responses to a range of attempts that vary in their invasiveness and romantic character, and that vary in the nature of the relationship. I also explore ways in which women's emotional responses to forcible interaction are mixed, or ambivalent. Then, I look closely at how individual women account for forcible interaction and how they respond to it (in the questionnaire and in their own lives), linking these accounts to the relational, romantic, and ambivalent themes already articulated.

The Range of Attempts

Table 4.1 presents the mean emotional responses (with standard deviations) to each hypothetical attempt at forcible interaction in which an un-

Table 4.1. Mean Emotional Responses (With Standard Deviations) to Each Type of Forcible Interaction Attempt, Undergraduate Sorority Women (*N* = 260)

	Leaving a Gift	Waiting w/Flowers	Leaving Messages	Showing Up	Following	Suicide Threats
Flattered*	3.56(2.27)	3.42(2.32)	3.05(2.18)	2.27(2.02)	0.40(0.91)	0.08(0.46)
Romanced	2.92(2.29)	3.15(2.48)	1.30(1.60)	1.21(1.58)	0.22(0.61)	0.01(0.11)
Annoyed	4.55(2.46)	4.96(2.52)	6.32(1.72)	6.00(1.91)	6.82(1.75)	6.26(2.68)
Frightened	3.20(2.66)	3.70(2.80)	4.22(2.41)	4.07(2.49)	6.80(1.73)	7.82(0.62)

*scales range from 0–8 points

wanted suitor might engage, following a woman's attempt to terminate all interaction. The six types of attempt are grouped into three categories: the two right-hand columns represent relatively unambiguous behaviors, while the two columns on the left represent romantic attempts. The middle two columns are nonromantic attempts that are not explicitly threatening. Not surprisingly, following and threatening suicide elicit the least positive or neutral and the most negative emotional responses. Among the less extreme attempts, the infusion of an overlay of "hearts and flowers" produces a more receptive response from these women. Overall, the explicitly romantic behaviors are the most flattering and the most romantic—as well as the least annoying and the least frightening—of the behaviors a date or an ex-boyfriend might choose. The similar, but less courtly attempts (leaving messages or showing up without flowers) are perceived less positively and more negatively. While percentages are not presented in these figures, over half the women found leaving a gift (52 percent) and waiting with flowers (56 percent) to be at least moderately romantic, as compared with leaving messages (22 percent) and showing up empty-handed (20 percent).

The effect of romantic imagery appears to counter increasing levels of "invasiveness." Table 4.1 indicates that waiting with flowers, which involves contact with the pursuer, is only a little more annoying and more frightening than leaving a gift. Following the same logic, the romantic strategies seem intuitively more invasive than leaving messages on a computer or phone because of the physical presence of the gift or the unwanted suitor, but nonetheless the accompanying romantic symbolism makes them more acceptable for this group of women. Over 75 percent of the women found the e-mail or voice-mail messages moderately to extremely frightening. In contrast, only half of the women found the gift moderately to extremely frightening, as did just one-third of the women responding to the flower-bearer on their doorstep. Additionally, while both the man who merely shows up and the man waiting with flowers are physically present, the romantic attempt remains less frightening than the similar (but less love-symbolic) attempt (34 percent and 70 percent, respectively). Thus, the infusion of romantic imagery into a representation of forcible interaction alters women's perceptions, as Table 4.1 shows. Despite the escalation of incursion represented by evidence of physical presence, or the presence of the man himself, romantic attempts with this character do not engender a correlated escalation of annoyance or fear.

However, it should be noted that Table 4.1 also shows that following someone and threatening suicide are both the least flattering or romantic of the attempts, and are the most annoying and frightening behaviors. Mean "flattered" scores of .40 and mean "romanced" scores of .22 for following, and .08 and .01 for suicide threats indicate that only a very small percentage of the women (between 1 and 6 percent) found being followed in their cars or a suicide threat to be even moderately romantic or flattering. Very few women were only a little annoyed or frightened by being followed (fewer than 4 percent), and the mean scores were 6.82 for annoyance and 6.80 for fear. The suicide threat was seen as moderately to extremely annoying by 86 percent of the women (the mean score was 6.26) and frightening by almost all of them (99 percent), with a mean score of 7.82. Thus it appears that for the group as a whole, it is only when an escalation of "invasiveness" is not accompanied by the trappings of romance, or is unambiguously threatening, that women's perceptions of violation escalate in tandem.[1]

This finding is reinforced when we consider the variability of responses to the hypothetical scenarios. With the exception of how annoyed by a suicide threat these women were, the attempts at forcible interaction in which responses are most diverse are the romantic attempts. The highest standard deviations from the mean are in how frightening the flower-bearer and the leaving of a gift appear (about 2.8 and 2.7 points on a nine point scale), and the standard deviations in annoyed responses to these behaviors are among the highest (about 2.5 points for each). In contrast, flattered and romantic responses to being followed and the suicide threat have the least variability, ranging from .11 points for finding the suicide threat romantic to .91 points for being flattered by being followed. Hearts and flowers elicit a range of responses, invasive but not explicitly threatening attempts induce less variance, and being followed or threatened with suicide engenders almost uniform, distinctly negative responses.

Relational Circumstance

Relational circumstance here refers to the duration of the hypothetical relationship prior to attempted termination, described in half the questionnaires as following a single date and in the other half as following the ending of a long-term relationship. Is the confounding effect of romantic imagery altered in any fashion by the degree of intimacy of the unwanted relationship? Table 4.2 compares women's responses in both groups to the series of attempts at forcible interaction in which their hypothetical pursuers engaged. In this table, the data are summarized by presenting numerically the mean scores shown for the group as a whole that appeared in Table 4.1.

Table 4.2 indicates that even though simple romantic strategies alter the perceptions of both well- and little-known pursuers, there are differences in emotional responses to all of the attempts when the dating scenario is compared to the intimate relationship scenario. In general, the women re-

Table 4.2. Mean Emotional Responses to Each Forcible Interaction Attempt By Type of Relationship, Undergraduate Sorority Women (*N* = 260)

	Flattered		Romanced		Annoyed		Frightened	
	Date	Intimate	Date	Intimate	Date	Intimate	Date	Intimate
leaving a gift*	3.27	3.83	2.47	3.35	4.94	4.15	4.14	2.24
waiting/flowers	3.28	3.56	2.80	3.48	5.30	4.61	4.53	2.85
leaving messages	2.86	3.23	0.97	1.63	6.90	5.71	5.21	3.21
showing up	2.04	2.49	0.95	1.46	6.43	5.56	4.98	3.14
following	0.33	0.47	0.16	0.26	7.22	6.42	7.28	6.33
suicide threat	0.07	0.09	0.00	0.01	6.61	5.90	7.93	7.70

*Differences between means in bold-face are significant at the .05 level.

sponding to unwanted pursuit by a date were less flattered and romanced, and more annoyed and frightened by any form of forcible interaction than the women responding to a former intimate engaging in the same behaviors. Looking at the romantic attempts of leaving a gift and waiting on the doorstep with flowers, there are significant differences between all of the emotional responses of both groups of women—except in how flattered they are by the flower-bearer. There are also significant differences in the emotional responses of women with different versions of the questionnaire to the less romantic, but not explicitly threatening, attempts of leaving messages and showing up. And while there are only small differences in the mean responses to being followed and to the suicide threat, the feelings of annoyance and fear these women express are significantly different between groups.

Table 4.2 shows that where the date and ex-boyfriend differ most, is not in how positively their forcible interaction attempts are viewed, but in how negatively these behaviors are viewed. The differences between the casually acquainted pursuer and the once-loved partner are larger for the negative responses (annoying and frightening) than for the positive ones (flattering or romantic), particularly when the behavior is less ambiguous.

In sum, relational circumstance clearly alters women's perceptions of forcible interaction, even in the most "unambiguous" situations. Women look more positively upon all of the attempts used by a hypothetical ex-boyfriend, and are more annoyed and frightened when a hypothetical date engages in the same behaviors. While women's responses are generally more varied for the romantic attempts, explicitly threatening behaviors elicit more diverse emotional responses when the danger is posed by an intimate. Women who are made acutely uncomfortable by unwanted attention from a person in whom they have little invested, are inured to the hazards represented by the person whom they know well.

Ambivalence

The ambivalence suggested by the responses to romanticized forcible interaction described above is highlighted when the group's emotional responses along positive dimensions (feeling that an attempt is romantic or flattering) are cross-tabulated with their responses along negative dimensions (feeling that an attempt is frightening or annoying). Table 4.3 illustrates ambivalence for the aggregate by cross-tabulating each of the two negative emotional responses with each of the positive responses, for the "waiting with flowers" attempt. This is a summary of how, for the group, it is possible to experience multiple, diverse emotional responses to each of the attempts at forcible interaction.

As one might expect, there is a negative association between finding this attempt frightening and finding it romantic. At the same time, however,

Table 4.3. Distribution Of Finding Waiting With Flowers Romantic and Flattering By Finding It Frightening and Annoying, Undergraduate Sorority Women ($N = 268$)—Percentages

	FRIGHTENED Response to Attempt			ANNOYED Response to Attempt		
	Slightly*	Moderately	Extremely	Slightly	Moderately	Extremely
ROMANCED Response to Attempt						
Slightly	25.0	38.2	74.7	17.9	27.8	67.2
Moderately	38.5	42.1	17.7	33.9	45.8	25.4
Extremely	36.5	19.7	7.6	8.2	26.4	7.4
Totals**	100.0	100.0	100.0	100.0	100.0	100.0
($N = 251, 250$)						
FLATTERED Response to Attempt						
Slightly	14.4	31.6	63.3	10.5	17.8	56.1
Moderately	50.5	52.6	25.3	43.9	58.9	34.1
Extremely	35.1	15.8	11.4	45.6	23.3	9.8
Totals	100.0	100.0	100.0	100.1	100.0	100.0
($N = 252, 253$)						

*Response categories are coded as follows: scores between 0 and 2 are labeled "slightly," between 3 and 5 "moderately," and between 6 and 8 "extremely."
**Totals vary slightly due to the percentage (approximately 5% of the sample) who failed to provide indicators for all of the emotional response categories.

there are a considerable number of women whose feelings are mixed. Many respondents reported that the attempts in question seemed *simultaneously* flattering or romantic as well as annoying and frightening. While almost two-thirds of the women found the presence of an unwanted suitor on their doorstep to be moderately or extremely frightening (despite the flowers he holds), those flowers apparently lead many of the women in this subgroup simultaneously to perceive this behavior as moderately or extremely romantic. One-quarter of the women who said this attempt was extremely frightening also reported it to be at least moderately romantic.

The women were even more likely to combine flattery with fear for this attempt. More than two-thirds of the women who are moderately frightened are moderately or extremely flattered as well, and about a third of the women who are extremely frightened remain moderately or extremely flattered. Thus, although the overall tendency of the women is to find this particular attempt less romantic or flattering as their fear and annoyance increase, large percentages of the women have mixed feelings. Over one-quarter of the women are both moderately or extremely romanced *and* at least moderately frightened, and almost half the sample are both moderately or extremely flattered *and* at least moderately annoyed. It is apparent, then, that romantic cultural imagery creates ambivalence in these women's definitions of forcible interaction situations, even when they recognize the attempts as problematic. To probe the meaning of these results, I move from presenting the quantitative data that summarizes the women's aggregate responses, to these and other young women's own accounts, in which they describe and explain their individual responses to actual forcible interaction as well as the hypothetical situations with which they were presented.

TRUE ROMANCE: ACCOUNTING FOR FORCIBLE INTERACTION

The data described above suggest that men who use symbols of courtship, romance, and love—when paying unwanted attention to women who have made clear their desire not to interact with them—shape these women's perceptions in ways that diminish interpretations of forcible interaction as invasive or threatening. This is particularly true when the relationship the woman is attempting to dissolve is long term and intimate, but even the relatively unknown pursuer is less annoying or frightening when he draws from romantic cultural repertoires. By examining the sorority women's explanations of their responses to the hypothetical scenarios, their descriptions of their own experience with forcible interaction, and what some of the undergraduate women interviewed had to say, definitions of situations and relationships can be explored in greater detail. The ways in which women account for the attempts of their pursuers and their own interpretations of these attempts, further illustrate the interpenetration of cultural and hierarchical frameworks for forcible interaction—and some women's vulnerability as a consequence.

I return to the themes of relational circumstance, varied attempts, and ambivalence, in the process of exploring how these women characterize pursuit as representative of love, men as active pursuers, and themselves as passive objects of pursuit. These vocabularies of emotion and role—including those in which they frame themselves as nurturing and men as implicitly unromantic—make sensible the use of romance within a coercive interaction. The accounts of the women confirm that intimates who force interaction are less problematic than acquaintances who do so, but also that this relational context is less salient than the cultural context supporting romantic attempts—when used by either a date or an ex-boyfriend. The data demonstrate the effects of romantic strategies in various ways, ranging from ambivalent and/or guilty feelings on the part of women, to questioning the decision to disengage, to continuing interaction and, in some cases, to returning to the unwanted relationship.

In the following analysis of the survey data, I have chosen to discuss the sorority women's responses to their dates or ex-boyfriends waiting on the doorstep with flowers, the most romantic attempt, and the attempt in which romantic imagery appears to render physical presence less threatening than when the same pursuer shows up at work or class, without being so "armed."[2] When appropriate, I also include accounts of women's self-reported experiences of a broad range of forcible interaction, romantic and sometimes otherwise. In response to an open-ended question in the questionnaire, half the women in the sample reported being in a situation in which someone engaged in behaviors similar to those in the hypothetical scenarios, and many described their experiences in some detail. There are excerpts from the interviews with undergraduate women, in addition. I begin by looking at the effect of intimacy alone. Then I examine some ways in which romance influences interpretations, paying special attention to the ambivalence it can generate.

Relational Circumstance: "It's Not Like He's Your Boyfriend."

The means and percentages indicate that the type of hypothetical (and real) relationship (long-term or a single date) between the pursuer and the woman influences her perceptions of how romantic, flattering, annoying or frightening his behavior has become. In responses to open ended questions, about 20 percent of the women who received the dating version of the questionnaire referred to some aspect of the relationship in their explanations of their negative or ambivalent responses to this romantic strategy. One woman said "I think in all of the above scenarios how I felt would depend on the extremity of the situation and who was involved," suggesting, as Goffman predicts, the importance of relational context for understanding interpretations. The gift of attention a woman bestows on her suitor as a sign of favor is an affront when it is wrested from her by force. "If he's only a date, why would he do all of this. It's not like he's your boyfriend," said one woman, as did another who added "[i]t would be different if I had ended a three-year relationship," affirming not only the difference relationship makes but implying that such behavior is acceptable when engaged in by an intimate, even when interaction is undesired.

In one interview, it was only after redefining a relationship she described as coercive, manipulative, and emotionally neglectful as *non*intimate that one young woman was able to disengage. As long as she was able to imagine that the man involved was still her "boyfriend," Kendra continued to have sex with him despite her better judgement and the urgings of her friends to end the relationship. After one final interaction, in which she allowed him to come to her office even though she had said, "I can't believe this jerk is calling me!" she explained:

> I think he did, for a long time, take total advantage, and I was willing, and it was real clear that I wasn't so [anymore]. But at the same time, he still followed up the visit with a call a month later. I was like, God, didn't you get the picture? But, I don't know he'd always say, "We should be friends." Well, I don't want to be your *friend*, you don't know how to be a friend.

Of a violent relationship in which she remained long after wanting to leave, another young woman said,

> It was something I was used to, it was, I mean, we basically knew each other, and, it was comfortable. So, I think the relationship was over like a year, a couple, actually, six months into the relationship, but I think we stayed together longer 'cause it was convenient.

This woman tolerates abuse in part because her abuser is her boyfriend. His otherwise unacceptable actions are altered in their meaning by her acceptance of him as a continued presence in her life.

However, even the date, when romantic, is seen in a more favorable light. "He's starting to grow on me," was one woman's comment. In the case of such strategies, as the following quote makes clear, it is the relationship that changes interpretations of attempts that are drawn from a common cultural frame: "Receiving flowers is always nice but if I didn't like the guy, I would feel annoyed and want him to leave me alone," commented a woman who recognizes precisely the reverse tension—that between the acceptable act engaged in by an unacceptable actor.

The Range of Attempts: "It's Obvious He's Sane" and "He Went Out of His Way"

Romantic attempts are subject to multiple, interrelated interpretations. Because receiving flowers is always nice, this and other trappings of love may cloud women's sensitivity to violations of the boundaries she has set with both intimates and acquaintances in hypothetical scenarios as well as in real life situations. As the scaled responses cited earlier suggest, routine wariness can dissipate when physical presence—ordinarily perceived as threatening—is accompanied by flowers. This finding is illuminated by the women's accounts: "These actions are not as pushy and forceful," said one woman, explaining why she was less annoyed or frightened by the romantic attempts of leaving a gift and sitting on the doorstep with flowers than by leaving messages or showing up empty-handed. "These outcomes or situations don't seem as aggressive and I think I would know how to handle them better than the first," said another, and, in the same vein: "[Because] of the manner in which [he] is trying to see me," a third woman said, "maybe it is less intimidating, I'm not sure." The "manner" is that of the courtier, the supplicant, thus the intrusiveness of the more powerful into the realm of the less powerful is disguised.

Moreover, as the quantitative data indicate, this is even true of a pursuer about whom the woman knows very little. A person who is violating the boundaries of acceptable behavior given the relational context, and is therefore threatening in most circumstances, becomes less so. "This is taking a lot of time and effort on his part for just a first date—I hate to have someone just show up at my house, but flowers are nonthreatening and thoughtful," said a woman who reminds us of the invasiveness of physical presence, but for whom the violation is softened by its romantic accouterments.

Other respondents make clearer yet the revelation that flowers can render the stranger innocuous. "These are harmless, nice gestures and it's obvious he's sane so maybe he should be given a second chance," said a woman "obviously" favorably impressed. Another is completely won over by this strategy: "He's getting more and more endearing, " said the woman whose imaginary pursuer was starting to "grow" on her. "This is progressively cute," she continued, alluding not only to the success of persistence when romantically framed, but also using a term ("cute") that minimizes the threat this person represents. "Just seems a bit more acceptable," commented one woman, and another, recognizing precisely the power inherent in such symbols, said that "cultural elements of the flower gesture make it less intimidating than the display of desperation shown in [leaving messages]."

One of the undergraduate women interviewed in an earlier study of coercive dating experiences described an incident in which a man with whom she had a brief affair, but no longer wanted to be involved with began to come over to her house unannounced. "He would come over to my house when I wasn't expecting him, just be here," said "Terra," and continued:

> Fred [her boyfriend] was gone for Christmas, and I was home. He knew Fred was gone and he was at my door. He'd done this one day before, and then he, he just came over to like hang out, and then one day I came home from work, and he was at my door! And I just. Um, and I, I was really mad but I let him in, and he said, I said "What do you want? I'm tired." "Well, I just wanted to come over for a little bit," and um, I said, "Fine, but I've go to do this, this and that, so I'm just going to leave you alone and you can hang out in my house," you know, "but I'm not going to be at your beck and call because I just came home from work." So I did. I don't remember what I did, but I left him alone in the living room, and um, and then we, I came back and we talked a little bit. About a week later he left a present on my doorstep, or in my Christmas wreath or something, um, and it was a little pin that he had made, of my cat that he had sketched while he was—that's why he came over, was to sketch my cat. So in a way I felt like, oh he's, so he's trying to make me feel guilty [she laughed] you know, but on the other hand it could have been, um, innocent. It could have been.

Even though Terra already had decided that this man was "dangerous" and "crafty," she was nonetheless confused because of the character of his violation. "See, you could look at this two ways," she said, as either manipulative ("trying to make me feel guilty") or as genuinely romantic ("innocent").

Ambivalence: "It Made Me Doubt if I'd Made the Right Decision."

The confusion that characterizes Terra's experience arises when pursuit that would otherwise be unambiguously annoying or threatening draws upon cultural repertoires commonly associated with ordinary courtship. That many of the sorority women appeared to feel frightened and flattered, or frightened and romanced, or flattered and annoyed, at one and the same time, is an important finding in the scales describing their responses. These women's responses to the open-ended question asking them why they thought they would feel this way about such strategies further articulate this ambivalence; over one-quarter (27 percent) of these responses can be categorized as both negative *and* positive, and also suggest some outcomes that might follow from these uneasy emotional companions. This is important because ambivalence may not only confound her perception of violation of the boundaries a woman has set, but may also cause her to question her definition of the situation and of the relationship, increasing her vulnerability to further incursions. In some cases, it may even contribute to the ultimate success of an attempt at forcible interaction.

The women demonstrated ambivalence by pairing emotions in their responses, using the conjunction "but" again and again. "It's nice to know he still cares, but I'd feel he should move on," said one. "It's a nice gesture and it's good to feel someone cares about you, but again—get the hint," said another, and, "It makes you feel good that someone likes you that much but it's annoying because you asked him to stop," responded a third. Others alluded to their perception of the tactical character of romantic overtures: "He is trying to be sweet and win me back but it is annoying if I made myself clear" and "I do find it very romantic since I am a sucker for gifts, but he is annoying me because he will not leave me alone." The women found the attempts compelling even when their first reaction was negative: "Although I said I didn't want to see him, it's still a nice gesture," said one respondent. "I would be annoyed, as it is a situation I wouldn't want to deal with," said another, adding "but I would also be flattered and think it was romantic because of the (excessive) attention." This woman pointed both to the inappropriateness of the attempt, calling it "excessive," but at the same time she acknowledged her mixed feelings regardless.

It is not only the hypothetical scenario that stimulates this conflation of flattery and fear, love and wariness, however. The sorority women's descriptions of their own experiences are similarly complex. "A former boyfriend sent flowers and called constantly. I was extremely annoyed, but I felt sorry for him too," said one. Another respondent reported the following:

> It was a four-year relationship that I broke off because [he] started to become physically abusive. He would sit outside my bedroom window every night to see if I would go out and then follow me wherever I went. He would often threaten to hurt me if I didn't go back with him. I was extremely upset and wished he would go get some help. I wanted to see him happy.

An undergraduate woman I call "Corinne" described unwanted interaction with a former boyfriend who continued to call her and profess his love for her after a violent incident that led Corinne to end the relationship. The calls, she said, caused her

> a lot of stress, a lot of emotional burden. Like, I didn't want to be at home, cause I didn't want to answer the phone. Annoying. At first, annoying wasn't how I felt. At first, it was very emotionally hard, every time the phone rang, well, God, [she sighed], and after a couple weeks it was continuing to hap-

pen, it was becoming, God damn, is he ever going to stop? I don't need to talk to you, you're only making things worse for me, and for yourself. Then it became annoying, then it became a nuisance in my life. And he became, he himself became a nuisance. And it felt like, a part of me, at times, I can remember at times going, well maybe it won't happen again. Maybe I should give it a try again. I do love him and even this, this, this, and that, so it just dragged out that pain even longer, by him continuing to call. If he had just walked out and left and I never heard from him again, that would have been easier to deal with, but every time he'd call, it was like it happened all over again.

Corinne is describing emotions that vary widely over the course of time; she is annoyed, but initially she is sad, and even though her ex-boyfriend became a "nuisance," she still felt love for him and considered returning.

"Bella" described a similar experience, again based on repeated, pleading phone calls from a former boyfriend who had begun hitting her prior to their breakup. At first she was "flattered" by the calls and said: "I think the first couple calls, it was okay, and I guess I could understand it, but that was—I was feeling really bad, too, like I wanted to stay with him, but I knew it wasn't going to work out and I knew things were only gonna get worse." Despite her stated understanding that the relationship was properly over, the calls made her feel "bad," and she sympathized with her former boyfriend: "I wasn't willing to go back with him. But I was willing to talk to him and be his friend." All of these women expressed contradictory emotional stances that could encourage rather than discourage continued interaction. Their concern for the well-being of their partners might well limit the range of responses available to them, including that of simply ignoring attempts at forcible interaction.

Another consequence of the ambivalence resulting from the incorporation of romantic repertoires into pursuit is that women may doubt their understanding of the situation, as the following explanations of responses to waiting on the doorstep with flowers illustrate. "I can see that he really cares, but really it's hurting me because it makes me wonder if I did the right thing," said one respondent. Another commented, "That is so sweet, but it would be hard to see him and accept/be reminded that he's a good guy." A third woman implicitly refers to the cultural expectation that women respond positively to attention, however unwanted, and the problems associated with this: "I naturally would be flattered," she said, "but his actions do not help make the break up any easier for me, and might spark doubts about our separating." Describing the experience of having an ex-boyfriend beg her to reconsider breaking up, a woman wrote plaintively, "It made me sad and lonely and doubt if I'd made the right decision." "I'm a very strong person," said Corinne, saying of her experience with her violent, pleading former boyfriend:

[It] knocked me down the most with my strength, who I am the most. I didn't, for a while you know it was my fault, if I hadn't done this or hadn't done that, maybe he wouldn't have reacted like he would have but I sought help for this.

Given this apparent tendency toward self-doubt, and the active construction of romantic realities by persistent pursuers, it is not surprising that some women might define forcible interaction, albeit unwanted, as nonetheless acceptable in the context of courtship. This gives the "bring flowers" tactic considerable efficacy, in both imagination and fact. When asked in the open-ended questions why women found this attempt less frightening or annoying than less love-laden actions, they said: "Because flowers are somewhat romantic and get to a girl's heart in one way or another," and, repeating the cultural motif, "Because flowers are the way to a girl's heart. It is very romantic and special," and simply, "It would make me melt"—all comments that suggest surrender and capitulation. In real life, these attempts sometimes do cause women to reconsider their decision to disengage. One sorority woman said:

> When he wanted me to accept his apology when I broke up with him, he flooded me with flowers, cards, stuffed animals and things. I was flattered, however I knew this was something materialistic and when we got back together the romance and flattery stopped.

This woman, like the women whose interpretations of forcible interaction shift from annoyance to romance in the hypothetical scenario, was dissuaded from her initial inclination by a pursuer drawing from well-honed cultural tools. Another survey respondent described breaking up with a boyfriend as follows:

> He was definitely stunned—he called me at least twice a night, sent me flowers at work, walked me to class, etc. Actually I interpreted his behavior as him showing me he cared about me—something I never saw before. His behavior actually made me realize we should get back together.

This example clearly illustrates how choosing from a romantic repertoire alters the meanings this woman confers upon the relationship with her ex-boyfriend and shapes the decisions she then makes about her own course of conduct. Corinne said that when her former boyfriend called, saying things like "I'm back, I'm sorry, I need you back in my life" it was "hard, because I can remember a couple times almost going back to him." Bella said that when her former boyfriend "needed" to see her every day,

> And I was just kind of like, gosh, I really don't care to see you every day (she laughed), but it seemed like I really had to, and I guess the thing too was that

he would show up sometimes at my house without calling or anything, if I'd tell him, even my mom would tell him, no, you can't come over, it's late, he would still show up, which made my mom really upset and he basically I guess he kept doing these things, and I went to lunch with him a couple of times, and then he said "you have to go out with me," and I guess I had a hard time telling him "no," that I couldn't go out with him.

WHAT LOVE HAS TO DO WITH IT

Each survey response, each victim narrative, each interview, and each conversation that contributes to this study takes place within a gendered cultural context that molds and channels the direction these interpretations take. In this section I follow some of these cultural pathways, beginning with the idea of "vocabularies of motive" (Mills 1940). Mills argued that "[t]he differing reasons men give for their actions are not themselves without reasons" and used this term to describe "typical vocabularies having ascertainable functions in delimited societal situations" (1940:904). Because motives are the only empirically available explanation for behavior and "[t]he only social items that can 'lie deeper' are other lingual forms," Mills treats vocabularies of motives as constraining, inducing, and as "significant determinants of conduct" (Ibid. :908–909). But vocabularies are always historically and culturally located; this is what Mills means when he says, "Motives are of no value apart from the delimited societal situations for which they are the appropriate vocabularies. They must be situated." (Ibid. :913) The researcher thus works to delineate the "typal frames of normative actions and socially situated clusters of motive" (Ibid. 1940:913) that meaningfully direct social action. Simply put, we can begin to make sense out of the choices young women (and the stalking victims in the Domestic Violence Unit) make in forcible interaction and stalking situations by examining the cultural frameworks from which they draw their explanations of what they do.

A "culture of romance" shape women's interpretations of hypothetical scenarios and of their own experience of forcible interaction in dating situations. In addition, gender-specific "feeling rules" (Hochschild 1979) constitute part of this interpretive framework, or the "cultural toolkit" (Swidler 1986). Because unwanted romantic attention so closely mimics the persistence associated with "normal" male courtship, it is sometimes difficult for women to distinguish between the acceptable and the inappropriate, the ordinary and the extraordinary. It is hard for women to trust their own emotions when these are confused by a romantic ideology that tells them they ought to be flattered by such pursuit, unwanted or not. It is also hard for women to set the boundaries they are instructed they must, when the source of coercion and confusion is someone they once loved—

in part because women are taught to be the caretakers of the emotions of men. This is a cultural prescription that reinforces an emotional inequality along the dimension of gender, in which power to force interaction may accrue on the basis of feeling rules.

What makes women so susceptible to these expectations? First is the symbolic environment that surrounds young men and women. What are women taught about love and romance that might make them interpret the actions of boyfriends and husbands, of coercive pursuers and intimate stalkers, in the ways that they do? Second are normative expectations governing how women ought to feel. Last is the emotion work they feel compelled to do as a consequence.

Fairy Tale Romances: Intersections of Culture, History, and Gender

Consider first the "love story." Of the many versions of such narratives in popular culture, I have chosen an archetypal form, the fairy tale, to explore. These are "didactic" (Zipes 1984:15) stories told to young children; feminist analyses of fairy tales (Lieberman 1986; Zipes 1984) focus both on their socializing presence in the nursery and the influence of the stories on adult interpretations of the world. Lieberman argues that fairy tales are "primary channels of acculturation" of gender roles (Ibid. :187). As the stories are read and reread over time, children learn "behavioral and associational patterns, value systems, and how to predict the consequences of specific acts or circumstances" (1986:187). When children learn how to predict the end of the story and the fate of the protagonists based on gender, they learn gender limitations and goals, and the tales become "the repositories of the dreams, hopes and fantasies of generations of girls" (Ibid.).

Ultimately, the tales constitute part of adult cultural repertoires as well. Karen Rowe (1986) points to the "mass popularity" of romance and gothic novels as an indicator of a "pervasive fascination with fairy tale romance in literature not merely for children but for twentieth century adults" and claims that because fairy tales "portray basic human problems and appropriate social prescriptions," they are not merely "innocuous fantasies" but instead, " are powerful transmitters of romantic myths" (1986:210–211). Zipes affirms this position:

> Over the centuries the influence of folk and fairy tales has not diminished. On the contrary, they continue to exercise an extraordinary hold over our real and imaginative lives from childhood to adulthood. The enormous amount of scholarship testifies to this as does the constant use and transformation of this material in novels, poetry, films, theatre, TV, comics, jokes and everyday conversation. The motifs and stories appear to be so well known and so much part of our lives that mere allusion is all that is necessary to provide pleasure and stimulate interest. (1986:22)

We can easily find the "motifs" Zipes refers to in popular romantic movies, and in what follows, I connect these contemporary forms back to the original tales. I cite as exemplars scenes from some movies that were extremely popular at the time the sorority women were in high school, but the reader is invited to substitute filmic love stories from any generation. In either, I argue, there is no great difficulty identifying the characters and themes from *Cinderella, Beauty and the Beast,* or *The Glass Mountain.* The point is that both fairy tales and popular romantic movies provide resources from which young people draw as they struggle to make sense of courtship and union in a real-life social world that is sometimes violent and ambiguous. They provide "equipment for living," as Burke says (1957:262); and are part of what Swidler argues are "symbols, stories, rituals, and world-views, which people may use in varying configurations to solve different kinds of problems" (1986:273).

Table 4.4 lists the movies I have chosen for this discussion, the year in which they were made, and their directors.

With the exception of *Fresh Horses*, these movies were cited as particularly important by one or more women in a small group of sorority informants. (Again, however, readers are free to substitute lists of their own. If the movie is a love story, the conventions will be markedly similar). Their plots or subplots deal with courtship and romance, and their protagonists are young (ranging from high school students to recent college graduates).

The movies explored are almost all centrally motivated by the attraction two fundamentally mismatched people feel for each other and the obstacles they must overcome in order to achieve some sort of union in the end. In *The Breakfast Club, Dirty Dancing, Say Anything, The Sure Thing, The Cutting Edge,* and *Reality Bites,* the male protagonist embodies some aspect of the Beast in the fairy tale *Beauty and the Beast.* He is portrayed as some combination of the following attributes; he is violent, or rebellious, or he is of a lower social class than the female protagonist, or less educated, or he is sexual in opposition to her virginal character, or unwilling to be in a "com-

Table 4.4. Romantic Movies

Director	Title	Year
John Hughes	The Breakfast Club	1985
Rob Reiner	The Sure Thing	1985
John Hughes	Pretty in Pink	1986
Emile Andolino	Dirty Dancing	1987
David Anspaugh	Fresh Horses	1988
Cameron Crowe	Say Anything	1989
Paul M. Glaser	The Cutting Edge	1992
Ben Stiller	Reality Bites	1994

mitted relationship" so important to her. In two of the films (*Pretty in Pink* and *Fresh Horses*), the male protagonist is from the upper class, the American cultural equivalent of a young Prince, who desires a working-class girl, a Cinderella figure who may or may not get to go to the prom/ball.

The female protagonist is typically represented as a prize to be won, most frequently as a girl who is Princess-like and unattainable, either by virtue of her upper class background, or her beauty, or her intelligence, or her "betrothal" to another, or her controlling and overprotective father, or some combination of the above. Like Sleeping Beauty and Snow White, she awaits the sexual awakening bestowed by Prince Charming's kiss, and like Rapunzel or the Princess on the Glass Hill, she presents barriers that require wit and persistence in his pursuit. If the male protagonist is Beast-like, he must usually undergo some transformation before winning his prize. Despite the obstacles thrown in the path of the young lovers by the filmmaker, they are destined to be together and, with the exception of the protagonists of *Fresh Horses*, are eventually joined happily ever after.

Young Lovers: Beauties, Beasts and "Highnesses"

Movies about courtship and romance among teenagers and young adults allude to and refer explicitly to fairy-tale characters in their depictions of protagonists. In *The Breakfast Club*, which opens with a voice-over narration by one of the youthful characters explaining that they are a "brain," an "athlete," a "basket case," a "criminal," and a "princess," Molly Ringwald plays the role of Claire, who is first viewed being dropped off in front of the high school by her father, who is driving a BMW. The first reference anyone makes to her is when John, the "criminal" or Beast-like character played by Judd Nelson, suggests the group close the door and "get the prom queen impregnated." Later John calls Claire "fucking Rapunzel" in a caustic allusion to her social class and privilege, signified by the diamond earrings she has been given by her "Daddy." In *The Cutting Edge*, social class similarly confers Princess status on Kate (played by Moira Kelly), who lives with her widowed father in a huge mansion and skates alone on her private ice rink, dressed in the gauzy white of diamonds, ice, stars and purity, surrounded by mirrors reflecting her cold beauty, as classical music plays in the background. In *Dirty Dancing*, Baby (played by Jennifer Grey) is the idealistic younger daughter of a physician who forbids her to spend time with the working class dancer with whom she falls in love.

Female protagonists become sought after because they are beautiful and intelligent, destined for bright futures, and moving in social circles beyond the reach of the young men who ardently desire them. The Princess in *Say Anything*, played by Ione Sky, is Diane Court (a nice use of name to convey the idea of aristocracy), valedictorian of her high school class and "a brain trapped in the body of a game show hostess" who "doesn't go out with boys like [Lloyd]" (the clever "commoner" who woos her, played by John Cusak). When she goes to the party with Lloyd, dressed in a white summer dress with a gardenia in her dark hair like an island girl, people are amazed that she is with this ordinary guy. "How did it happen?" a friend asks Lloyd, and when Lloyd says "I called," the friend says "This gives me hope." Later Diane tells Lloyd that before the party, "nobody knew me— I feel like I fit in for the first time" as he steers her around the broken glass on the pavement, perhaps a chivalrous allusion to Sir Walter Raleigh and the cloak across the puddle, or the glass slippers of Cinderella fame? Then she tells Lloyd he is a great date; she has never gone out with someone so "basic" before. When Diane's father tells her she should stop seeing Lloyd, it is because he thinks they have nothing in common, and when she breaks up with Lloyd, his friends call her a "show pony" and insist that he never had a chance with her. They invite him to find another girl at a party but Lloyd says "You don't find a girl like Diane Court at a kegger."

Winona Ryder plays Lelaina, also valedictorian, in *Reality Bites*, a privileged child given a BMW as a graduation present and much more upwardly mobile than her roommates and Troy, the rebellious, Beast-like character played by Ethan Hawke. In *The Sure Thing*, Daphne Zuniga plays Alison, and tells Gib (another John Cusak character) that when she was little, she wanted to be a Princess when she grew up. "She'll never go out with you, I hear she goes for the intellectual type," says Gib's friend.

Sometimes the female protagonist is Cinderella, and becomes a prize by being desired by a male beyond her social reach. In *Pretty in Pink*, Molly Ringwald plays Andy, a motherless young woman who is first shown taking care of her single father, a child-wife who makes her own clothes and lives in a house near the railroad tracks (read: the "wrong side of the tracks"), who wonders what it would be like to "go out with a guy with money," and who is awed by the "amazing houses" in Blaine's (played by Andrew McCarthy) neighborhood. We know Andy is Cinderella because her friends refer to the upper-class Blaine as "Prince Charming," the plot revolves around the prom (the modern-day equivalent of a ball), and Andy makes her own ball gown out of a friend's old dress and an inexpensive dress her father buys her—he would have bought shoes but he didn't know her size! Molly Ringwald and Andrew McCarthy are again paired as working class girl and upper-class lad, as Jewel and Matt in *Fresh Horses*, a dark version of Cinderella in which the seductive, passionate child Jewel is rescued from her marriage to an evil older man by Matt, who isn't "the Prince that's going to carry her off" after all, in the one movie in this group in which the protagonists don't end up in each other's arms.

If the women in these movies are most often the unattainable Beauty, it fits within the cultural logic that young men are so frequently represented as the Beast. Sometimes a male protagonist is the Beast because he is vividly and unreservedly wild; such a character is John in *The Breakfast Club*, the "criminal" the youthful narrator typifies in the opening voice-over. We first see him walking defiantly against traffic, almost getting hit in the process, wearing a trench-coat, shades, and gloves with the fingers cut out, a literal as well as a metaphoric Artful Dodger who is deliberately rude and quintessentially rebellious. John is a semi-permanent resident of "Saturday School" who gets a carton of cigarettes from his abusive father for Christmas, who shows Claire the cigarette burn on his arm, and whose Beast-like status is signified not only by his antisocial behavior (lighting his shoe on fire, destroying a book, rigging the door so it won't stay open, pulling a knife on the athlete, defying the authority represented by the Dean, and supplying the others with pot) and appearance, but also by his opposition to the others in terms of social class. Andrew tells him "You don't even count. You could disappear forever and it wouldn't matter," and John himself echoes this when he tells Claire not to compare herself to him, because she has everything, and he has nothing.

As Beast, John represents authenticity, danger, and passion. He is the truth-teller who refuses to let the other young people maintain their illusions about themselves, especially Claire, whom he predicts will be a fat society matron, and whom he accurately reads as the uptight virgin she is, commenting ironically, "You won't let a guy put his tongue in your mouth but you'll eat [sushi]?" He recognizes that she is a "poor girl" whom everybody loves, but that it is a false popularity because it doesn't reflect the real Claire, the sad little prize in a bitter custody battle. He also points out that if Claire hasn't had sex, she is a "prude," if she has, she is a "slut," or perhaps she is a "tease," using sex as a "weapon." He is dangerous because he refuses to kowtow to the sadistic and hypocritical dean, he takes a fall for the others, and he signifies his sexuality by mesmerizing Claire (as when he lights his shoe on fire), by his constant sexual references, by putting his head between Claire's legs when he is hiding under her desk, and by saying "being bad feels pretty good."

Ethan Hawke plays a similar character, Troy, in *Reality Bites*. Troy is an intelligent but underemployed musician / philosopher working in a newsstand and possibly going nowhere; Lelaina says he is "on the road to loserville," and lives in "the den of slack." Troy too represents untamed sexuality, dangerousness, and authenticity. In an early scene he is shown leaving a girl's bedroom, tossing her phone number aside, so we know he is casual about sex or unwilling to make a commitment. This impression is confirmed the morning after he and Lelaina finally have sex, when he rushes off to his gig rather than linger with her. He further exhibits his Beast nature in the argument that follows, in which he tells Lelaina that he might do mean things, but he is the only real thing that she has (perhaps a reference to the title of the movie)—after which he sings a vicious song that prompts her to run away.

Passionate sexuality and working class origins combine in the character of Johnny Castle (a good name for a Prince), played by Patrick Swayze, in the film *Dirty Dancing*. He is a Beast because he comes "from the streets" and because he is the embodiment of male sensuality in the "dirty dancing" that gives the movie its name. Baby first sees him dance like this when she makes her excursion to the staff quarters, past the "NO GUESTS" sign reinforcing the social distance between her and Johnny. We get a sense of the roughness of this man in a scene where he is teaching Baby to dance, and his black shoes and blue-jeaned legs are shown aligned with her white tennies and tights. He is all controlled passion as he puts her hand on his heart and tells her to feel the music. Johnny is treated as someone who doesn't "count" by the owner of the hotel and Baby's father assumes that he is responsible for impregnating his dance partner, and thus orders Baby to stay away from "those people." Johnny tells Baby, "The reason people treat me like nothing is because I am nothing." (But Baby responds: "No, you're everything.") And when Johnny locks his keys in his car, he breaks a window with a fence post and Baby, laughing, tells him he is "wild."

Like Johnny Castle, Doug, the hockey player played by D. B. Sweeney in *The Cutting Edge*, is a character combining male sexuality with a working-class background. We first see Doug engaging in casual sex with a woman whose name he doesn't remember, one of the several women other than Kate who find him attractive. He plays a violent sport, works as a construction worker, and helps out his brother in "Dorsey's Penalty Box," the family bar and restaurant. Kate refers to him as a Neanderthal and wonders if he has ever read a book. In this way we learn that he was on a sports scholarship and learned very little in college. He wants to skate to the pounding rhythms of heavy metal, goes "whoring" on his break from an intense training regimen, and, when drunk, has sex with a rival skater. Like John in *The Breakfast Club*, Doug is authentic and brave. He is unimpressed by Kate's wealth and holds his own with Kate's father, winning a crucial wager that grants him permission to pursue the Princess. This is much like the riddle the proverbial youngest son, a "Clever Lad" whose only resources are his wits, answers in some fairy tales.

As Gib in *The Sure Thing*, John Cusack's free-wheeling male sexuality confers on him the Beast character. He tries very hard to seduce the elegant and sexually repressed Alison, but dreams nightly of the blonde, bikini-clad "sure thing" of the title. He also eats fried pork rinds and punches holes in beer cans to drink "shotgun," tells Alison after rescuing her from the advances of a creep that he likes "living on the edge," and endears himself to her by getting drunk.

The other character played by Cusack has Beast-like attributes, but also represents another archetypal figure, the Clever Lad who wins the heart of the Princess through his wit and persistence. Lloyd in *Say Anything* is the Beast based mostly on his lack of ambition to do more than be a kickboxer, certainly a marginal and violent calling. But more importantly, he is defined by his singleminded desire for the aristocratic Diane, who has won a fellowship to some prestigious university overseas. When asked at dinner what his future plans are, he tells Diane's father, "To spend as much time as possible with your daughter before she goes away" and later he informs the father that "what I want to do for a living is be with your daughter." He is princely in his attentiveness to Diane, making her laugh, "checking up" on her at a party, and sending a card the morning after they first have sex that says, "I'll always be there for you." When Lloyd first calls Diane she is dubious and he fast-talks his way into their first date. This persistence sets the tone for their relationship and is sustained throughout the breakup that occupies the second half of the movie, culminating in his emotional availability when Diane needs him most.

Glass Mountains and Briar Bushes: Antagonism and
Other Obstacles

As in the mythic tales from which they draw their inspiration, contemporary stories of young love present their protagonists with a series of obstacles to overcome before the resolution of the dramatic tension thus created. The problems that separate the Princess from her Prince, such as their differing social class backgrounds or the hostility of parents and peers, direct attention to the desirability of the female protagonist and to the qualities the hero possesses that will enable him to win his prize in the end. Generally the two are quite mismatched, as the following descriptions reveal.

In *The Breakfast Club*, the obstacles to their eventual union faced by Claire and John are their vastly different social class backgrounds and their antagonism toward each other—which is based on their different backgrounds. Claire is the type of person who won't speak to someone outside of her clique and John is contemptuous of this snobbery, this artificiality. John insults Claire, telling her she will be fat, that she is pristine and still a virgin. This prompts one of the other characters to defend her honor and tell John to leave her alone, saying, "You don't talk to her, look at her, even think about her." But John is trying to "help her"; he is the one who will ultimately rescue her from her virginal state, freeing her repressed sexuality. After Claire responded to his first attack on her (the "impregnation" remark) by suggesting the others ignore him, he says, "Sweet, you couldn't ignore me if you tried." And we see that she is mesmerized by his violence; the camera shows her transfixed by the fire he lights on his shoe, and he will similarly spark her passion. Although they fight each other until the final scenes, these obstacles are overcome by propinquity and confrontation, group therapy style.

Kate and Doug in *The Cutting Edge* are similarly at odds. Their oppositions are continually emphasized in camera shots depicting her in the filmy pale costume of a ballerina skating with him clad in blue jeans or wearing a hockey uniform, her gift to him of *Great Expectations* and his to her of a hockey jersey, her ease in the company of the very rich, and his attempt to explain his figure skating career to the boys in Dorsey's Penalty Box. Like Claire and John, Doug and Kate are hostile to each other throughout much of the movie, as are Alison and Gib in *The Sure Thing*; the only sign that these couples are attracted to each other is the jealousy they express when they see the other in the company of a rival.

In *Reality Bites*, the sexual tension between Troy and Lelaina similarly takes the form of hostility and antagonism, as in the scene when Troy confronts Lelaina after he has seen her kissing her (boring but "suitable") boyfriend. When she walks in to the apartment she reluctantly shares with Troy, he starts insulting her "yuppie cheesehead." This sets up a confrontation in which she asks him why he is acting like a jealous boyfriend "all of a sudden," and he says, "I am really in love with you," pauses while she absorbs that, and then retracts it by saying, "Is that what you want to hear? Don't flatter yourself." This encounter is followed shortly by a poignant scene when the two are being friends, and although they kiss, there is still the obstacle presented by the male foil: "I can't," Lelaina says. "I'm talking about evolving," Troy says, but Lelaina replies, "I can't evolve right now." "Because of Michael?" "No—yes."

In addition to hostility and the presence of a rival, Troy and Lelaina have differing aspirations and backgrounds, a common theme in these films and the fairy tales they retell. The predominant problem in *Pretty in Pink* is the differing social locations of Andy, who dresses oddly in the clothes she makes herself, and Blaine, who is best friends with a guy who refers to Andy as a "mutant." When Blaine asks Andy out, she won't tell him where she lives (in the house by the railroad tracks). Andy's friends, as well as Blaine's, disapprove of their relationship, and after a disastrous first date, Andy says, "It's too weird; maybe it shouldn't happen," but Blaine says, "Would you feel any better if I asked you to the prom?" prompting her to kiss him. But he prolongs the tension by changing his mind, in spite of telling Andy, "This is going to happen, I really want this to happen," apparently deferring to the friend who says "The girl was, is, and always will be *nada*."

The obstacles in *Dirty Dancing* are also social class differences. The owner of the resort where the action takes place tells Robbie, the college boy, to "show the girls a good time," but tells Johnny to "keep your hands off." Not only does Baby have to secretly learn the dance, but her affair with Johnny must also be covert, as her father has ordered her to stay away from the dancers. When Baby comes to Johnny's room he is conscious that it is not a "great" room like the one Baby must be staying in. When Johnny's regular dance partner realizes what is going on, she asks "What are you doing? How many times have you told me never get mixed up with them?" When Robbie finds out, he tells Baby, "That's okay, Baby, I went slumming too." In spite of Johnny's dream of acceptance by Baby's father, her father, who mistakenly thinks Johnny has irresponsibly impregnated a woman, sees only the Beast. When Johnny is falsely accused of a theft, the resort owner pressures Johnny to leave in spite of Baby's alibi and the discovery of the true thieves.

Last, in *Say Anything*, the differing aspirations of Lloyd and Diane lead, through the intervention of her father, to the major obstacle to their union, their breakup. After spending the first half of the movie courting and winning Diane, Lloyd spends the second half regaining her. When Diane says, "Let's not put things on this level," Lloyd says, "This is a good level," and this represents his inability to accept the breakup. He drives around in the rain, calling a friend from a pay phone to ask how to get her back. He tells his friends hanging out at the AM/PM that "she won't talk to me, she won't look at me" and explodes in a kick to the fence, knocking over a garbage can and scattering the guys. Then he decides he will be "the new me, Iceman, Power Lloyd" and draws the line at seven phone calls. When Lloyd's friends tell him to visit Diane, he says, "No, I'm a guy." But they tell him to "be a man," so he calls again to tell her this is the eighth and final call. She doesn't answer the phone, and we next see her tossing and turning in bed, then going to the window where he is standing outside her house, the boom box raised high playing their song, him silent and offering her his love, and still she turns away. It is only when her father goes to jail, and thus is removed as a barrier to their relationship that she can finally respond as she wishes to Lloyd.

Love Conquers All: Beasts Redeemed
and Beauties Awakened

The last fairy-tale theme I want to consider, before turning to the implications of this enculturation into norms of courtship and romance, is the "happily ever after" outcomes in the sample. With the exception of *Fresh Horses*, all the movies end when the young protagonists overcome the disapproval of parents and peers, discover that the hostility and confusion they feel is actually attraction, and learn to love each other in spite of their vast differences in personality, aspirations, or social standing.

In *Pretty in Pink*, Andy goes by herself to the prom—wearing the dress she has cobbled together—and dazzles Blaine with her beauty, forcing him to see that she is the girl he should be with in spite of being ostracized by his upper-class friends. Even though Andy has been unsure all along if this can work, given the differences in their backgrounds, she is in love with him after all, and they end up kissing under the stars in the parking lot. Cinderella goes to the ball and ends up with Prince Charming.

Say Anything ends when Diane finds out her father is a criminal and he goes to jail, and she realizes that she needs and loves Lloyd, who sees her walk into his dojo and, distracted, is knocked down by his opponent. Battered and bloodied, he asks Diane, "Do you need someone or do you need me?" but before she can answer, says, "Forget it, I don't care." He loves her so much it doesn't matter if she really loves him. Even though her father says, "You're not a permanent partner, you're just a distraction," Lloyd and Diane board the airplane together, and we see that he will protect her from her fears (earlier we learn that she screams on airplanes), even if that is his only job in life. The Clever Lad thus wins the hand of the Princess in the end.

Even more romantic are endings in which the Beast is transformed by the Sleeping Beauty he has sexually awakened. The final scene in *Dirty Dancing* shows the return of the banished, leather-jacketed Johnny to the ball (the end-of-the-season dance put on by the resort) where Baby is sitting with her parents against the wall, grieving. Johnny pulls her from her seat, saying, "Nobody puts Baby in a corner!" and informs the crowd that he is going to do *his* kind of dance with *his* kind of partner, thus triumphantly and publicly affirming their relationship even as he explains that Baby has taught him about the kind of person he wants to be. She has transformed him from Beast into Prince, as the father, apologizing, is shown to recognize. The Beast is also redeemed by the Princess in *Reality Bites* when, after Troy runs off and behaves cruelly to Lelaina, he goes to the hospital where his father is dying, symbolically taking care of unfinished business and growing up. In the final scene, he returns and stands humbly outside the apartment, wearing a suit that signals the shift he has made and his new willingness to commit to Lelaina, who runs into his arms.

Finally, the closing scenes of *The Breakfast Club* are a particularly striking invocation of this kind of fairy-tale resolution: the "princess" Claire is drawn to the "criminal" John, who has revealed her true self to her and who is thus an authentic male, and she goes willingly to him in the end to be freed from the spell of her virginity and wealth. When Claire finally goes to John in the office/dungeon where, like the Minotaur, he is being held, and takes him in her arms, he again tells a truth; in the same way her parents use her in their war against each other, she could be using him, in a self-conscious recognition of his Beast status and hers as Princess. This opposition is the final metaphor, represented in the last frames by close-up shots of Claire's small, beautifully manicured hand placing the diamond from her ear into John's black-gloved hand, his fist closing upon the jewel, and then putting the earring in his ear as he marches triumphant across the playing field. In the end, the Truth Teller turns out to be the True Love, a Beast whose very charm resides in his dangerousness.

True Romance: Courtship, Love, and Danger
in the Real World

What contribution might such media portrayals make to the experiential understanding of particular violent relationships, and in what ways might such representations be "realized," that is, made realistic and incorporated into definitions of real world situations?"

When a young woman is faced with a hypothetical situation such as those that were posed to the sorority sisters in this chapter, or a woman trying to escape a violent relationship receives a card, flowers, and a tearful message on her answering machine, what resources does she bring to her interpretation of these behaviors? If her understanding of these scenarios or actualities is shaped by her understanding of courtship and romance, and if these more general meanings are learned in part from depictions of ideal romances in romantic movies, what might these movies be teaching her that contributes to the ambiguous interpretations indicated by the survey results and stalking victim narratives?

The movies I have described, like the love stories in other media and times, use fairy-tale plots and characters to resonate with their young viewers. I have focused on the obstacles placed in the path of various Beasts, Prince Charmings, and Clever Lads in their quest to win the affections of the Beauties, Princesses, and Cinderellas with whom they ultimately enter into relationships. Courtship is the central theme of many, if not most, famous fairy tales, "magnified into the most important and exciting part of a girl's life" (Lieberman 1986:199–200). Male protagonists actively pursue females who sleep passively or who are chosen simply because they have been observed (Lieberman 1986). These threads are picked up and transmuted in literary romances (Cawelti 1976). Modleski puts it thus:

> [a] young, inexperienced, poor to moderately well-to-do woman encounters and becomes involved with a handsome, strong, experienced, wealthy man. The heroine is confused by the hero's behavior since, though he is obviously interested in her, he is mocking, cynical, contemptuous, often hostile, and even somewhat brutal. By the end, however, all misunderstandings are cleared away, and the hero reveals his love for the heroine, who reciprocates. This formula is, of course, as old as the novel itself. (1982:36)

In the literary romance, as in the fairy tale, the narrative structure is organized around courtship, the clearing of whatever hurdles the protagonists face (whether they be glass mountains, differing social classes, or the apparent Beastliness of the hero) and the joining together of two people who are destined to be one. The same conventions structure romantic movies. Heroines may be prized for their intelligence and potential as well as their beauty, and while they are not so "passive, submissive, and helpless" (Lieberman 1986:191) as Sleeping Beauty or Snow White, they are nonetheless the "waiting prize" for the suitor who perseveres, or who sees her true worth, or who is transformed by her surrender from Beast to Prince.

This last convention is particularly important for understanding forcible interaction. In the fairy tale, when Beauty is willing to love the Beast for what he is, he is able to show his "gentler form" (Lieberman 1986:200). The enigmatic hero of contemporary romance novels is mocking and angry, and his very brutality indicates his love (Modleski 1982; Radway 1984). He is also singleminded and determined to gain possession of the heroine in the end. Like the Beast who will die if he is not transformed in time, the hero in the romances Radway's readers enjoyed most was one whose "recognition of his own deep feelings for the heroine and his realization that he could not live without her" was best portrayed, a hero who finds the woman "so desirable that he will not take 'no' for an answer"(1984:76–77, 81), a hero who, in what Modleski describes as a "very potent feminine fantasy," is obsessed with her and thinks of nothing else (1982:16).

We have seen these characters in the movies I have reviewed. He is the "criminal" John in *Pretty in Pink*, the brilliant rebel Troy in *Reality Bites*, the sexual and adventurous Gib in *The Sure Thing*, and Doug in *The Cutting Edge*, the clever and persistent Lloyd in *Say Anything*. He is an incorporation and a contemporary rendering of an archetypal hero, and it is this reference to the fairy tale in conjunction with the modernness of his translation that makes him so potentially attractive and interesting to the young women who watch him on the screen, and perhaps imagine themselves in the gentling role. We have also seen the kind of conventional antagonism between protagonists that Radway calls the romance genre's

> characteristic preoccupation with what is typically termed a "love-hate relationship" [in which] hero and heroine are shown to despise each other overtly, even though they are "in love," primarily because each is jealous or suspicious of the other's motives and consequently fails to trust the other. (1984:65)

Like the briar bushes that the Prince must cut through to reach the sleeping Princess, the hostility toward each other expressed by Claire and John in *The Breakfast Club*, by Gib and Alison in *The Sure Thing*, and by Troy and Lelaina in *Reality Bites* serves as obstacle to and proof of love. In *The Cutting Edge*, Doug and Kate snipe and fight until the final moments of the movie, when their recognition of the feelings the audience has known they had for each other from the start enables them to conquer the ice, like the glass hill that separates the Prince and Princess in the tale

If, as Rowe contends, such tales "exert an awesome imaginative power over the female psyche" (1986:218), the sorority women (and the stalking victims in the Domestic Violence Unit) may have learned that courtship is the central, defining characteristic of life for teenagers and young adults. In the stories "they tell themselves about themselves" (Geertz 1991:266), the plots of their own lives may be organized in terms of the drama of love, to the exclusion of other possibilities. If courtship and romantic relationships in real life are understood to be—like courtship and romance in fairy tales, novels, and movies—the most important series of events in a woman's life, it might make perfect sense to her that the disruption of a courtship could engender the resistance and even the desperation that the survey questions were designed to evoke, and that we have seen in some of the stalking cases.

Then, when a woman imagines herself and her former boyfriend or husband in the situation of the scenario or interprets her experience of stalking, she might do so in terms of the archetypal characters that model gender roles in such vivid and *familiar* ways in the films described above. If she has watched these and similar movies, or heard the stories from which the movies draw their resonance, she will have seen that women are objects of desire to be ardently pursued. Their worth derives from their desirability and in many cases their unattainability. If a beautiful woman, like a Princess in a fairy tale, necessarily inspires the passionate, obsessive, and persistent attentions of male suitors, the kind of behaviors described in the survey or reported in the victim narratives could well be interpreted by a respondent or a victim as indications of her own desirability. Thus we find the common interpretation of the behavior as flattering, despite its threatening character. However difficult the hero may seem, he is controlled by his love for her, thus conferring a kind of power upon her that she is unlikely to experience in real life.

But more importantly, we should ask ourselves what kind of suitor this woman imagines in the scenario, or even hidden underneath the living Beast of her experience. If she hasn't been in a forcible interaction or stalking situation, she may think of the romantic heroes in movies. If she has been in a similar situation, and imagines a person like her own former boyfriend or spouse, it is possible that the suitor she pictures is similarly violent and/or obsessive. Nevertheless, this imagined or real person is not merely frightening, but is sometimes or to some extent a romantic figure as well. This image is entirely consistent with the romantic heroes we see on the screen. Remember the Beast, who is really gentle underneath, whether he is the Beast of the fairy tale, the "forcefully persuasive" hero of the literary romance, or the wildly sexy movie antihero.

Think of the persistent suitor, steadfast in his refusal to be dissuaded from his love. In this context, a former boyfriend or spouse who won't give up, or who threatens to kill himself, or even one who is violent, is simply demonstrating the depth of his need and love. Therefore he may not be perceived as merely manipulative, controlling, or dangerous, but also as romantic. And sometimes he is merely foolish, a comic figure in his desperation until he is redeemed by the heroine.

The obstacles that are so crucial in the structure and content of fairy tales, romantic literature, and movies occupy a similar slot in women's cultural repertoires. First there is the notion that love conquers all, even the apparent dislike of two people for each other. In the fairy tale, the suitor who wins the hand of the Princess is the one who climbs the glass mountain. In the romantic movie, the hostility that characters express functions as a signifier of their attraction to each other, and adds to the narrative's appeal. If a woman then imagines or faces a situation in which her protestations of disinterest are ignored, but her suitor persists rather than desists, and she interprets this as romantic as well as frightening, or flattering and frightening both, it could be because her understandings follow the same cultural logic from which our expectations of romantic formulas derive. Seen in this light, the survey results and victim narratives are not so puzzling after all.

We have seen that some women have quite mixed feelings about forcible interaction and stalking. Here, I have looked at one possible source of some of those mixed feelings: the fairy-tale representations of romance and love with which popular culture is imbued. We have seen how women make use of these cultural repertoires: in sorority women's explanations of their ambivalent emotions and in stalking victims' explanations of their compliance with their former partners' coercion and use of force. There is another facet of cultural repertoire that may also come into play. This consists of normative expectations governing feeling and expressing emotions in intimate relationships, and merits some discussion as well.

Feelings Rule: Being Desired and Being Responsible

The accounts of these women also suggest that gendered "feeling rules" (Hochshild 1983) come into play in matters of the heart and of personal space. The normative expectations that men are not given to expressing romantic feelings, that women ought to feel flattered by romantic attention no matter the source, and that women are responsible for managing the emotions of men all may influence women's interpretations of imagined and real interactions. These interpretations, then, guide the decisions they make about how to proceed.

Women gauge the strength of men's feelings toward them by how romantically the men act, important because of the cultural expectation that men are less emotionally expressive than women. In an environment such as sororities where traditional gender roles hold sway (Risman 1982) men are expected to pursue women who are made desireable by virtue of being pursued. And it seems that men who employ romantic strategies are attractive in part because while pursuit is expected of men, the incorporation of romance (and the emotionality romantic imagery signifies) is less so. Thus the sorority women felt that a pursuer who brought flowers had done more than the ordinary, despite the clear understanding that this was a common indication of romantic love. A little over 10 percent of these women volunteered that the romantic attempts represented a special effort undertaken by their imaginary pursuers. One woman found the attempt highly flattering and romantic "[b]ecause he went out of his way to wait for me and to get the flowers," while another suggested the uniqueness of this approach by saying the following: "It is flattering when a guy puts more effort into you than most do." Similarly, "I would be totally flattered that he would go to such an extent and I really wouldn't be annoyed how could you be. I would wonder why he hasn't been so romantic before." This woman implies that the men of her experience have been less than artful in their ardor, and another is even more explicit about her appreciation of this effort: "Flowers are not expensive," she says, "but they are thoughtful which is more important. Usually when I have broken up with someone it was because the guy was not thoughtful, interested anymore, or attentive to my needs."

One woman interviewed sardonically described the actions of her former boyfriend, whose first reaction to the news that she wanted to break up with him was "What do you mean, it's over? I don't think you're considering how I feel about this!"

> And he paid me the money he owed me, he sent me flowers, something he'd never done, he sent me flowers, he dropped into my house, he dropped by when I wasn't there my birthday's in September and he sent me a short letter and a book.

Her tone of voice, and the comment that these were things that he had "never done," indicate not only that in this case, the actions come too late, but also imply that they might have been effective had they been made earlier.

That the emotive fellow is extraordinary was often very clear. "I have never had a boyfriend do that for me, i.e., sitting and waiting plus flowers," wrote one flattered woman. "He brought me flowers and for the guy to put down his pride is a big deal to me," said another, and a third explained her positive responses thus: "This is the most flattering I guess because he's trying so hard to show how he feels—not so easy for lots of guys.

This would encourage me to reconsider." This woman points to not only the cultural expectation that men hide their feelings, but also to the effectiveness of revealing them when she says that doing so might change her mind.

If men are expected to be unromantic, making the use of romantic imagery all the more effective, women's role expectations may require that they be flattered by this imagery even when pursuit is undesired. This expectation interacts with the notion that women are responsible for men's feelings when they are fortunate enough to elicit them. Thus, flattery was the single emotion in which there are no significant differences overall between responses to the dating and ex-boyfriend versions of the questionnaire. What characterizes the feeling of flattery is that it signifies that one is desired, and thus desirable. Waiting with flowers "would show how much he cares and would make me feel pursued, wanted," said one respondent.

Even unasked for expressions elicit this response: "It would be annoying because he hadn't listened to what I had said," offered one woman, who went on to say "[o]f course,"—a reference to the cultural toolkit constituted by what "everyone knows"—"I think I'd still be a little flattered." Another woman explained the ambivalence of her own responses:

> It is nice of him to bring flowers and flattering that he wants me back so bad but it would be annoying that I would have to hurt his feelings again & turn him down. It is hard enough to turn them down once.

This woman not only reveals that her feelings are mixed but also suggests the reason—it is difficult for women to assert themselves in the face of unwanted attention. And while this difficulty may well also characterize relationships from which men are attempting to disengage themselves (Goffman 1952; Vaughan 1986), some researchers suggest a gender imbalance in reliance upon physical attractiveness as the basis of self-worth (Holland and Eisenhart 1990) that could make men less susceptible to the complication introduced by flattery.

Studies of emotion management cast women as the nurturing gender (Cancian 1987; Clark 1997; Clark, Kleinman and Ellis 1994; Hochschild 1983). The women I surveyed often expressed feelings of guilt for attempting to disengage, and, perhaps in an attempt to alleviate their own discomfort as well as that of their pursuers, sought to "cool out the mark" (Goffman 1952) by maintaining friendly relations. Several women (about 7 percent of the sample) spoke of the guilt and sense of responsibility engendered by forcible interaction, both hypothetical and real. "It's so cute the way he is making such an effort," one respondent said of the scenario, and added: "I would feel bad," indicating that for her, the suitor she defines as childlike evokes a perhaps maternal response. Another woman, clearly drawing upon her own experience, articulated increasing feelings of discomfort as romantic imagery comes into play, particularly in face-to-face interactions: "Just talking after class is okay. It's easy to deal with. A card and a gift are nice but then I would have more to deal with and I'd feel guilty. Him with flowers is a lot to deal with; I would feel very guilty 'cause I'd have to disappoint him."

Attributions of responsibility to self in the situation can have distressing consequences, as a woman describing real-life forcible interaction indicates:

> I felt scared and very out of control—like I could not take control of my life. It just goes to show you that many males do not think women are capable of making decisions and can be bought or manipulated if they are persistent. It is a horrible situation that makes you feel guilty for not 'liking' them".

Both this woman and the one in the preceding paragraph allude to an interesting feature of flattering romantic attempts at forcible interaction. While the pursuer enacts the role of supplicant, the feelings of responsibility engendered by his attentions—albeit unwanted—take on coercive power. This may place the woman in an uncomfortable position where her personal power to choose is eroded by the expectation that she not disappoint, and that she is somehow obligated to manage the emotions of her suitor. This can translate, ironically, into feelings of powerlessness. "I would feel scared and annoyed because obviously there is nothing else I could do if he kept being so persistent," said one respondent. Other women described their actual experience thus: "It was almost like my opinion didn't matter," said one about a classmate who "didn't take [her] lack of feelings for him at face value," and "[w]hen I told him I wasn't interested," another woman said of her suitor,

> he pursued calling me and writing me letters, having my physics teacher deliver them. He gave me a necklace which I tried to give back but he kept telling me to keep it. I felt totally voiceless in this relationship.

A gender-appropriate vocabulary of emotional role may also underlie the frequent mention of the need or wish to maintain friendships with former boyfriends. Some women offer friendship as a consolation, saying things like, "I basically told him that I didn't want anything more than just a friendship from him" in an apparent effort to soothe offended feelings and repair damaged self-esteem. One woman had this to say about her own experience:

> I never really wanted to make a clean break from anyone because if I feel they were special enough to be my boyfriend I always want to remain friends. Being obsessive is scary and my boyfriend was like that, and he also used sui-

cide guilt trips, but you have to work at being friends and so you deal with it and help them so they won't do it to anyone else. Sooner or later they will realize their mistakes.

This woman's desire to protect other women from similar discomfort suggests the extent to which she takes responsibility for both managing and instructing her ex-boyfriend. Similarly, another respondent offered:

My high school boyfriend of three-and-a-half years and I broke up. He couldn't accept my decision to see other people. I wanted to remain friends but thought it best not to be in contact for a while. He kept calling anyway and would cry and say things that made me think he was suicidal. Eventually we were able to be friends but it took a lot of patience on my part.

It is clear from this example that this woman, like the first, takes her responsibility for the feelings of her former boyfriend as requiring her to maintain interaction, even though forcible—indicated by his refusal to respect her desire to discontinue interaction, and her reference to the patience that (presumably) enabled him to disregard her wishes.

While I do not have comparable data on men's interpretations of unwanted pursuit by women, or on the experiences of nonheterosexuals in intimate and dating relationships, it is fair to say that respondents' accounts for their emotional responses to forcible interaction are consistent with feeling rules in romantic, courtship situations dictating reserve and "emotional unavailability" on the part of men and, by virtue of this, flattery and guilt for women who elicit professions of love. These accounts help us to make sense of the scales indicating that romantic imagery in combination with relational context alters women's attributions of danger and invasion when faced with unwanted attention, by bringing our own attention to the influence of vocabularies of emotion and role. The scales also suggest substantial ambivalence, as we have also seen in victim narratives. I conclude this chapter with a brief exploration of this ambivalence and its consequences.

MILIEUS, MIXED EMOTIONS, AND (VOCABULARIES OF) MOTIVE

I constructed a survey of undergraduate sorority women and interviewed a few of their peers to find out how gendered cultural constructions of romance, courtship and love shape women's definitions of forcible interaction, both mild and extreme. The objective was to identify how cultural definitional frameworks influence meaning conferral and thereby action in such situations. I found that while forcible interaction is a distressing phenomenon that annoys and frightens young women in the context of dating relationships, when their pursuers choose strategies from romantic repertoires, an interpretation of attempts to force interaction as coercive and intrusive becomes significantly complicated. Symbols of love and romance such as cards, gifts, and flowers are powerful, emotion-laden images that alter women's sense of invasion by triggering ambivalence and confusion, just as they appear to do for stalking victims in real life.

This may happen as a result of the fairy-tale meanings we attach to such symbols and gender-appropriate vocabularies of emotion and role, in which even violent actions, as part of the active pursuit of women, demonstrate love—and women assess themselves and the significance of their relationships in terms of the lengths to which men go to signify desire. This is especially true when the relationship is an intimate, long term relationship, like the relationships from which the stalking victims were attempting to disengage themselves. While the sorority women were almost equally flattered by floral attention from lesser- and better-known partners, their heartstrings were much more susceptible to the tug of the former lover, however unwished for. This helps to explain why the stalking victims do what they do.

That the sorority women found even relatively innocuous forms of intrusion annoying and frightening supports arguments that both explicitly violent and less extreme forms of forcible interaction are a problem for some young women, defined as "real" and thus become real in their consequences (Thomas 1978). That many of the respondents' feelings about forcible interaction were nonetheless markedly ambivalent is consistent with findings (reviewed in Cate and Lloyd 1992) that victims of relationship violence have various interpretations of the abuse they experience, mentioning love and confusion as well as anger and fear when asked to give their perceptions of violent acts. That women tolerate indignities bestowed by lovers they do not suffer from more casual partners adds weight to the argument that intimacy and violence are anything but mutually exclusive states (Gelles and Strauss 1998; Jackman 1994).[3]

An interactionist analysis of these women's own accounts sheds light upon what Cate and Lloyd (1992:104) call a "romantic veneer." The relational context of intimacy alters women's response. As Goffman (1983:4) says,

> many of the forms of behavior through which we can be offensively treated by one category of others are intimately allied to those through which members of another category can properly display its bondedness to us.

It is thus this very "duality of use" (Goffman 1983:4) of tools from a romantic stock in trade, that confounds women's sense of invasion in the situation they imagine in the questionnaire scenarios. In real life it may increase women's vulnerability to violation of their expressed desire to be left alone and it may be partially responsible for the mixed feelings and compliance so common in the stalking cases reviewed.

Moreover, these attempts fall into gendered categories of appropriateness that contribute to what I have called "complicity" in acts of incursion. They help to explain what Goffman terms a "disheartening capacity" for cooperation exhibited by disadvantaged categories (1983:6). If women think that "of course" they should be flattered by gifts and flowers, it becomes less salient that the offerings are unasked for and that there are emotional strings attached, such as in the form of the guilt and responsibility they inspire—another feature of women's emotional role as nurturers and managers of men's emotional states. Emerson, Ferris, and Gardner point out that the ambiguity that makes the recognition of stalking problematic resides in the "overlap between stalking and normal romantic or relational moves and actors" (1998:291). This "overlap," and the ambivalence it engenders, is a feature of the cultural construction of women as the romantic objects of pursuit so that a persistent male pursuer simply enacts "normal" courtship routines. While ambiguity may well be a general feature of human relationships, this particular ambiguity draws upon gendered romantic moves; unwanted pursuit of men by women is more likely to be represented by Glenn Close in "Fatal Attraction" than some female version of Prince Charming. I suspect that the men whom Emerson, Ferris, and Gardner (1998) found much less likely to be alarmed by pursuit than the women they interviewed are also much less likely to interpret attempts at forcible interaction in romantic terms. This is so because women who pursue are acting inappropriately, and inspire annoyance and pity.[4]

Therefore, when women are confronted with situations in which they have asked or begged to be left alone, and their requests or pleas are ignored, they may sometimes use vocabularies of romance and love to account for the damage to their definitions of situations and relationships that occurs. They align the behavior of pursuers with normative expectations in an effort to ease the discomfort these disruptions create. Courtship becomes a "vocabulary of motive" (Mills 1940) in which aggressors are redefined as suitors and supplicants. Cultural prescriptions that require women to feel flattered by romantic overtures make unwanted pursuit confusing, and the degree to which it is a violation is not always clear. "Feeling rules" (Hochschild 1979) associated with romantic love justify forcible interaction and encourage compliance, rather than resistance, on the part of women; this is another way in which culture shapes these women's actions.

The question remains whether the ambivalence and associated acquiescence to coercion observed in these sorority surveys and interviews might also come into play in intimate, violent relationships. I have described and discussed the perceptions of intimate stalking victims of this phenomenon report. While the language of threat and the symbols of the emotional terrorist dominate the accounts of these women, we also see the infusion of a culture of romance in many cases. Cards and flowers and entreaties and demonstrations of passion, however edged with danger, act to make women question their own subjective reality. And like the sorority women, the stalking victims' confused definitions of the situations in which they found themselves shape their responses. These women take the role of emotional caretaker as if their lives depend on it—sometimes, perhaps, they do. They placate and pacify and plead even as they seek desperately to flee. Again, cultural prescriptions conflating jealousy with love and control with desire and rage with ardor may conspire to make women uniquely vulnerable to this crime in which the vast majority of offenders are men—men whom they once loved and to whom they are still bound.

I have also sought to examine and explain some of the practical consequences emerging from this emotional maelstrom once women are cast upon the hard cold shores of rational-legal systems. In the next, concluding, chapter, I return once more to how the criminal justice system interprets the actions of stalking victims within the same gendered cultural frameworks victims draw upon. At the heart of the matter are social and legal constructions of agency and accountability tremendously complicated by intimacy. I explore some complexities for the theorizing of victimization and other kinds of symbolic interaction and discuss what those of us interested in social policy might make of all this.

NOTES

1. While it may be argued that following and threatening suicide are not only different in *degree* of invasiveness and threat from the other attempts, but also different in *kind*, they occur within the same context, both in the hypothetical scenarios and, as we will see, in real life. In the questionnaire, they stand out in contrast to more ambiguous attempts at forcible interaction. In real life, women draw upon more complex interpretive frameworks in which they also share histories with former intimates that can create ambivalence even here.

2. While it is possible that sorority women are unlikely to be particularly threatened by anyone showing up at a shared residence such as a sorority house or dormitory, they are nonetheless more frightened by the person who shows up sans flowers at a presumably even "safer" place, that is, work or class.

3. As Joel Best points out (2001: personal communication), "Intimacy always carries cost." It is not my intention to imply that dating relationships are

unique in this respect, but rather, to affirm that it is naive to believe that romantic feelings insulate relationships from violence.

4. When I initiated this study, I attempted to survey fraternity members in addition to sorority members, but gave up due to lack of cooperation. However, I was able to obtain 18 completed questionnaires from one fraternity. The men who responded almost unanimously characterized women who "continued to pursue" as "desperate," "insecure," and "annoying." Such a woman is "worthless and has no life," said one, and others described real life pursuers as "ridiculous," "pathetic," and "a loser." Other terms indicated definition more equivocal than not: "disturbed" was one characterization; "stalker!" said one respondent, "sick bitches," said another; and "she's a freak," said yet another.

5

Damned If You Do: Social Problems Work, Emotion Work, and the Worthy Victim

INTRODUCTION: WHEN A VICTIM IS NOT A VICTIM

In this chapter, I briefly review the findings in this exploration of women's feelings about and experience of intimate stalking and the criminal justice system. I begin by explaining how stalking, victimization, and prosecution are each in their own way "courting disaster," and I discuss the identity dilemmas women face as a result. I explore what this explication of the experience of intimate stalking victims adds to our understanding of victimization processes and, especially, the revictimization that is so frequently reported by women who become involved with the criminal justice system, whether they are victims of stalking, sexual assault, or domestic violence. It is also important to consider the larger sociological agenda of which these issues are a part, that is, what this study reveals about the interrelatedness of the everyday "work" through which actors constitute emotions, identity, and social problems. Finally, I will propose some ways in which the criminal justice system might begin to address the complexity of victimization that occurs in complicated human relationships that do not always fit neatly into legal assignations of responsibility and agency.

Courting Disaster and Disasters in Court

Sometimes stalking is courtship gone awry; when overtures are unwanted or when they alternate with communications that are clearly coercive, definitions of interaction as "normal" heterosexual romance are called into question. These "definitional disruptions" (Goffman 1959:13) can become a courting disaster ranging from mild dis-ease (the annoyance imagined and experienced by some of the sorority women I surveyed) to a redefinition of the situation as dangerous and criminal in nature (the perspective of the women claiming victimization in the Domestic Violence Unit). The

data (cards, letters, telephone answering machine messages, and the narratives of victims) in the case files reveal that real-life stalkers often seem
to use interactional strategies much like those in the hypothetical scenarios presented to the sorority women. The scenarios, in turn, clearly res-
onated with the lived experience of even those women who did not assert
that they were stalking victims but who were merely the objects of romantic pursuit taken to an extreme.

While it seems fairly obvious that the *men* who annoy and especially
who terrorize women by refusing to give up pursuit or let go of relationships are courting personal disaster, many of the women whose cases were
prosecuted in the DVU courted disasters of their own. They did so, in part,
precisely because of the romantic and intimate elements of the stalking
documented. That is, the protestations of undying love and need their former partners expressed, using the imagery of romance and symbols of traditional courtship, sometimes induced women to continue interacting
with these men. This was true even when the women reported being
deathly afraid of their pursuers.

Whether women complied in such ways out of fear, love, or ambivalence, and no matter the urgency of a perceived need to keep the emotions
of their former partners under control, their own actions had unintended
results. Sometimes they became unable to convince police officers to make
reports, or to respond to 911 calls, or to refer cases for prosecution. Sometimes advocates, both victim-witness advocates and prosecutors, dis-
counted claims of victimization and chose in various ways to invest less in
these cases, from spending less time on them to seeking lesser charges. In
the few cases that actually went to trial instead of being resolved with negotiated plea bargain, or dismissed, this compliance led on occasion to dramatic disasters in court, the worst being acquittal of the defendant on all
charges, as in Winnie's case.

Winnie's case also exemplified other potential traps in continued interaction; resistance to stalkers in the form of expressions of anger and
"fighting" back were similarly counterproductive. In the eyes of the jury,
the fear that Winnie was required to show to establish a "credible threat"
was undermined by the emotional strength she displayed for her former
partner's benefit. Both resistance and compliance hinder the ability of a
woman to convincingly demonstrate the emotions victims "ought" to feel,
and thus call their "victim" identities into question. For these reasons, a
woman who cannot successfully present herself as a victim has in a sense
courted disaster merely by becoming involved with the criminal justice
system. Being discredited is uncomfortable under any circumstance; being publicly humiliated on a witness stand is an experience few would
wish to undergo.

Walking Fine Lines: Participants, Victims, and Survivors

We have seen that the very actions women take to cope with stalking victimization (as a condition they face) interfere with their ability to "accomplish" victimization (Holstein and Miller 1997), that is, to socially construct themselves as victims. Many of the women attempt to cope with extremely frightening situations that circumscribe their entire lives in ways that are hard for the unitiated to comprehend. Often these situations continue for excruciatingly lengthy periods of time. Moreover, the possibility of getting real help from the criminal justice system seems faint indeed. Nonetheless, the ways in which others interpret the actions of stalking victims frequently fail to take these circumstances into account. No matter what course of action a woman takes, she risks being unable to establish that she is a victim, or that she continues to be victimized, or that she continues to need help.

A stalking victim is not a victim when she violates the expectation that women who are truly afraid of their former partners will have nothing further to do with them. This means that she cannot succumb to pleading even for a moment, no matter how deeply she has cared for her former intimate or how well she knows that pleading quickly becomes raging when unsatisfied. Nor can she send an irate letter, or rush over to the house where her pursuer is staying to confront him about the latest vandalism—because no matter how safe she feels at the time (he is in jail, or staying with his mother), women who are legitimately afraid do not take such actions. Compliance is almost always framed as complicity and victims become participants and participants precipitate, in these constructions.

Victims are expected to be passive but not compliant. On the other hand—and this is another identity dilemma these women face—victims should be proactive but also cooperative. That is, they must not have done anything to bring their situation upon themselves or to encourage it to continue, so they must not ever do as their former partner demands. They must resist the stalker *and* be active in their own defense, taking responsibility for their own safety, and at the same time willingly cooperate with the requests of prosecutors. No matter how frustrated they become, they must not be too needy or too demanding, too emotional or too unemotional. Furthermore, even after they have established that they are, in fact, victims, and even if stalking continues, they cannot claim victim identities too intensely or too long. They can be "too much" the victim and fail to "move on." Victims must become "survivors" if they are to stay in the good graces of their advocates and others, and if they are to feel positively about who they are and what has happened to them. And even this accomplishment, should it occur, may not meet the conflicting expectations to which victims try to conform. This is because survivors take responsibility for their own situations, confounding the very logic of what it means to be a victim in the first place.

These are the situations in which women who claim to be stalking victims find themselves. While their experiences may seem to be unusual or even bizarre, there is a great deal we can learn from what they undergo and endure, however frantic or graceless they are at times. To begin, we can understand more about processes of victimization, especially those that involve intimates. We also can see how the misery that advocates have termed "revictimization" occurs and, importantly, how it is related to victimization.

CONTRIBUTIONS TO VICTIMOLOGY: THE LIVED EXPERIENCE OF VICTIMIZATION AND REVICTIMIZATION

The history of victimology as a social science appears to be inextricable from its history as a moral and political stance taken toward victims. This is partially due to the nature of the task victimologists have traditionally set themselves. The first researchers in the field looked for the part that victims play in their own victimization as a means of explaining why some people are more likely to be victimized than others. Thus Mendelsohn (1956), who named this subdiscipline of criminology in 1947, studied resistance to rape, and early efforts to explain victimization were profoundly influenced by Wolfgang's (1958) conceptualization of "victim precipitation"—in homicide cases in which the violence was initiated by the eventual victim. "This issue of shared responsibility captivated the first criminologists who became interested in victimology" (Karmen 2001), shaping not only their research but the uses to which it was put.

The search for the contributory or causal role of victims in criminal events appears to have slipped easily into a tendency to attribute responsibility for victimization to victims and shift blame from offenders (Mannheim 1965; Reckless 1967; Schafer 1968; Shultz 1968; von Hentig 1941, 1948). Amir's (1971) study of rape victimization exemplified this trend and is perhaps the most widely criticized work in this area. Much of the "victim defending" (Karmen 1991, 2001) literature argues most strongly against the application of the idea of victim precipitation to rape (see, for example, Anderson and Renzetti 1980; Brownmiller 1975; Clark and Lewis 1977; Kennedy and Sacco 1998; LeGrande 1973; Reiff 1979; Symonds 1980; Weis and Borges 1973). Some social science responses to this controversy have been to question the utility of the idea of precipitation (Kennedy and Sacco 1998), to create typologies of victims that recognize degrees of responsibility (see Fattah 1967, 1991; Lamborn 1968; Schafer 1977; and Sheley 1979), and to argue for a shift in focus away from the "microscopic" level of analysis toward "the larger social and cultural context and the institutional sources of lawlessness" (Karmen 1991).

I would argue that it is possible and important to distinguish between and disentangle the explorations of social scientists from the moral evaluations that often follow from our findings. Setting aside (temporarily) the claims of victims' and defendants' advocates, symbolic interactionists will argue that in order to understand victimization from the perspective of the actors involved, we must treat it like any other complex social interaction. That is, none of the actors are passive, but all are actively engaged in observing, defining, feeling, and acting on the basis of their interpretations of each other and themselves (Blumer 1969). Suspending for the moment the terminology of "responsibility, culpability, guilt, and blame" that critics such as Karmen (2001:86) claim are "routinely" used in interactionist models of victimization, we consider, as Luckenbill (1977) does for murder, that any crime

> is the outcome of a dynamic interchange between an offender, victim, and, in many cases, bystanders. The offender and the victim develop lines of action shaped in part by the actions of the other. (185)

This approach allows us to do several crucial things. First, we can begin to understand victimization as an emergent process rather than a more-or-less static event—especially important in the consideration of a crime such as stalking that continues over time and involves multiple violations. Second, we can address some of the complexities of real life crimes in which the actors know one another and both share and contest understandings of their situation. How actors define what goes on is influenced by a multiplicity of factors, including the immediate context for what is happening; the history of the relationship between the parties; and historical, cultural, and structural frameworks for establishing meaning. Furthermore, we extend our analysis to include the responses of others to victimization, as an integral part of these definitional processes (Kennedy and Sacco 1998). This processual analysis confers agency upon *all* of the actors involved. Attributions of blame themselves can then be analyzed as part of processes of victimization—even those made by social scientists.

Dancing with Wolves: Interactions with Former Intimates

Although this study focuses on victims' perspectives of intimate stalking victimization, it clearly illustrates these emergent, complex, situated, interactive definitional processes. Although stalking is a variant of interaction that is forcible rather than engaged in with mutual consent, it is interaction nonetheless. Women find themselves in situations they must define before they can respond; they must determine whether or not they are being stalked and assess the dangers they face. They must figure out if and when to seek help, and what to say to criminal justice actors when they do. They must decide if professions of love and remorse are believable and if so, whether they can let down their guard or even redefine the relationship from which they are trying to flee. Is this just because he loves me too much? Or is it a trick to get me to come back? Will he calm down? Are his threats to kill me and the children serious? Why is he telling me he loves me one minute and threatening to beat me to a pulp the next? Is he going to follow me everywhere I go? Will he ever give up?

Once a woman arrives at a definition of the situation, she then can and must choose how she will respond and the actions she will take. While the data collected here do not allow me to determine with any certainty how victims' responses to stalkers influence the process of stalking, it is certain that they do. Keeping in mind that the cases studied here are only those in which the actions of former partners were frightening enough and persisted long enough for victims to define them as stalking and exclude cases in which women were able to deter stalking without criminal justice system assistance, we can imagine ways in which the choices women make shape this crime. Some of these may be problematic, both immediately and later on. For example, women who make themselves harder to find (avoidance) could discourage some stalkers from their pursuit. However, that so many women reported screening phone calls, hiding, changing their phone numbers and moving—and yet stalking continued—suggests that if anything, this response might result in an escalation of stalking behaviors in cases like those studied. Compliance is a response in which virtually all of the women engaged, in some form, and in all but the cases where the women returned to the relationship, stalking continued or escalated. Resistance appears to have angered stalkers, judging from the threats and violence that often resulted when women responded in this way.

To say that what a victim does likely affects what a stalker does is not affixing blame, but characterizes an interactive process. Moreover, what the data do reveal is the degree to which victimization is a process that includes the responses of yet more actors—some of whom assuredly *do* assess causality in evaluative ways. As Kennedy and Sacco, speaking of interactionist analyses of victimization more generally, put it:

> The victimization interaction does not end with the violent attack. [T]his situation continues. [Criminal justice system] responses are important in understanding the stages following the event, which include the determination

of blame, the extent of harm done, and the actions that need to be taken to deter future victimization." (1998:108)

We have seen that the criminal justice system response to intimate stalking is profoundly influenced by interactions between victims and stalkers, as well as between victims and their various advocates and adversaries. The actions women take in response to their definitions of stalking situations shape how family members, friends, police officers, victim advocates, prosecutors, judges, juries, and the media interpret what has taken place. These definitions of situations then play a major role in whether women will be able to successfully claim, maintain, and transcend their victimization, whether they will get help, and perhaps even whether stalking will continue. This brings us to the topic of the "revictimization" processes attendant upon the victim blaming that matters most. These are the attributions of "responsibility, culpability, guilt, and blame" (Karmen 2001:86) in which the criminal justice system actors involved in intimate stalking victimization engage.

In the Lion's Den: Interactions in the Domestic Violence Unit

The term "revictimization," sometimes called the "second assault," refers to situations in which crime victims feel harmed by the treatment they receive at the hands of the criminal justice system actors they encounter, usually as part of prosecution processes. It appears most often in discussions of rape victims' experience, and researchers argue that it is a consequence of questioning the credibility of victims, thereby implicating them in their own victimization (Frohmann 1994; Holmstrum and Burgess 1983; Kerstetter 1990; Kerstetter and Van Winkle 1990; Konradi 1996, 1997; Madigan and Gamble 1989; Martin and Powell 1994; Rose and Randall 1982; Stanko 1982). Like the victims cited in this literature, stalking victims described feeling as if *they* were on trial.

Stalking victims sometimes feel like rape victims, who, prior to the introduction of "rape shield laws," could be questioned about their past sexual conduct. Ellen Nichols, whose husband was convicted of spousal rape, described her interactions with her ex-husband's defense attorney thus:

> Testifying at the trial, as far as the defense, the way they approached me was pretty nasty, [the defense tried to make it appear that] I was denying, I wanted him in my life, I liked it, and I liked it that way. It was the only way I could enjoy sex, and it was the only—I was lying now, to try to make it look like it was a rape, but I really wanted him to live with me, be with me, because I was a typical, you know, want him in my life kind of victim, is the way the defense was portraying me.

In Ellen's narrative, the defense attorneys appeared to link together for the jury vintage assumptions about rape victims "wanting it" and a freshly minted construction of a stalking victim who likewise "want[s] him in my life." Kathy Felson's case didn't go to trial, but she felt similarly mischaracterized during a preliminary hearing. Of her experience, she said:

> And of course, the court process itself is ugly. I mean, to go through that preliminary hearing, and have you know, [my former husband's] PD [public defender] turn everything around, it's like, you know, "You set him up." Um, um, which—that's what he's supposed to do. But that whole process, I mean, [you are] at the point where you are probably your most vulnerable, and you're getting attacked from all sides.

Kathy suggested that the public defender was attempting to portray her as a vindictive ex-wife in a custody battle, and Ellen alluded to a framing relying on similar stereotypes of gender, relationships, and sexuality (Frohmann 1994). During cross-examination, the attorney defending Winnie's former boyfriend tried to establish that Winnie only claimed to have ended the relationship, was inviting the defendant over to her house, and was still having "sexual relations" with him even while he was being arrested for violating the restraining order.

> Q: Isn't it true that you have several men friends?
> A: No. It is not true that I have several men friends that come over. The one man friend that comes over is [the name of her friend].
> Q: Would it surprise you—your neighbor indicated that you had many boyfriends come over to your house?
> A: Yeah. It would surprise me that I had many boyfriends. I got a play family of eight guys in the family.
> Q: Do you recall Easter Sunday in April of '97 having sexual relations with [the defendant]?
> A: No, I did not.
> Q: He did not pay you $30?
> A: Let me tell you, if somebody was going to pay me to have sex with him, it is more than $30. I guarantee you that.

Winnie's unshaken, matter-of-fact demeanor seemed to defeat what was quite clearly an attempt by the defense to portray her as both promiscuous and as still attached to her former boyfriend. Like Winnie, Kathy and Ellen were also relatively unfazed by their court experience, despite the unpleasantness of the tactics chosen by the defense, and both of these women chose to return to make victim impact statements at sentencing.

Not all victims are so resilient, however. One victim refused to prosecute her former boyfriend a second time, even though he appeared to have resumed stalking her after his conviction. She told the police officer who responded to her father's request for aid that

> [My former boyfriend] needs some help. Going to jail isn't going to help him. I don't want to go to court and testify. I was ridiculed and put through too much the last time I had to testify. I was treated very rude by the court system. I don't want to do this again.

According to the victim advocate who interviewed her later, this victim said that testifying against this same defendant was the "worst experience of my life." For her, having the defendant show up at her house with a gun (the incident that prompted her father to call police) was less frightening than going back to court, a process that she believed would only demean her. The transcript of Caity Ingall's former boyfriend's preliminary hearing illustrates the misery some victims experience. It is almost painful to read, and must have been horrible to witness. Even without a visual image to attach to the computer-generated words, it is clear that Caity was stumbling through her interrogation by the defense. For example, when asked if the relationship had ended at a particular point, she responded:

> No. That was the last—that was—that was the final time that we were around one another. It was—he—that was in response to when was the last time, but before that [the DA] asked me about four or five times that we were broke up before that it was in the sense where I would—I would see him maybe once. Not a—when you say "back together," it wasn't a back together. Back together was not back together.

Then, as part of a strategy to further reframe their interaction as consensual rather than forcible, the defense attorney asked Caity about letters she had written to the defendant after the "final time." Regarding one of these, when Caity was asked if she had typed it, she said, "This is—this is not— no—well, yes—yes. I guess I did type it, but not sitting at a typewriter by myself," an evasive-appearing answer that her later explanation (of being forced to write the letter) did little to dispel. Of the other letter, in which she apologized to the defendant and professed her continued love, she said:

> You're—you're—you don't understand the context. My meaning is different than the way that you are taking it, and so I really can't—I can't answer that because you're taking that to mean something that it did not mean.

It is responses such as this, under circumstances clearly stressful for Caity, that later enabled the defense attorney to tell the judge that "it never really became clear during the course of this witness's testimony when in time [the relationship] was over with," and that "[h]er memory became a little spotty when I asked her the context or why she wrote those letters." It also appears that the defense was successful in its attempt to portray Caity as paranoid; the judge told the attorneys that when a victim had emotional and psychological problems the standard of "reasonable fear" may be at issue, before adding,

> Normally you take your victims as you find them. If you have a victim [who] is a bleeder, that is no defense that the conduct might not have resulted in death or serious injury if there is criminal behavior towards that victim.

The district attorney who prosecuted this case told me that Caity had been "completely out of her body" during the testimony, but "bleeding" remains an apt metaphor for the "dissection" she described in the carefully composed statement cited earlier.

Kennedy and Sacco, in their discussion of "secondary victimization" in the context of rape, suggest that sexual history is still salient in "certain situations," claiming that "[i]n the case of rape, extralegal factors such as court officials' own beliefs of morality and proper behavior; not only the evidence provided in the case," can affect prosecutorial outcomes, and further claim that "this type of judgment does not occur in other types of court cases" (1998:184–185). The cases I studied suggest that markedly similar "extralegal factors" come into play in stalking cases as well. From the perspective of stalking victims, they too suffer the indignities of questioning about their sexual relations with defendants and others, and defense attorneys, at least, seek to give these relations credence as evidence for the court to ponder.

It is not only defense attorneys whom victims characterize as problematic. Both Ellen Nichols and Kathy Felson described the ongoing construction and maintenance of their credibility as central in their efforts, and reported frustrations with even those prosecutors and advocates that were most helpful. Their cases were actively prosecuted, but any victim whose case is not referred for prosecution, or dismissed, or even negotiated with an unsatisfactory plea bargain, has grounds to feel that her claims about her experience of stalking, and therefore her identity as a victim, are disbelieved. She may not be aware that the plea is a result of her own divergence from normative expectations of the "ideal" or "worthy" victim, but she likely feels the sting of rejection regardless.

In sum, this study reveals that for stalking victims, "revictimization," like "victimization," is a complex definitional process in which the actions, or imputed actions, of victims form the bases of the judgment of others'. Identities are fundamentally at stake. And the phenomena are intimately related. If victimization is something that victims must "accomplish" (Holstein and Miller 1991, 1997) by successfully claiming victim identities, then revictimization appears to hinge on the dismantling of the edifices victims have constructed with such effort. While processes of revictimization may lack the intentionality of constructions of victim status, criminal justice system actors nonetheless call victims' definitions of situation and self into question and propose alternate, discredited definitions in explanation. Revictimization, then, is the failure to achieve victimization. Moreover, it is the quintessential experience of "stigma," as Goffman put it: "An undesired differentness from what we had anticipated" (1963:5) that causes us to profoundly redefine and thereby discount victims.

CONTRIBUTIONS TO SOCIAL PROBLEMS THEORY AND THE SOCIOLOGY OF EMOTIONS: SAINTS, SINNERS AND THE SOCIAL CONSTRUCTION OF STALKING VICTIMS

Throughout this analysis, I have worked to show that stalking victimization is a process in which the "objective" condition of being coerced or forced to interact with former partners is defined and redefined by victims and their advocates. Women go to great lengths to construct themselves as victims, and we have seen many of the dilemmas they face as they negotiate both stalking and the criminal justice system response to it. While doing so, they not only construct themselves as victims, but construct stalking as the social problem to which they have fallen prey. Thus they are doing what Holstein and Miller call "social problems work":

> We accomplish social problems as we communicate about, categorize, organize, argue, and persuade one another that social problems really do exist. Thus, we produce the practical reality of social problems." (1997:ix)

This examination of the accomplishment of stalking victimization not only illustrates the workings of these interpretive practices for a particular social problem, but also highlights the interconnectedness of emotion work, identity work, and social problems construction more generally. The study of stalking victims shows us that when women work to establish themselves as such, they manage their own (and sometimes others') emotions as part and parcel of the identities they are claiming. The interrelationship of these constructive activities is consequential; attributions of responsibility are inexorably linked to the success or failure of the "work." This happens because the creation of emotions, identities, and social problems I have described influences the social construction of agency and choice. This is the crux of the matter, and a discussion of stalking victimization as an exemplar of these generic processes follows. Stalking is not only a situation, however, but is situated. Thus I will also attend to the definitional frameworks upon which victims and their advocates draw as they create the problem of stalking and constitute themselves as victims before concluding with a few of the implications of this research for those who would be advocates.

The Making of Victims: Socially Constructing Problems, Identities, and Emotions

Following Holstein and Miller (1997) we can conceptualize the activities of victims and those who act on their behalf as the "work" of convincing others of their claims to be victims of stalking. A victim who successfully constructs herself as a victim has "accomplished victimization" (Holstein and Miller 1991). She has become "a particular kind of person who is affected by, and is an example of, a particular type of social problem" (Ibid. 1997:x). Consistent with Holstein and Miller, stalking victims illustrate that this kind of social problems work involves assignations of responsibility, the "public articulation and dramatization of injury and *innocence*" (Holstein and Miller 1991:105, emphasis added). This study fleshes out this conceptualization, illuminating for us the particulars and especially the problems associated with becoming and being a stalking victim in the eyes of the law. Stalking victims must possess a number of attributes, many of which reflect contradictory normative expectations, in order to be defined as victims and thus get help. As we have seen, victims cannot be too strong or too weak, too compliant or too resistant, too passive or too proactive, and so on. We have seen what constitutes this type of victimization, because we have observed both women who succeeded and thus exemplify "typical" victims, and women who failed and thereby became recast as "deviants." We have constructed a generic "stalking victim," shown what a woman must do to achieve this identity, and shown how hard this often is. We have even explored, in brief, the stigma that attaches to accomplishment—hinting at "the myriad ways that the 'victim' image debilitates those to whom it is applied" (Holstein and Miller 1991:120). The articulation of this particular victim identity ("stalking victim", as central to the definition of this particular social problem ("intimate stalking") reveals the degree to which social problems work in everyday life involves identity work.

"Emotion work" (Hochschild 1979, 1983) is important too. As women struggle to control their fear and not allow guilt, ambivalence, or love to sway them from their course, they must convince others of the legitimacy of their feelings in order to achieve victim identities. Hochschild argues that emotions are socially conditioned. That is, they are subject to normative expectations governing not only which emotions are appropriate to display under particular circumstances, but even which emotions people "ought" to feel. Thus actors "work" to manage their own and others' emotions to bring them into conformity with these expectations.

Clark (1990:305) brings our attention to the political content of emotions, theorizing that felt and displayed emotions "mark and claim place" or establish the rank of actors relative to one another in an interaction. She elaborates this theme as part of her extended discussion of sympathy in which she articulates the feeling rules governing sympathy and elaborates a relationship between sympathy and deviance (Clark 1987; 1997). As Clark characterizes this, people can become deviant by asking for sympathy when it is unmerited, for example, or by asking for more sympathy than is merited, in a "socioemotional economy" that "create[s] the microlevel equivalent of stratification, or microhierarchy" (1997:143). In these exchanges, actors only allocate sympathy to those they deem worthy recipients, in particular those people thought to be "free of responsibility" (Ibid.:207) for the situation that places them in need of sympathy.

Clark also points out that deviance, by definition, attaches to sympathy recipients.

> Because people receive sympathy only when something goes wrong, even the most innocent people are *potentially* labelable as "deviants." Plights are nonnormal and nonroutine, and people in plights may slip in others' esteem for the mere fact of undergoing them (1997:197, emphasis in original).

This study of stalking victimization illustrates and expands upon these themes. It illuminates a set of feeling rules, governing both what women in this circumstance ought to feel and the emotions they are permitted or expected to publicly display. It shows the role that these rules play in the construction and maintenance of identities. In addition, it demonstrates some micropolitical consequences of feeling and displaying certain emotions, and lends weight to the notion that sympathy is a central and highly evaluative emotion influencing social interaction.

The penal code criminalizing stalking in the state where this research took place codified a feeling rule; it required victims to experience *fear* (a "credible threat"). Thus, stalking victims display this emotion as part of their presentation of the victim self. It is part of claiming and "managing" (Goffman 1963) a victim identity. Like the attribute of "innocence," however, the emotional normative expectations associated with stalking victimization are not always easy to conform to. Identity dilemmas are often emotion management dilemmas. The appropriately fearful woman cannot be too fearful, or she becomes "hysterical." Nor should a stalking victim express her anger too vociferously, whether it is with her former husband or towards her criminal justice system advocates. Anger is discrepant with the fear she is expected to feel for the former, and gratitude for the latter.

If a woman still feels love for her former partner—or even ambivalence—
and worse, expresses it, this too calls her claims to be a stalking victim into
question.

In addition, the management of her own emotions is not the only emotion work that can discredit a victim. First, it seems clear that stalkers' efforts are directed to inducing emotions in victims—primarily fear, but also
guilt and romantic feelings. Sometimes, these efforts are successful. Many,
many actions that women take, even if they are a direct result of profound
and intense terror, or specifically intended to calm former partners and
prevent further violence, belie their fear. Those who judge victims, whether
they are her friends or a jury of the defendants' peers, construct compliance with demands or pleas (no matter how it is inspired) as an indication
that women are not truly frightened. Therefore, they are not truly who they
are claiming to be. Instead, they are participants, and following the logic
of attributing responsibility, not victims.

When stalking victims violate feeling rules in these ways, and are then
discredited through the revictimization processes I have described, they
have cause to feel shame. This "marks" their place (Clark 1990) in the criminal justice system. As Goffman (1963:7) puts it, they are "intimately alive
to what others see as [their] failing" and perceive themselves as having little value within, much less power or control over, prosecution. Sympathy
is lost to them; their failure to accomplish victimization leads inevitably to
definitions or redefinitions of whether they merit it. And even women who
meet emotional expectations for victims mark their inferior place, because
fear is associated with weakness. Sympathizing with a stalking victim thus
demeans her, ultimately robbing her of her self-efficacy and making the
fruits of her emotional labor bittersweet. Victims are deviants by virtue of
their victimization, and their efforts to recast themselves as "survivors" attest to their awareness of this fact. They take on new identities in ongoing
processes in which they work to transform fear and shame into pride and
confidence in their own resourcefulness. Through this, they continue to
construct stalking as a social problem. As in the accomplishment of victimization, their social problems work rests upon their identity work, of
which some significant piece is emotion work.

Unhappily Ever After? Structures, Interpretations, and Further Research

Thus far I have examined the stalking victimization situation primarily
within the definitional frameworks and constraints represented by the district attorney's office, arguing that women navigate treacherous waters
there. I have looked at some ways in which cultural expectations of courtship
and romance influence stalking victims, thereby sometimes confounding
their presentation of innocence in the interactions that take place within

this organization. This analysis only scratches the surface of this complicated situation. Here I briefly explore some possibilities for further research and theoretical development of relationships between persistent social structures beyond the confines of the Domestic Violence Unit and the claiming of these often-contested identities. Whether definitions of victimization are those of prosecutors or sociologists, "the differing reasons [humans] give for their actions are not themselves without reasons" (Mills 1940:904)—that is, they are situated within particular intersecting social arrangements that shape the realities we create. How might the definitional processes I have described be influenced by the time during which they take place, and where do representations of stalking victimization fit within our culture? What do our ranking systems of gender, race, and social class have to do with the travails of the women whose stories appear here? These are questions yet to be addressed.

In some ways, the historical moment for stalking victims is fortuitous. Stalking has been "institutionaliz[ed] as an enduring crime problem rather than simply another focus of short-lived media attention" (Best 1999:56), resulting in new social movements and support groups as well as legislation. Additionally, advocates have successfully defined the problem of stalking as a problem of domestic rather than stranger violence, thus gaining the powerful sponsorship of the crime victims' movement and the battered women's movement (Best 1999; Lowney and Best 1995). Victim advocates now work within the criminal justice system, ostensibly to meet victims' needs as well as prosecutors, and victims are far more involved at all stages of prosecution than previously (Karmen 2001; Kennedy and Sacco 1998; Lurigio and Resick 1990). Best (1997:13) argues that victimization "has become fashionable" and that an entire industry has sprouted from ideology that is fundamentally supportive of victims and victimization.

> [This ideology] defines victimization as common, serious, morally unambiguous, yet largely unrecognized; it justifies methods to identify individuals (and help those individuals recognize themselves) as victims; it delegitimizes doubts about victims' claims; and it provides new, nonstigmatizing labels for those who have suffered.

That the district attorney's office in which this research was conducted not only had a prosecutor designated to handle stalking cases, but a victim advocate as well suggests that stalking was "fashionable" at the time, and victims were well supported within the organization.

On the other hand, the victims I interviewed and those who talked about their criminal justice system experience in case files felt far from privileged. One possibility is that there is a cultural/organizational lag here: criminal justice systems have yet to fully implement victim advocacy in ways that truly reflect the "victim ideology" Best (1997) describes, especially when organizational constraints conflict with victims' needs. Another possibility is that victims have actually fallen *out* of fashion because in the contemporary United States we are saturated with them. If, as Hilgartner and Bosk (1988) argue, we have a limited "carrying capacity" for social problems, the current omnipresence of victims clamoring for our attention can create a climate in which audiences are increasingly jaded or, at least, skeptical. Presently there are a number of critical voices, ranging from those who decry the alleged advent of a "victim feminism" that frames all women as helpless in the face of multiple oppressions (Roiphe 1993; Wolf 1994), to writers such as Best, who points to the ironies of classification systems in which "the [posttraumatic stress disorder] label is now applied to victims whose experiences range from battering and incest to receiving contaminated fast food," and a widely read book about codependency "lists more than 230 characteristics of codependents" (Best 1997:11, 12).

Moreover, the redefinition of stalking as a domestic violence issue (rather than primarily a problem for celebrities with obsessed fans), while solidifying the importance of stalking in legislative arenas, might be a double-edged sword. It is possible that the social problem of domestic violence has passed its peak in popularity, and that association with it gives stalking a mundane character that detracts from the strangeness which attracted public attention to it in the first place. Research that traces how representations and interpretations of victimization have changed over time would add to our understanding of the current difficulties stalking victims face convincing others that *they* are victims.

In addition to weariness with the abundance of available victims in general, there may presently be widespread ambivalence toward domestic violence victimization in particular. There is an image of the battered woman in contemporary popular culture that could hinder stalking victims in their pursuit of legal help. This image is derived from legal and social-scientific discourse that frames domestic violence as frequently reciprocal (Gelles and Straus 1988), domestic violence "disputes" as the major source of law enforcement injury and death, and domestic violence victims as abusing the criminal justice system (Jones 1994). This is seen in narratives describing the police officer who is injured by the *victim* when responding to the domestic violence (who is enraged by his intervention), or the victim who has "second thoughts" the morning after and asks that the case be dismissed. The accuracy of this imagery, while arguable, is not at issue here: it is simply that the "battered woman" is not the "morally unambiguous" figure to whom Best (1997) refers. If a stalking victim is a variant of a domestic violence victim, she too may be tarnished by association.

Thus there is not only a culture of romance within which stalking victims struggle to define their situation and make their claims, but also, perhaps, a culture of intimate violence that intersects with the historical moment. It is a kind of "backlash," as Faludi (1991) would put it, in which the gains the battered women's movements and victims' rights movements have made in the last few decades are offset somewhat by countering arguments and alternate, unflattering constructions. Women who are being stalked have to distinguish their experience from "normal" courtship and relationship. They also have to set themselves apart from the legions of sometimes pathetic, sometimes tawdry, sometimes sordid images of battered women with which the public, and the criminal justice system, have been inundated. Research illuminating constructions of intimate violence victimization in current popular (and social scientific) discourses would add to the sophistication of our understanding of the context for interpretations of intimate stalking.

There are also systems of stratification to consider. Criminal justice systems reflect the hierarchical arrangements of societies both in their organization and by differential treatment of offenders. It is probable that ranking affects victim advocacy too. First, as I have noted, the Domestic Violence Unit was not a prestigious Unit in the district attorney's office at the time of the research, although that changed somewhat with the increased funding obtained by Laura Lennox and the advent of Domestic Violence Court. There were more women deputy district attorneys in the DVU than in higher status units such as Major Crimes and Homicide, and with the exception of the district attorney herself and Laura Lennox, the lead attorneys were primarily male, as were the judges. All but one of the Victim Advocates were women, and the sole male Advocate did not work in the DVU.

Gender disparities in law enforcement are rapidly changing (Miller 2000; Morash 2000), but the district attorney's office still mirrored these professions in the larger culture. Domestic violence victims and stalking victims are predominantly women, and thus rank low not only because of their victim status but also because of their gender. In addition, the victims whose cases were resolved in the DVU, like violent crime victims (and offenders) nationwide, were disproportionately minority women and of lower socioeconomic status. If it is true, as many feminist social critics (Belenky et al. 1986; Lashgiri 1985; Taylor et al. 1995) argue, that women in the contemporary United States are "silenced"—and all the more so when they are facing multiple oppressions—then it is likely that it is harder for these victims to make themselves heard than for others who are more privileged. The stalking victims I interviewed were middle-class and white, for the most part. A research program that looked more closely at how race, ethnicity, and social class shape the accomplishment of victimization would make a significant contribution toward understanding relationships between social problems work, identity work, and emotion work in settings like the DVU.

Finally, in revealing some of the complexities of intimate stalking victimization, certain theoretical as well as empirical tensions become apparent. There are dilemmas victims face, and in their disentangling, they pose problems for analysts. These are related to the social construction of agency or choice. I have argued, consistent with Clark (1997), Goffman (1963), Holstein and Miller (1991, 1997), and Loseke (1999) among others, that attributions of responsibility are at the core of judging whether victims are in "fact" victims or deviate from the identities they claim. Following Holstein and Miller (1991; 1997), and Loseke (1999), I have also worried about ways in which successfully achieving victim identities diminishes the worth of the women who accomplish this, by casting them as essentially powerless. Put otherwise, victims, by definition, cannot be agents, and therefore deviate inherently from expectations that individuals are autonomous, self-efficacious, and have control over their own lives.

Not only do these constructions stigmatize victims (Goffman 1963), but from an analyst's perspective, they tremendously oversimplify the lived experience of stalking. Stalking is an interactive process in which women make decisions based on their definitions and redefinitions of the situation in which they find themselves. They choose whether to comply with or resist their former partners, and their actions appear to shape victimization processes in multiple ways. Are they then somehow fundamentally "responsible" for their victimization, as the victim precipitation theorists would have us believe? If they are not (as the victim advocates argue), is it possible to be a victim and an agent both?

In previous research on sexual coercion (Dunn 1998), I have argued that structures of tradition and cultural imagery and gendered inequality profoundly constrain women's choices. However, casting actors as solely victims or agents obscures the interpenetration of structure and agency in everyday life. Thus (following Thomas and Znaniecki 1951:162) women are neither the product of their circumstances (victims) nor the producers of their situations (agents), rather, they are both. Here, my argument is that these same structures profoundly influence *interpretations* of women's choices as well. If "victim" is a social construction, an identity that is the product of interactions between women and criminal justice system actors, by the same token, so is "agent." Further research that explores historical, cultural, and hierarchical definitional frameworks for the representation and understanding of agency in violent intimate relationships would complicate our understanding of stalking victimization—and reality construction more generally—in fruitful ways.

MAKING A CASE: POLICY IMPLICATIONS FOR VICTIM ADVOCACY AND PROSECUTION

In this book I have considered what happens to women who are being stalked when they seek assistance from the criminal justice system. The "victim contests" (Holstein and Miller 1991) that take place in legal arenas are such that stalking victims rarely emerge the winners, it seems. Cases are never referred for prosecution, or charges are not filed, or charges are dismissed, or defendants plead "no contest" to reduced charges, or defendants are given sentences that barely permit victims time to gather their belongings and flee, or cases go to trial and defendants are acquitted. The most bitter of ironies reside in the cases where it is the woman's own decisions that create the disaster in court, especially when she takes the actions she does to protect herself, most especially when she does so because the help she has been seeking was not forthcoming. There are many costs paid by the losers of such struggles. The dearest toll paid, perhaps, is the loss of credibility and the feeling of revictimization that results. What does this research offer those who would help stalking victims?

First, we have seen that the compliant and resistant acts in which stalking victims engage become comprehensible when we examine them from the perspective of these women. An interactionist approach to lived experience teaches us that in order to understand what people do we need to know their definitions of the situations upon which they act (Blumer 1969). People who deal with stalking victims, whether they are police officers responding to 911 calls or juries assessing the guilt or innocence of defendants, should be educated in the dynamics of stalking as an interactive process. Advocates at all levels need to be taught how to take the point of view of victims. If these actors can use their imaginative and empathetic capacities to get a sense of how persistent, omnipresent, and threatening—but also occasionally endearing—the stalker appears to the victim, her "bad judgment" makes more sense. Also, if legal professionals know more about what stalking is like for victims, they can better advise victims at early stages of stalking processes. Thus they might let victims know to document and to keep love letters as well as threatening letters, to expect both, and to expect to feel differently upon the receipt of one rather than the other.

This last point is particularly critical for educators to emphasize and for advocates to tell victims and prosecutors to explain to juries. Crimes involving intimates are complex rather than simple and emotional as well as rational. Crimes such as stalking are a process that occurs among people who have histories with each other and who have multifaceted, variable, and volatile relationships. Stalking brings our attention to the ways in which the legal discourse of statutes fails to capture the complexity of human violence and violation. How can we judge the emotions ("credible threat") a "reasonable person" ought to feel when she is subject to such an onslaught of wildly varying communications from someone she once loved, and may still care for? For that matter, how can someone who is terrified be reasonable?

In the case of intimate stalking, it seems more likely that a victim's emotions fluctuate than not, and that some of her emotions violate normative expectations. In particular, if we expect that a woman who is terrified does not also feel and express anger, or even love, toward her tormentor, the experience of stalking victims calls our assumptions into question. These are characteristics of the lived experience of stalking. Donileen Loseke (1992) found, in her study of the social construction of battered women by shelter workers, that the "official reality" of workers and the public did not fully encompass the "lived reality" of domestic violence victims. Legal and other "official" definitions of stalking victimization could be significantly broadened, to victims' benefit.

This research has also brought to the fore a central feature of the revictimization processes with which victim advocates have been concerned. This is the demolition and collapse of the "victim" identities women have worked hard to accomplish, under such difficult conditions. This happens when the behavior of the victim, rather than the stalker, is held up to the harsh glare of (as yet) uneducated assessment, as we saw most dramatically in a few of the preliminary hearings and trials described here. Defense attorneys make victims responsible for what has befallen them, often because women have complied with the demands of their former partners. Sometimes this is framed as "precipitation."

This is much like accusing a rape victim of not saying "no" loudly enough or fighting hard enough, or even "encouraging" the advances of her attacker. Strategies that prosecutors use to separate acquaintance rape from the previous sexual history of a couple might be of use in separating stalking from the previous relationship history of a couple. Laws similar to rape shield laws that prevent defense attorneys from questioning the sexual history of victims to discredit their testimony might offer similar protections to stalking victims.

If this is not possible, advocates who understand that identity is at stake in a victim contest can at least prepare victims better for the questioning they will face. Based on her study of prosecutors' precourt preparation of rape survivors, Amanda Konradi (1997) argues that revictimization is a consequence of lack of preparation or understanding of what will be expected of victims in court. My research suggests that stalking victims could be prepared for assaults on the identities they claim, even at very early stages of law enforcement involvement in stalking processes. Police officers, for example, could advise women that their actions will be subject to evaluation should their former partners ever be prosecuted. Not only does a decision to comply with a stalker or to fight back create problems in enforcing a restraining order, officers could tell women, but it is a choice that may later come back to haunt them. Like the rape survivors of whom Konradi writes, stalking victims are "constructed for public consumption in the courtroom," (Ibid.:50) and forewarned, could be better witnesses and suffer less as a result.

Of course, stalking victims do not have to face the cross-examination of defense attorneys to feel revictimized. Most victims, in fact, will never see the inside of a courtroom, no matter how extensive their involvement with the criminal justice system. Even so, there are lessons for victims and their advocates here. For those who seek to help, it may be useful for them to remember that victims have more to lose than might be evident at first meeting. It is not only a case in the making, but a person—for selves are at stake and depend upon what transpires in those interactions. The "facts of the case" and the facticity of victimization are not always the same, because "victim" is simply (and complexly) a label. If a victim says that she is frightened, pay heed, because who she is in some sense rests on how she feels. Popular injunctions to "honor" the emotions of victims get right at the heart of what happens in revictimization processes. By understanding that the very actions that seem to contradict the representation of fear are *based* on fear, and that muddled thinking and feeling are the consequences of terror, and finally, that fear and love are not mutually exclusive emotions, advocates can treat victims with the same regard any person who is claiming an identity deserves.

For those who are seeking help, the advice that emerges from this analysis is to consider carefully not only one's interactions with former partners, but interactions with potential advocates as well. Treat police officers, advocates, and prosecutors as the evaluative audiences they are, because they too are judge and jury and they too may have the power to decide one's fate. Keep in mind that the emotions one reveals to that audience may aid or dissuade, for people will treat them as windows to the soul. There are rules for when and what and how much to feel, and they matter despite how hard it is to meet them. Understand that even when one is feeling the most trapped, there are still choices to make. Choose carefully, though, for they *all* have consequences.

Bibliography

Altheide, David L. 2000. "Identity and the Definition of the Situation in a Mass-Mediated Context." *Symbolic Interaction* 23(1):1–27.

Amir, Menachem. 1971. *Patterns of Forcible Rape*. Chicago: University of Chicago Press.

Anderson, Margeret L. and Claire Renzetti. 1980. "Rape Crisis Counseling and the Culture of Individualism." *Contemporary Crises* 4(3) (July):323–341.

Beck, Melinda. 1992. "Murderous Obsession: Can New Laws Deter Spurned Lovers and Fans from 'Stalking'—or Worse?" *Newsweek* 120 (July 13):60–62.

Best, Joel. 1997. "Victimization and the Victim Industry." Society 34:9–17.

———. 1999. *Random Violence: How We Talk About New Crimes and New Victims*. Berkeley: University of California Press.

Blumer, Herbert. 1969. *Symbolic Interactionism: Perspective and Method*. New Jersey: Prentice Hall.

Bechhofer, Laurie and Andrea Parrot. 1991. "What Is Acquaintance Rape?" In *Acquaintance Rape: The Hidden Crime*, edited by A. Parrot and L. Bechhofer, pp. 9–25. New York: John Wiley and Sons, Inc.

Belenky, Mary Field, Blythe M. Clinchy, Nancy R. Goldberger, and Jill M. Tarule. 1986. *Women's Ways of Knowing: The Development of Self, Voice, and Mind*. New York: Basic Books.

Boeringer, Scot B., Constance L. Shehan, and Ronald L. Akers. 1991. "Social Contexts and Social Learning in Sexual Coercion and Aggression: Assessing the Contribution of Fraternity Membership." *Family Relations*. 40:58–64.

Bohmer, Carol. 1991. "Acquaintance Rape and the Law." *In Acquaintance Rape: The Hidden Crime*, edited by A. Parrot and L. Bechhofer, pp. 317–334. New York: John Wiley and Sons.

Bradburn, Wayne E. 1992. "Stalking Statutes: An Ineffective Legislative Remedy for Rectifying Perceived Problems with Today's Injunction System." *Ohio Northern University Law Review* 19:271–288.

Bradfield, Jennifer L. 1998. "Antistalking Laws: Do They Adequately Protect Stalking Victims?" *Harvard Women's Law Journal* 21:229.

Burke, Kenneth. 1957. *The Philosophy of Literary Form*. New York: Vintage Books.

Brownmiller, Susan. 1975. *Against Our Will: Men, Women, and Rape*. New York: Simon and Schuster.

Burt, Martha. 1980. "Cultural Myths and Supports for Rape." *Journal of Personality and Social Psychology* 38(2):217–30.

Cancian, Francesca M. 1987. *Love in America: Gender and Self-development*. Cambridge: Cambridge University Press.

Cate, Rodney M. and Sally A. Lloyd. 1992. *Courtship*. Newbury Park, CA: Sage.

Cawelti, John G. 1976. *Adventure, Mystery and Romance: Formula Stories as Art and Popular Culture*. Chicago: The University of Chicago Press.

Charmaz, Kathy. 1987. "Struggling for a Self: Identity Levels of the Chronically Ill." *Research in the Sociology of Health Care* 6:283–321.

———. 1991. "Translating Graduate Qualitative Methods into Undergraduate Teaching: Intensive Interviewing as a Case Example." *Teaching Sociology* 19: 384–395.

———. 1999. "Stories of Suffering: Subjective Tales and Research Narratives." *Qualitative Health Research* 9(3):362–382.

Clark, Candace. 1987. "Sympathy Biography and Sympathy Margin." *American Journal of Sociology* 93:291–321.

———. 1990. "Emotions and Micropolitics in Everyday Life: Some Patterns and Paradoxes of 'Place.'" In *Research Agendas in the Sociology of Emotions*, edited by T. D. Kemper, pp. 305–333. Albany, NY: State University of New York Press.

———. 1997. *Misery and Company: Sympathy in Everyday Life*. Chicago: University of Chicago Press.

Clark, Candace, Sherryl Kleinman, and Carolyn S. Ellis. 1994. "Conflicting Reality Readings and Interactional Dilemmas, Part 2: His, Hers and Theirs." In *Social Perspectives on Emotions* (Volume 2), edited by W. M. Wentworth and J. Ryan, pp. 125–146. Greenwich, CT: JAI Press.

Clark, Lorenne M. G., and Debra Lewis. 1977. *Rape: The Price of Coercive Sexuality*. Toronto: Women's Press.

Diacovo, Nanette. (1995). California's Antistalking Statutes: Deterrent or False Sense of Security? *Southwestern University Law Review* 24:389.

Dunn, Jennifer L. 1998. "Defining Women: Notes Toward an Understanding of Structure and Agency in the Negotiation of Sex." *Journal of Contemporary Ethnography* 26(4):479–510.

Elias, Robert. 1990. "Which Victim Movement? The Politics of Victim Policy." In *Victims and Crime: Problems, Policies and Programs*, edited by A. J. Lurigio, W. G. Skogan, and R. C. Davis, pp. 226–250. Newbury Park, CA: Sage.

Ehrenreich, Nancy S. 1990. "Pluralist Myths and Powerless Men: The Ideology of Reasonableness in Sexual Harassment Law." *The Yale Law Journal* 99(6):1177–1234.

Eisenman, Russell. 1995. "Dubious Value of the 'Reasonable Woman' Standard in Understanding Sexual Harassment." *Psychological Reports* 77(3):1145–1147.

Emerson, Robert M., Kerry O. Ferris, and Carole Brooks Gardner. 1998. "On Being Stalked." *Social Problems* 45(3):289–314.

Estrich, Susan. 1987. *Real Rape*. Cambridge, MA: Harvard University Press.

Faludi, Susan. 1991. *Backlash: The Undeclared War Against American Women*. New York: Doubleday.

Fattah, Ezzat A. 1991. *Understanding Criminal Victimization: An Introduction to Theoretical Victimology*. Scarborough, Ontario: Prentice-Hall Canada.

———.1967. "Toward a Criminological Classification of Victims." *International Criminal Police Review* 209:162–169.

Faulkner, Robert P. and Douglas Hsiao. 1994. "And Where You Go I'll Follow: The Constitutionality of Antistalking Laws and Proposed Model Legislation." *Harvard Journal on Legislation* 31:1–62.

Fein, Robert, and Bryan Vosschuil. 1994. "Stalking Behaviors: An Intoduction to What is Known." Unpublished manuscript.

Felson, Richard B. 1991. "Blame Analysis: Accounting for the Behavior of Protected Groups." *The American Sociologist* 22:5–23.

Ferraro, Kathleen J. 1993. "Cops, Courts and Woman Battering." Pp. 165–177 in *Violence Against Women: The Bloody Footprints*, edited by P. B. Bart and E. G. Moran, pp. 165–177. Newbury Park, CA: Sage.

Forell, Caroline A. and Donna M. Matthews. 2000. *A Law of Her Own: The Reasonable Woman as a Measure of Man*. New York: New York University Press.

Frohmann, Lisa. 1994. "Discrediting Victims' Allegations of Sexual Assault: Prosecutorial Accounts of Case Rejections." In *Constructions of Deviance: Social Power, Context, and Interaction*, edited by P. A. Adler and P. Adler, pp. 210–228. Belmont, CA: Wadsworth.

Furio, Joane. 1993. "Can New State Laws Stop the Stalker?" *Ms.* 3 (January/February):90–91.

Gardner, Carole Brooks. 1995. *Passing By: Gender and Public Harassment*. Berkeley: University of California Press.

Geertz, Clifford. 1991. "Deep Play: Notes on the Balinese Cockfight." In *Rethinking Popular Culture: Contemporary Perspectives In Cultural Studies*, edited by C. Mukerji and M. Schudson, pp. 239–277. Berkeley: University of California Press.

Gelles, Richard J. and Murray A. Straus. 1988. *Intimate Violence*. New York: Simon and Shuster.

Goffman, Erving. 1952. "On Cooling the Mark Out: Some Aspects of Adaptation to Failure." *Psychiatry* 15:451–63.

———. 1959. *The Presentation of Self in Everyday Life*. New York: Anchor Books.

———. 1963. *Stigma: Notes on the Management of Spoiled Identity*. New York; Simon and Schuster.

———. 1983. "The Interaction Order." *American Sociological Review* 48(1):1–17.

Hentig, Hans von. 1948. *The Criminal and His Victim: Studies in the Sociobiology of Crime*. New Haven, CT: Yale University Press.

———. 1941. "Remarks on the Interaction of Perpetrator and Victim." *Journal of Criminal Law, Criminology, and Police Science* 31 (March-April):303–309.

Henton, June, Rodney Cate, James Koval, Sally Lloyd, and Scott Christopher. 1983. "Romance and Violence in Dating Relationships." *Journal of Family Issues* 4(3): 467–82.

Hilgartner, Stephan, and Charles Bosk. 1988. "The Rise and Fall of Social Problems: A Public Arenas Model." *American Journal of Sociology* 94:53–78.

Hochschild, Arlie Russell. 1979. "Emotion Work, Feeling Rules, and Social Structure." *American Journal of Sociology* 85: 551–75.

———. 1983. *The Managed Heart: Commercialization of Human Feeling*. Berkeley: University of California Press.

Holland, Dorothy C. and Margaret A. Eisenhart. 1990. *Educated In Romance: Women, Achievement and College Culture*. Chicago: University of Chicago Press.

Holstein, James A. and Gale Miller. 1997. "Introduction." In *Social Problems in Everyday Life*, edited by G. Miller and J. A. Holstein, pp. ix–xxi. Greenwich, CT: JAI Press.

————. 1990. "Rethinking Victimization: An Interactional Approach to Victimology." *Symbolic Interaction* 13(1):103–122.

Holmstrum, Linda L., and Ann W. Burgess. 1983. *The Victim of Rape: Institutional Reactions*. New Brunswick: Transaction Books.

Hughes, Everett. 1945. "Dilemmas and Contradictions of Status." *American Journal of Sociology* 50:353–359.

Ingrassia, Michele. 1993. "Stalked to Death?" *Newsweek* 122 (November 1):27–28.

Jackman, Mary R. 1994. *The Velvet Glove: Paternalism and Conflict in Gender, Class, and Race Relations*. Berkeley: University of California Press.

Jones, Ann. 1994. *Next Time She'll Be Dead: Battering and How to Stop It*. Boston: Beacon.

Karmen, Andrew. 1991. "The Controversy Over Shared Responsibility: Is Victim Blaming Ever Justified?" In *To Be a Victim: Encounters with Crime and Injustice*, edited by D. Sank and D. I. Caplan, pp. 395–408. New York: Plenum Press.

————. 2001. *Crime Victims: An Introduction to Victimology*. Belmont, CA: Wadsworth.

Kennedy, Leslie W., and Vincent F. Sacco. 1998. *Crime Victims in Context*. New York: Roxbury.

Kerstetter, Wayne A. 1990. "Gateway to Justice: Police and Prosecutorial Response to Sexual Assault Against Women." *The Journal of Criminal Law and Criminology* 81:267–313.

Kerstetter, Wayne A., and Barrick Van Winkle. 1990. "Who Decides? A Study of the Complainant's Decision to Prosecute in Rape Cases." *Criminal Justice and Behavior* 17:268–83.

Kingsnorth, Rodney. 1999. Personal communication.

Konradi, Amanda. 1999. "I Don't Have to Be Afraid of You: Rape Survivors' Emotion Management in Court." *Symbolic Interaction* 22(1):45–77.

————. 1996. "Understanding Rape Survivors' Preparation for Court: Accounting for the Influence of Legal Knowledge, Cultural Stereotypes, Personal Efficacy, and Prosecutor Contact." *Violence Against Women* 2(1):25–62.

————. 1997. "Too Little, Too Late: Prosecutors' Pre-Court Preparation of Rape Survivors." *Law & Social Inquiry* 22(1):1–54.

Kurt, J. Leslie. 1995."Stalking as a Variant of Domestic Violence." Bulletin of the Academy of Psychiatry and Law, 23(2):219–30.

LaFree, Gary. 1989. *Rape and Criminal Justice: The Social Construction of Sexual Assault*. Belmont, CA: Wadsworth.

Lamb, Sharon. 1999. "Constructing the Victim: Popular Images and Lasting Labels." In *New Versions of Victims: Feminists Struggle with the Concept*. Edited by S. Lamb, pp. 108–138. New York: New York University Press.

Lamborn, Leroy L. 1968. "Toward a Victim Orientation in Criminal Theory." *Rutgers Law Review* 22:733–768.

Lashgiri, Dierdre. 1995. "To Speak the Unspeakable: Implications of Gender, 'Race,' Class, and Culture." In *Violence, Silence, and Anger: Women's Writing as Transgression*, edited by D. Lashgiri, pp. 1–21. Charlottesville: University Press of Virginia.

Lieberman, Marcia K. 1986. "'Some Day My Prince Will Come': Female Acculturation through the Fairy Tale." In *Don't Bet on the Prince: Contemporary Feminist*

Fairy Tales in North America and England, edited by J. Zipes, pp. 185–200. New York: Methuen.

Leland, Dorothy. 1994. "Hurrah for the Reasonable Woman." *Initiatives* 56(3):1–7.

LeGrande, C. 1973. "Rape and Rape Laws: Sexism in Society and Law." *California Law Review* 61:919–941.

Lofland, John and Lyn H. Lofland. 1995. *Analyzing Social Settings: A Guide to Qualitative Observation and Analysis*. (3rd ed.). Belmont, CA: Wadsworth.

Lorber, Judith. 1975. "Good Patients and Problem Patients: Conformity and Deviance in a General Hospital." *Journal of Health and Social Behavior* 16:213–25.

Loseke, Donileen. 1992. *The Battered Woman and Shelters: The Social Construction of Wife Abuse*. New York: State University of New York Press.

———. 1999. *Thinking About Social Problems: An Introduction to Constructionist Perspectives*. New York: Aldine de Gruyter.

Lowney, Kathleen S. and Joel Best. 1995. "Stalking Strangers and Lovers: Changing Media Typifications of a New Crime Problem." in *Images of Issues: Typifying Contemporary Social Problems*, edited by J. Best, pp. 33–57. New York: Aldine de Gruyter.

Luckenbill, David. 1977. "Criminal Homicide as a Situated Transaction." *Social Problems* 25:176–186.

Lurigio, Arthur J., and P. A. Resick. 1990. "Healing the Psychological Wounds of Criminal Victimization: Predicting Postcrime Distress and Recovery." In *Victims of Crime: Problems, Policies, and Programs*, edited by A. J. Lurigio, W. G. Skogan, and R. C. Davis, pp. 50–68. Newbury Park CA: Sage.

Madigan, Lee, and Nancy Gamble. 1989. *The Second Rape: Society's Continued Betrayal of the Victim*. New York: Lexington Books.

Mahoney, Martha R. 1991. "Legal Images of Battered Women: Redefining the Issue of Separation." *Michigan Law Review* 90:1–64.

———. 1994. "Victimization or Opression? Women's Lives, Violence and Agency." Pp. 59–92 in *The Public Nature of Private Violence: The Discovery of Domestic Abuse*, edited by M. A. Fineman and R. Mykitiuk, New York: Routledge.

Mannheim, Hermann. 1965. *Comparative Criminology*. Boston: Houghton Mifflin.

Martin, Patricia Yancey and Robert A. Hummer. 1989. "Fraternities and Rape on Campus." *Gender and Society* 3(4):457–73.

Martin, Patricia Yancey. and Marlene Powell. 1994. "Accounting for the 'Second Assault': Legal Organizations' Framing of Rape Victims." *Law & Social Inquiry* 19:853–890.

Mendelsohn, Benjamin. 1956. "The Victimology." Cited in A. Karmen, (2001), *Crime Victims: An Introduction to Criminology* (4th edition). Belmont CA: Wadsworth.

Miller, Susan L. 2000. "Gender and Policing." In *Encyclopedia of Women and Crime*, edited by N. H. Rafter, pp. 93–94. Phoenix: Oryx.

Mills, C. Wright. 1940. "Situated Actions and Vocabularies of Motive." *American Sociological Review* 5(6):904–913.

Modleski, Tania. 1982. *Loving With a Vengeance: Mass-produced Fantasies for Women*. New York: Methuen.

Morash, Merry. 2000. "Women Professionals in the Justice Workplace." In *Encyclopedia of Women and Crime*, edited by N. H. Rafter, pp. 295–300. Phoenix: Oryx.

Morin, Karen S. 1993. "The Phenomenon of Stalking: Do Existing Statutes Provide Adequate Protection?" *San Diego Justice Journal* 1:123–162.

Morville, Dawn A. 1993. "Stalking Laws." *Washington University Law Quarterly* 71: 921–935.

National Criminal Justice Association. 1993. *National Institute of Justice Project to Develop a Model Anti-Stalking Code for States*. NIJ Research Report No. 144477, October. Washington, DC: U.S. Department of Justice, National Institute of Justice.

National Institute of Justice. 1996. *Domestic Violence, Stalking, and Antistalking Legislation: An Annual Report to Congress Under the Violence Against Women Act*. Washington, DC: U.S. Department of Justice.

Pinkston, David L. 1993. "Redefining Objectivity: The Case for the Reasonable Woman Standard in Hostile Environment Claims." *Brigham Young University Law Review* 1993(1):363–384.

Radway, Janice A. 1984. *Reading the Romance: Women, Patriarchy and Popular Literature*. Chapel Hill: University of North Carolina Press.

Reckless, Walter. 1967. *The Crime Problem*. New York: Appleton-Century-Crofts.

Reiff, Robert. 1979. *The Invisible Victim: The Criminal Justice System's Forgotten Responsibility*. New York: Basic Books.

Risman, Barbara J. 1982. "College Women and Sororities: The Social Construction and Reaffirmation of Gender Roles." *Urban Life* 11(2):231–242.

Roiphe, Katie. 1993. *The Morning After: Sex, Fear, and Feminism on Campus*. New York: Little, Brown.

Rose, Vicky McNickle and Susan Randall. 1982. "The Impact of Investigator Perceptions of Victim Legitimacy on the Processing of Rape / Sexual Assault Cases." *Symbolic Interaction* 5:23–36.

Rowe, Karen E. 1986. "Feminism and Fairy Tales." In *Don't Bet on the Prince: Contemporary Feminist Fairy Tales in North America and England*, edited by J. Zipes, pp. 209–226. New York: Methuen.

Russell, Diana E. H. 1991. "Wife Rape." In *Acquaintance Rape: The Hidden Crime*, edited by A. Parrot and L. Bechofer, pp. 129–139. New York: John Wiley and Sons.

Ryan, William. 1971. *Blaming the Victim*. New York: Vintage Books.

Schafer, Stephan. 1968. *The Victim and His Criminal: A Study in Functional Responsibility*. New York: Random House.

Scheppele, Kim L. 1991. "The Reasonable Woman." *Responsive Community* 1 (fall): 45.

Schulhofer, Stephan J. 1998. *Unwanted Sex: The Culture of Intimidation and the Failure of Law*. Cambridge, MA: Harvard University Press.

Schultz, Leroy G. 1968. "The Victim-Offender Relationship." *Crime and Delinquency* 14:135–141.

Sheffield, Carole J. 1989. "The Invisible Intruder: Women's Experiences of Obscene Phone Calls." *Gender and Society* 3(4):483–8.

Sheley, Joseph. 1979. *Understanding Crime: Concepts, Issues, Decisions*. Belmont, CA: Wadsworth.

Spitzberg, Brian H., and William R. Cupach, 1996. "Obsessive Relational Intrusion: Victimization and Coping." Paper presented at the Annual Meetings of the International Society for the Study of Personal Relationships in Banff, Canada.

Stanko, Elizabeth A. 1981. "The Impact of Victim Assessment on Prosecutors' Screening Decisions: The Case of the New York District Attorney's Office." *Law and Society Review* 16:225–39.

———. 1982. "Would You Believe This Woman? Prosecutorial Screening for "Credible" Witnesses and a Problem of Justice." In *Judge, Lawyer, Victim, Thief*, edited by N. H. Rafter and E. A. Stanko, pp. 63–82. Boston: Northeastern University Press.

———. 1993. "Ordinary Fear: Women, Violence and Personal Safety." Pp. 155–164 in *Violence Against Women: The Bloody Footprints*, edited by P. Bart and E. G. Moran. Newbury Park: Sage.

Stombler, Mindy. 1994. "'Buddies' or 'Slutties': The Collective Sexual Reputation of Fraternity Little Sisters." *Gender and Society* 8(3):297–323.

Stombler, Mindy, and Patrica Yancey Martin. 1994. "Bring Women In, Keeping Women Down: Fraternity 'Little Sister' Organizations." *Journal of Contemporary Ethnography* 23(2):150–84.

Sudnow, David. 1979. "Normal Crimes: Sociological Features of a Penal Code in a Public Defender's Office." Pp. 473–496 in *Social Interaction*, edited by H. Robboy, S. Greenblatt, and C. Clark. New York: St. Martin's Press.

Swidler, Ann. 1986. "Culture in Action: Symbols and Strategies." *American Sociological Review* 51:273–86.

Symonds, M. 1980. "The 'Second Injury' to Victims." *Evaluation and Change* 7(1):36–38.

Taylor, Jill McClean, Carol Gilligan, and Amy S. Sullivan. 1995. *Between Voice and Silence: Women and Girls, Race and Relationship*. Cambridge: Harvard University Press.

Thomas, W. I. 1978. "The Definition of the Situation." in *Symbolic Interaction: A Reader in Social Psychology*, edited by J. G. Manis and B. N. Meltzer, pp. 315–321. Boston: Allyn and Bacon.

Thomas, W. I., and Florian Znaniecki. 1951. "A Theory of Social Personality." In *Social Behavior and Personality: Contributions of W. I. Thomas to Theory and Social Research*, edited by E. Volkart, pp. 145–186. New York: Social Science Research Council.

Tjaden, Patricia and Nancy Thoennes. 1998a. "Stalking in America: Findings From the National Violence Against Women Survey." *National Institute of Justice Centers for Disease Control and Prevention Research in Brief*. Washington, DC: U.S. Department of Justice.

———. 1998b. "Prevalence, Incidence, and Consequences of Violence Against Women: Findings From the National Violence Against Women Survey." *National Institute of Justice Centers for Disease Control and Prevention Research in Brief*. Washington, DC: U.S. Department of Justice.

U.S. Senate. 1993. Antistalking Proposals. Hearing held by the Committee on the Judiciary. March 17.

Vaughn, Diane. 1986. *Uncoupling: Turning Points in Intimation Relationship*. New York: Oxford University Press.

Walker, Lenore. 1979. *The Battered Woman*. New York: Harper and Row.

Walker, Samuel. 1994. *Sense and Nonsense about Crime and Drugs*. Belmont CA: Wadsworth.

Weed, Frank J. 1995. *Certainty of Justice: Reform in the Crime Victim Movement*. New York: Aldine de Gruyter.

Weis, Kurt. and S. Borges. 1973. "Victimology and Rape: The Case of the Legitimate Victim." *Issues in Criminology* 8(2):71–115.

White, Jacquelyn W. and John A. Humphrey. 1991. "Young People's Attitudes Towards Acquaintance Rape." In *Acquaintance Rape: The Hidden Crime*, edited by A. Parrot and L. Bechhofer, pp. 43–56. New York: John Wiley and Sons.

Williams, Joyce E., and Karen A. Holmes. 1981. *The Second Assault*. Westport, CT.: Greenwood Press.

Williams, Willie, L., John Lane, and Micahel A. Zona. 1996. "Stalking: Successful Intervention Strategies". *The Police Chief*, February, 24–26.

Wolf, Naomi. 1994. *Fire with Fire: The New Female Power and How It Will Change the 21st Century*. New York: Random House.

Wolfgang, Marvin. 1958. *Patterns in Criminal Homicide*. Philadelphia: University of Pennsylvania Press.

Woody, William Douglas, and Wayne Viney. 1996. "Sexual Harassment: The 'Reasonable Person' vs. 'Reasonable Woman' Standards Have Not Been Resolved." *Psychological Reports* 78(1):329–331.

Zipes, Jack. 1984. *Breaking the Magic Spell: Radical Theories of Folk & Fairy Tales*. New York: Methuen.

———. 1986. "Preface and Introduction." In *Don't Bet on the Prince: Contemporary Feminist Fairy Tales in North America and England*, edited by J. Zipes, pp. xi–xiv, 1–38. New York: Methuen.

Zona, Michael, Kaushal Sharma, and John Lane. 1993. "A Comparative Study of Erotomaniac and Obsessional Subjects in a Forensic Sample." *Journal of Forensic Sciences* 38:894–903.

Index